C000292963

Juno Roche is a writer and ⟨...⟩ class, gender, sexuality and t⟨...⟩ 'provocative and innovative'. ⟨...⟩ Blair Peach Award in for the⟨...⟩ work has been supported by The Paul Hamlyn Foundation. Juno studied Fine Art and Philosophy at Brighton, and English Literature at Sussex, and has written for a wide range of publications including features for *Bitch magazine*, *Dazed*, *Vice*, *Broadly*, *Cosmopolitan*, the *i*, *The Independent*, *i-D*, the *Tate* magazine and *Refinery29*. They are the author of four books: *Queer Sex*, *Trans Power*, *Gender Explorers* and their memoir, *Roam*.

'[A] remarkable memoir ... An incredibly honest tale of survival, escape and resilience.' *Observer*

'Roche stands out as a memoirist of the highest calibre with a voice that teaches us how to live with emotional intelligence, wit and vigour, a voice that is sorely needed in this moment.' *Diva*

'[A] radically honest memoir . . . Roche's story is one of survival and what it means to stay alive.' *Bookseller*

'Few can write with such fresh analysis, whilst remaining so full of heart, wit and charm.' Travis Alabanza

'Juno Roche teaches us that our identity is not just about the past or the journey, but a future life built on our own terms and the discovery of a destination we can truly call home.' Natasha Carthew

'Such a powerful story, and so beautifully written.' Paul Burston

'A singular work of artistic genius.' Chance Czyzselska

*Also by Juno Roche*

Queer Sex
Trans Power
Gender Explorers

# ROAM

## JUNO ROCHE

dialogue
books

DIALOGUE

First published in Great Britain in 2022 by Dialogue Books as *A Working Class Family Ages Badly*

This paperback edition published in 2023 by Dialogue Books

1 3 5 7 9 10 8 6 4 2

A CIP catalogue record for this book
is available from the British Library.

ISBN 978-0-349-70233-9

Typeset in Berling by M Rules
Printed and bound in Great Britain by Clays Ltd, Elcograf S.p.A.

Papers used by Dialogue are from well-managed forests
and other responsible sources.

MIX
Supporting
responsible forestry
FSC® C104740

Dialogue Books
Carmelite House
50 Victoria Embankment
London EC4Y 0DZ

www.dialoguebooks.co.uk

Dialogue Books, part of Little Brown, Book Group Limited, an Hachette UK company.

*To the eight-year-old me who dreamt of climbing trees and hiding under leaves or flying away on my bed to some far-off sun-filled land as if it were magical, we did it, kiddo, we did, we escaped to these beautiful mountains.*

*We built our dreams, you, and me.*

'Follow your dreams, lad, don't be like me and waste your life.'

Dad, 1970 – in something of an odd moment of actually talking to me

# One

# My Family as an Archipelago

Tracing my family's history can be like looking at snail trails that you find in early spring or late autumn that poetically snake and whisper across paving slabs, stopping abruptly as if the snails have been lifted into the heavens, vanishing without a trace. Family histories, peppered with intergenerational trauma and the traces and imprints of difficult memories that arise from pain, often appear as disconnected clues across the chasm of time, across centuries. I've researched my family's history back over four hundred years. I made a map, an actual drawing of a map to try to make sense of things.

But making a map based on myths is as reliable as it sounds. As kids we were told falsehoods and exaggerated family legends. My dad, John, once told us that we were descended from the people who set up Barclays Bank. I looked. We're not.

There's a pudding called floating islands which is made of nuggets of Italian meringue on a sea of custard. Looking at the map of my family is like looking at a map of floating islands with only hints and clues about how to navigate the space between each distinct shore. How can you read the family's entire surface? Also, if you leave floating islands out for long enough, they take on board the lush, light custard and start to sink. That's my family's history: forever sinking, disconnected little islands in a vast Tupperware bowl.

Faint, fading dots and dashes lighting the paths to you, to me, to form us. Seemingly disembodied from us, from our bodies, like the snail trails they stop a distance away. How did we get from the path, from the lineage to us? So many clues, but no one wants to own them, to admit they belong to them.

Clues that you'd never see at street level, only from above, like a celestial map. To understand my family, you have to stop still and take the time to research, to look around, to find truth in scant clues. None of mine have the luxury of time, only me.

So, I search to try to find hidden truths.

Memories and events that surround us, circling us like soft winds, whispering to us, a few of them slipping in under our skin, to embed in our minds. Addiction in our family feels such. Violence in our family feels such. A fear of abject poverty in our family feels such.

Perhaps when mouths were aghast at the stuff that happened, we swallowed these embedded truths. They festered and grew into seeds of unhappiness that emerge as addiction; addiction runs in the family.

There are nuggets of truth. We come from hard work, addiction, violence and poverty. These nuggets shine brightly on my hand-drawn map, islands you can stand on. Reappearing time and time again, like their own sweet archipelagos.

We are told by polite society that whatever the trauma that we've experienced or are experiencing, we can always adapt, change, and move on to a better, brighter future. Find a perfect garden the other side of the fence with flowers and grass, grass that isn't peppered with dog shit and yellowing patches of seeping dog piss. Gardens inhabited by laughter and childish exploration rather than heavy silence, the aftermath of violence. We are led to believe that we can shuck off these layers of traumatic history like cotton-rich clothing on a sunny day, and emerge anew, different, changed, cleansed, transitioned into happy.

Perhaps some can, perhaps even most, I don't know any more. Maybe it's just me that can't even though I look like I have. The price of escaping has been to crawl inside me and create fantasies.

But the guilt I feel at failing to happily clamour upwards to brighter lands is immense. It shames me that I'm still trapped by my past. I'm still on this map.

The lines, the trails, the dashes that connect my family's different lines of history have disappeared over time, separating us, the different generations, different siblings, into distinct islands. Separately named. Living alone as singles. Lonesome spots, islets. Blips. Blips that don't understand what life's meant to be about, if it's always going to be this hard.

Dad forcefully explained to us on more than one occasion that our lives were like this because we were mental like our mum, we took after her. 'It's genetic,' he said.

That helped enormously.

Searching ancestry records only gives you a network of clues. At first nothing is emotional, far from it – just dates, places, names, jobs, births and deaths. But just occasionally I could join up two people or two generations and something would fall into place, and I'd be hit with the emotion of knowing these people, loving the names written in black and white.

My gran, my dad's mum Lou, appearing on the 1911 census in the Bethnal Green Workhouse. She was a kid. The same night, on the same census, her parents and some of their other children were just around the corner in a room in Russia Lane. Why was she there alone? I don't know if any of the other children were in this workhouse or one of the other workhouses in the East End. I couldn't find any other leads. Not that night.

My dad never knew. When I told him over the phone, he was silent, the kind of resolute silence that's holding back tears. I only remember him crying after he hit us and then, once, sobbing at his mum's funeral when they lowered her coffin into the ground. But I could feel tears close on that call.

Dad's neurological disease is a little like Parkinson's, phones are tough for him now, he can hardly talk, which is fine because we don't have a lot to say, but in his silence I sensed years of emotions catching up in his brain, like racing cars on the last lap. An actual piece of information, not supposition, or a family tale about a mythical banking connection, but an actual documented detail that allowed him an insight to his mum, a mum who left them, latch-key kids, day after day, night after night, as she went out to work in one factory after another, calling in for Guinness on the way home. Who was once a little girl left in the workhouse while the rest of her siblings were at home with their parents.

The Sunlight Laundry in Brixton, the Tate and Lyle factory in Silvertown. She worked in them all. All the big London factories.

I didn't mean the fact to be a gift, but it felt like I'd given him a single detail that explained so much about his own childhood. A childhood that had made him an angry, violent man. His mother would never forget the experience of being a child in a workhouse, possibly handed over when times were too tough for all the kids to be fed.

Her background informed and shaped my dad's lived experience, his background became the background to our foregrounds, and as I write, now my background, which if I'd had a womb would by now have become my children's foregrounds.

Single events shape generations, in exactly the same way that a moment of privilege does, privilege allowing space for simple things like breathing and thinking and dreaming.

A crown.

I found a history of alcoholism on both sides, of people dying prematurely of liver disease and bouts of hospitalisation noted on different censuses. Histories of fragile employment, the lowest paid employment possible – begging. On a census the words 'blind beggar' described my maternal great-grandfather. The words 'blind', 'beggar', 'labourer', 'servant' and 'workhouse' appeared numerous times on both sides. And just occasionally, the words 'prison' and 'crime'.

Through the contemporary cultural phenomenon of creating a family tree, a map, I connected the dots that I was told I could walk away from, because I'd read books and gone to university. Breezily walking away because I was the one in the family who'd done all right. But just because I embody new words for my family – 'queer', 'trans', 'HIV positive' – doesn't mean I can walk away from the ones I've inherited, the ones that shaped so much of my life.

I feel fraudulent because of what I hid when I said I was just reading books. The cocks I sucked for pounds, shillings and pence, the parts of me I sold – my arse and my soul, the deals I cut and the number of times I wanted to run away from running away because I missed my family and wanted to run back to them. I doubt that any of that will show up on any future ancestry research sites. I'll just look successful, purposeful, intentional. Textbook. Maybe I am, possibly I just can't find a high enough mountain to see where I stand in relation to the separate islands of my family.

But I want the spaces between my moments to be obvious, the connections to be clear. No one is one thing, no single act has been life changing – I went to university as an addict, and I remained an addict all the way through and after. I sold drugs, my arse, myself, and still got a good degree. Nothing's one thing. Nothing stands alone without vast conflicting emotions swirling around it, like trade winds around an island that both batter and cajole.

I hate the idea that we're only allowed to fuck up once or twice and always have to learn from it. I keep fucking up. This year I've slumped into my own minute battle with pre-scription addiction. A year of depressive relapses so deep I just wished for sleep, but sleep never came, just nights filled with anxiety and more pills.

The latticework of family and the endless generations that I've drawn together during this summer of pandemic and addiction has helped me to see who I am. Or at least how I might have been constructed from the different historical constituent parts to be this version of me.

Struggle, lapsed religion, addiction, alcoholism, crime

and the endless – and I mean endless – family breakdowns, people running away from each other to find security. These loom large in our family tree. People leaving people and often ending up alone.

Here is what I know for sure. We are descended from Huguenots (French Protestants who fled religious persecution) and Irish peasants who settled in London almost three hundred years ago.

Our first Huguenot, a single fellow, arrived in Shoreditch in 1742. Running from religious persecution, he left a beautiful village in south-western France to run to the slums of the East End. He wouldn't have carried much with him; travel light you run faster. A tradition that's been strongly upheld by each succeeding generation and come to a head in my family with us all running to different corners. I can see the past repeating itself, but I haven't yet been able to work out why.

Periodically, I get rid of stuff just in case I should have to flee. It feels hardwired into my brain. I came here to Spain with only a few boxes of things that seemed important at the time. Some seashells, a Chromonica, some books. Whenever I buy something, I feel that something else must leave, because of the irrational fear that I'll become overwhelmed, overrun by material possessions. Perhaps I thought coming here would only be temporary; I didn't realise it would become a home because I didn't understand the meaning of a home. A house maybe, but not a home. Isn't that a Luther Vandross song?

People glibly say that addicts need to hit rock bottom in order to rise up clean. Phoenix-like. Ready to move on with new, effective, stepped strategies to drug-free pastures.

This notion presupposes that life always starts away from the bottom, a rung or two up. I was born and raised as close to an emotional and dysfunctional rock bottom as you can imagine. I've forgotten much of what happened, because your head can only manage to hold in so much before it feels like it's imploding and you want to sleep for ever.

Holding inside what I do know has been exhausting. Especially as it's ongoing, it's a live event.

Setting out to write this book has created vistas back over my life in which events have popped up: some slight, a word here or there; some major, a full-on punch. Occasionally I've written down a memory, something that's so dysfunctional that I know as kids our brains must have been constantly whirring, trying to process what had happened while walking to school. Mum screaming, Dad punched, *must learn about triangles and verbs* (in a robot voice).

Little wonder that most of us dropped out and only I made it through the system, albeit on drugs. I was educated despite my addiction or perhaps through my addictions.

We were a working-class family forever scrambling upwards, never reaching above the first step, where we pointlessly squabbled, fought and fell out, arguing over whose head was just above the scum line, just above the parapet. Layers of violence and dysfunction gathering on that first step, dysfunctions we had to fight through to find space. Over the years that tiny space became so embittered and divisive that it separated us at first into factions, and then into singles. Blips in an ocean sky.

We are siblings only in name. I doubt that we will see each other again in this lifetime. Perhaps at the funerals of our parents. Perhaps not, if they're held on Zoom.

Our blood is not thicker or finer or more viscous than water. Sadly. But that doesn't mean that we don't want to love each other; we simply don't know how.

I still get two or three phone calls a week from my mum, Ann, about old or ongoing dramas, about my dad or something his new wife, also called Ann (the plot thickens), has said or done or not done or is going to do. About someone's drug intake (other than mine), someone's slip back into, or towards poverty, or new dramas, often age-old ones osmotically passed on, old behaviours that I've mapped through my research emerging in the actions of young nieces and nephews.

Bless them, some of them are already snared by the meagre offerings of comfort from a family in disarray. A family unable to put strong, protective arms around them. None of us has anyone to fall back on. Perhaps my mum has me. But the rest have no one.

There isn't a spare penny or ounce of emotional support. As I write, my sister Jack, my brilliant older sister, who taught me how to dance and how to be feisty, has two crisis teams looking after her; she struggles to dress or get up off the sofa. She shakes almost constantly, the stresses of our history manifest in her as a constant nervous quiver.

It's the way it is, the way it's always been.

Nothing spare to support any hardship that might arise, no advice, encouragement or soothing wise words are proffered, apart from my dad's 'follow your dreams', which I did. And of course, the classic, 'keep your pecker up', which I didn't, in fact I had it cut off and refashioned.

I mistrust support, because I have no frame of reference for unconditional, uncomplicated love. I'm suspicious of kindness, as if kindness itself is a malevolent trick that's out to get me, to trip me up. Like kindness is the enemy.

What a way to be. I'm aware that this huge flaw in me has dented my character, scarred it deeply. How could it not? Not being able to trust has led me to seek silent sanctuary in among ancient trees.

I witnessed violence that ended in blood and cuts, and the next day I'd have to go to school and listen to *care and share* moments about other kids' kittens and play-fights with their dad.

I once saw my sister dragged off by her hair by my dad because he was a racist and she'd been seeing a Black man. It was as violent as any action you'd see out on the street, but it was in the house. In the front room. Mum had hidden my sister's boyfriend in a cupboard in her room because Dad came in early, but he found him and violence ensued. A crowbar and a car door frame weaponised. Later that night, stitches in the back of my sister's head. We never talked about it. But I can still clearly see the congealed blood in her hair. She had a beautiful asymmetric stack perm weighed down like a sink hole with congealed blood.

I went to the school the next day, tried to smile and to focus on what was being said about learning and the value of learning. But I gave up and stared out of the window silently counting objects that didn't move and ones that did, counting down the minutes until I could return home, to a home that was the problem, but also the solution because it was home.

By the time I'd left school I'd discovered a myriad of ways to hurt myself – not eating, eating too much, throwing up, holding my breath under the bed-covers, holding my breath under the hand-me-down bath-water, scratching my hands and arms with a compass or a needle. By my teens I'd found cigarettes and then with increasing rapidity drink and a plethora of different drugs, and then pleasing men in dangerous spaces. Kids running away from harm often run into harm, running blindly, with arms open, desperate for a hug.

I found books.

A book was a physical thing that I discovered I could climb into; it could be an actual journey away from the place I was in. I crossed whole lands, getting lost in the words of a book. I could stand still, surrounded by noise, and still leave. No permission, just run.

I'm not sure if that makes writing a natural sanctuary for me, it actually always feels arduous and draining because of the stuff I write. But you do what you do.

I dreamt about becoming a Borrower and hiding under the floorboards or between the book-club books that we weren't allowed to read. I dreamt about still being able to see my family; I loved them, but needed to be apart from them, hidden from them, at a safe distance from them.

Me in a book, or perhaps them as a book?

Is this house here in the Spanish mountains a book?

Cognitive dissonance is a prerequisite for survival when a family isn't a place of safety.

# Two

# I'll Always Believe in Love

I grew up thinking it was normal for family members to beat the shit out of each other, to fight on doorsteps, on the streets, to have the police called and to fight collectively against anyone who dared to attack one of us, including the police. *The only people who knock at our door are the police with bad news about one of you, or someone wanting to fight*, my mum said, *I even dread picking up the phone.*

I thought it was normal for your fourteen-year-old sister to brawl with your mum on the doorstep, ripping out clumps of hair and biting chunks out of each other. I watched my sister sink her teeth into my mum's skinny leg as if she were taking a bite out of a chicken wing. The whole road watched them pummel each other and I watched and waited for Dad to step in and punch someone full on in the face. I thought that was a telling off. I thought a punch was a slap, a full stop.

Drug addiction in my twenties and thirties, however fraught with risk, felt like a holiday, a break from the intensity of my family life.

My relationship with drugs was formed early on. Drugs of one kind or another – prescription, alcohol, weed and Class As – permeated my childhood and teenage years. I grew up used to the smells, the sights, the paraphernalia and the sounds of drug taking. My older brother Nick once offered me a tray full of cocaine. I was fourteen and sat at my mum's ancient Singer sewing machine, trying to run up a top to annoy the fuck out of my dad. I found I could sew much quicker with a nose full.

Despite our childhoods, Nick is the most demonstratively loving person I've ever met. We hardly ever talk and never see each other but when our paths do cross he always says *I love you* and hugs me. I love him for that. My younger brother, Dom, hates being called little, he'll never talk about the family, and keeps a country's distance between him and all that was. He's a few years younger and took much of the brunt of what happened. Considering that, it's a miracle that he's still here, but he is, living by the sea somewhere, fishing occasionally and cooking the catch as an act of love for his partner and children. That he catches and cooks fish and believes in love is an act far greater than any moon landing.

I soon progressed from cocaine and speedy sewing and discovered a comfortable, weighty silence in the hibernation of a long cool heroin summer. A summer that dragged on and on like the midnight sun of an Icelandic day. For years I numbed with opiates. I still fight that desire to be numbed, my brain easily manifests in dreams that feeling of sweet emptiness.

My mum used to bake cakes called Coffee Kisses.

She'd hide them from us and eat them herself, one by one, often after we'd gone to bed. If we plucked up the courage when she wasn't around we'd climb up onto the kitchen worktop, take the tin down from the top of the cupboards, open it and try to work out if she'd notice if we each took one. Staring into an always near-empty tin we knew she'd notice.

They were called kisses but they felt like a punishment she'd baked, kisses withheld. The irony that she chose to bake cakes called kisses, which could have imbued love and knitted us together, but instead were weaponised and held back.

Her baking often happened during her spiky OCD phases when she was high on speeding, slimming pills. Baking and cleaning. She was tense in these phases, strung taut. We'd get in the way and on her nerves, we'd do nothing right.

She never seemed to sleep; my dad always went to bed alone.

Occasionally we'd find her asleep in the morning, curled up in the chair with orange thick wooden legs. It was an ugly chair but comfortable, Mum's favourite. She'd sleep with her legs over one arm. Her thick, flame-auburn hair pushed up against the cushion like a mud slide.

If she wasn't asleep it meant she'd been awake all night, and she'd probably wake us up at five in the morning hoovering our bedroom, flinging open the door, saying *don't mind me, carry on sleeping.* We'd rub our eyes and lie awake watching her manically vacuuming up every speck from the grey, hard-wearing, itchy carpet that you couldn't sit or lie on as it felt like a low-grade form of torture. The carpet became a weapon during sibling fights, causing carpet burns across your back or the backs of your legs.

*

There's a photograph of me that I have hanging opposite my bed in a wall of photographs. I keep questioning why I have a wall of black-and-white family photographs. What does it mean that I choose to wake up to look at my history? Is it punishment?

In the photograph I'm about five years old, I have a slight smile and big black bags under my eyes, there's already a sadness, a slight withdrawal, the dark circles look pencilled on like shelves for my eyes. I used to be called Simon, and Simon had worrisome eyes; we share those eyes, they weren't part of the transitional upcycling procedure that created Juno. I wish they could have been, as they haunt me. I could have an eyelift, a dark circle eradication, but I despise the capitalist core of the plastic surgery industry; it denigrates even when there are very good reasons for its usage.

My mum was part of the prescription-addiction generation. Every facet of her dysfunction solved and controlled by one doctor or another doling out a growing litany of pills with names like Purple Hearts, Blue Bombers and, of course, the ubiquitous Valium. Always bloody Valium.

Pills prescribed by general practitioners as the solution to womanhood, to bored womanhood, to unhappy womanhood, to overweight or underweight womanhood, to anxious womanhood, to struggling-to-feed womanhood, to rightfully-fucking-angry womanhood. To working-class women, to beaten women. To my mum.

For every broken or breaking emotion, a doctor gave my mum a pill. She takes so many now that it's a feat of endurance for her to organise them for the week. It worries m that none of us really know the whats and the whys of medication. If we had to look after her we wouldn't know the pills from the pills from the pills. I make a mental note to ask her to write it down.

No one offered a woman like my mum the chance to talk, the chance for therapeutic meanderings. There was no money set aside for Mum to talk about the struggles of being a mum. Even now, when there is scant money available, it is usually aimed at the children and parenting classes rather than at the women themselves and their hopes and aspirations.

Mum called the other day, upset about family stuff; it's been the story of her life, the trials of family stuff. I said, *Mum, you're a separate person apart from us, apart from being a mother, you were a human before becoming a mother, you can think about you, you're in your eighties, Mum, what do you want to do with these years?*

Silence. You can't change a mother's love, especially a mother like my mum who doesn't feel she's ever given enough or could ever give enough. It's love but it's also an obsession that avoids her addressing her unmet needs. Which has always loaded her love down with reciprocity. We must be there for the only thing that gives her purpose. Without us, she says, she'd die.

When she says, *my kids are more important than anything else*, she's also confirming that she's travelled through life not feeling worthy of a happy life. I've failed abysmally to ͨͧ͠ier. That's been my obsession, a trough I feed ͧ frequently avoiding my own unhappiness; ͨn.

r an attempted overdose, my mum's GP simply

prescribed more of the drug she'd overdosed on in her cry for help. Despite my screaming at him down the phone, he prescribed the very same drug and told me I was being hysterical. Like my dad, he gathered and inspected our hysterias as if they were DNA.

I said to him, *you should be struck off for being this lazy, my mum needs help, not more pills.*

*She doesn't want any help*, he replied, slapping me into my place.

He was right, she didn't and couldn't want any help; as a child she'd been too damaged by intrusive, interfering male hands and damaged by the unseeing eyes of her mother, Gertie, as she marched off to work, always looking the other way.

Valium was the drug that from an early age we were taught would solve anything and everything. Men, hardship, love, fear, bad dreams, insomnia, bad acid trips, school, work, life, heroin addiction, anxiety, the fear of anxiety, the fear of the fear of anxiety – yes it's a real fear. And OCD. I started taking them in my early teens to get through school, to be able to hold a pen or a pencil without shaking.

I loved my mum then; I love my mum now, but during those times her behaviour taught us to be scared around simple things. Everyday simple things, banal things. Things you wouldn't notice as things. Things that would become issues.

Food, clean things, finger-marks on glass, on surfaces, the surfaces themselves. Folded clothes, towels, tea towels. Washing-up sponges. The skirting boards. A used tea towel should never look like a used tea towel, so if you use it, return it to its pre-used state, i.e. cause a miracle to happen.

I'm not exaggerating: she was strung taut like a trip-wire waiting to catch us out. It was her only way to feel any control. If we did wrong, she'd punish us and feel like a mother.

At her absolute lowest, she was perpetually scratchy and angry, pecking at our behaviour like a fledgling eager to depart the nest. Nervously she'd pull at the skin that edged her fingernails until they became red with blood. She'd pull great chunks of skin off her heels until they bled and then she picked them some more.

She never seemed to sleep; she always cooked but she hardly ever ate, only small, sweet things like biscuits and Coffee Kisses. She ate like a child – I dream of that. Food was never simple for me; it became a thing of shared maternal complexity. Being close to her meant that her difficult relationship with food and with feeling full of food was passed on. I always felt chubby and clumsy and that made me feel vulnerable, so I too picked at the skin that bordered nails.

She'd look at photographs of film stars or models and say, *we can't all be as skinny as a rake but we won't stop trying.* I wanted to please her by being as skinny as a rake. I also wanted to please my dad by being a cowboy, this led me to anorexic delusions of Thelma, Brad and Louise.

I inherited her eating habits for years; sugar, jam, syrup on toast. A biscuit with a sweet cup of tea. Occasional blips of sugar to boost energy. Just a single slice to last the day; I didn't realise that she was also on a bevy of slimming pills, so when I tried to emulate her I felt faint. I smoked to fill the gaps in my belly, Number Six or Craven Black Cats.

Occasionally she'd open a can of condensed milk and

spoon it down, one sweet glutinous spoonful after the other. I'd watch her seal the can with tin foil with such fastidious detail that she'd know if anyone tried to break in. Then she'd go and throw it all up. I'd hear.

She ate like a very unhappy child because she was.

She was inconsistent: one minute strict and rigid, but then she'd let us smoke in the house as young teens. She took me out of school to see Bob Marley and The Wailers when I was twelve years old at the Hammersmith Odeon. By the time they played 'I Shot the Sheriff', we were both up dancing. I wore a green Levi's sweatshirt with my silver St Christopher necklace on the outside to make me seem older.

Her behaviour was terrifying but also fabulous. She was all over the place and loved us like a child would love other children or perhaps a puppy. She's always loved puppies, frequently dispatching them when they become dogs, grown-ups. She's always been good if we're in a mess but not great if we're not. It's easier for her if the whole world is messy, I think.

But Bob Marley at twelve years old and a day off school to recover, what a queen of a memory in among dark memories. How many other kids could say that?

I left home at eighteen, thinking I was leaving parts of me behind that I didn't need any more. A family, the family, the thing that resembled a family. The approximate family and the approximate family home. Apart from the drug years, I've really been alone ever since; it wasn't a stretch to move to live in isolated mountains.

But the isolation of COVID-19 has exacerbated my

aloneness, I now miss the idea of an idealised family more than ever. I don't want to die alone, although I imagine I will.

How else could it happen? I'm virtually isolated now. A few friends scattered far and wide whom I suspect wonder exactly the same thing, what will it be like to die alone. At least there'll be no fuss, no need to make plans or lists, just burn me and scatter me if you have to, I really don't care once I'm dead. I like the idea of being as light as a feather, some ashes swept up into the sky unfettered, without the baggage.

According to the chirpy, chipper narrative around working-class aspiration, I should be here thriving in the sun and not thinking about dying alone.

I should feel complete.

I have books that sit on the shelves of bookshops – people send me photos of my books.

I should feel a modicum of success, perhaps I do in my sun-splashed home.

I enjoy feeling the sun on my skin. Is that enough to define aspiration, that I have the time to feel sun on my skin? Is that enough? Is it enough that the sun shines and the flowers grow and I have the time to observe their beauty. That feels luxurious compared to what has gone before and compared to my siblings' lives. I no longer have to scurry around looking for pennies to make pounds to allow me to buy drugs. I'm clean of all those messy shackles.

I have time, which for a life condemned many years ago to die of AIDS, is an irony in and of itself: that I am the one who ends up with time I can waste looking at flowers in my fifties.

That does feel like a success, having the time to plant

flowers and watch them grow any day of the week I choose, but it's tinged with something because I've failed abysmally at the human touch and feel stuff. Intimacy, hugging, being held, holding, kissing, being kissed. Or just resting my head on another's shoulder, that would be enough for me now. But when I try to give my body the permission to let go and trust a willing shoulder it tenses into a shape which cannot meld. I become like chalky bones. Stiff, spiky, impossible.

In trying to reject the dysfunction of my mum, my dad and us as a family, I avoided owning the same, shared dysfunction that had already seeped into and lodged in each of my cells, to sit, watching and waiting for the HIV that would soon arrive, or some other calamity, my DNA hardwired to flourish in strife.

I walked away from my named family, my birth family, but I always miss them because they're my only blood people. My tribe. My clan. My peeps. I know them inside out and they me, I think. We were all there. I hide that loss behind a sunny veneer.

'Look, Mum, I got away.'

'Did you?' she asks knowingly.

Through the veneer of my obsessively curated Instagram feed, I proclaim contentment and happiness. A serene, steady stream of beautifully rendered functionality that exists on the side of happiness.

Pomegranate season distilled in single objects painted in shades of red. Blues, only blues, in this COVID-19 summer because I read and re-read *Bluets* by Maggie Nelson. Shades of yellow when the sun shines because that's happiness, that's

California meets Andalusia. That's joy, unquestionable joy. I live in the sun, I chased the sun here, I must be happy; I must be close to finding love, wrapped tightly in my whiter-than-white sheets.

'Look at this house, Mum, I must be happy.'

This house is the place I sketched and carried around in my head as the visual embodiment of dreams and safety. Light filled – the opposite of a Louise Bourgeois cell but crafted with the same dank, convoluted intent. A place so bright and light that my depression and darkness won't return.

Banished momentarily, it did return, it carried me over the threshold as its bride. But we're not there yet. Let's stay in the sun for a moment.

I have a beautiful house, honestly it's so beautiful it's perfect, I wish I could paint it. I've tried, I can't. I can only paint cups and vases quite badly, in fact very badly.

I write books. I've had therapy that I paid for with my money I earnt. I obviously prioritised my mental wellbeing at some point, not that it worked. I have a small amount of money; I have a teacher's pension, I was once a teacher – a decent one according to my pension.

I have some trappings of comfortable functionality. I should be happy, or I should shut the fuck up about being unhappy, I have no right to that voice in my beautiful house. I'm ungrateful.

But I did make this happen, this house, this place.

When I wake here, especially in spring, each day feels like the first day because eternally, it feels miraculous that somehow I got here. Somehow I seem to have left darkness for light. Grey, not French grey, but Old Kent Road grey, swapped for an expansive painted blue. The blue of Yves Klein, the blue of Moroccan nights, of the oil-paint pigment produced by old Holland that is so intensely blue that its price holds it aloft from the rack of other colours. A special blue. A dreamy blue. A Maggie Nelson blue. An old-monied blue.

The sky must be so pissed at me trying to drag my shady ol' greys into its mix. It's too simplistic and naive to try to reduce my mental wellbeing to some new-age colour-therapeutic equation, but I am aware of how grey my moods can feel splashed against the clarity of the whitewashed walls and rich blue sky. I wonder if I wouldn't feel more resolved on the Isle of Skye.

Here, trapped between the top of the white walls and blue sky, old traumas keep rising up like morning mists off my skin to surround me, how could they not? I kidded myself that I could run away. They come to me in words on the page, and then at night as fleeting visons in my dreams, traumas buried so deeply in my brain that they swim upwards with the speed and power of Olympic swimmers, swimming towards the light, smashing through any dermal resistance ('keep it in,' whispers Juno) to resurface and lie wilfully on the surface of my skin like sunbathers at Tooting Lido. My traumas lounge here in the sun.

My memories, my dysfunctions and my ideas about love shape and surround my being, like a shed skin held tight by a thousand hands pressed against my dermis. My skin holds all of me. These pages I write are like my skin, or perhaps another layer of skin that I shed in some kind of desperate need to find or create distance. I create to create distance. Is writing the sanest thing I do or just another layer of fucked-up-ness?

That's why I find being touched so difficult, maybe even impossible now. Touch hurts. I feel toxic, poisoned by having to hold it all in. As kids we grew up blaming ourselves, I know we did. So we swallowed it all down with drugs, alcohol and abusive relationships. The work of having to be good enough to exist in this world, to be seen, to be worthy of kind, sensual, loving touch, is all consuming. I ran here, albeit slowly, because I needed the sun to burn away the layers of unworthiness that scupper my skin.

Pup is my third dog; he's one dog too many, even two now is one too many. Perhaps even one is one too many. I love all my dogs but I'm exhausted and increasingly I dream about owning a cat who comes and goes as she pleases. A haughty independent madam of a cat with her own debit card and wheels. A cat who stays over at her tomcat's house three nights a week.

But, alas, Pup turned up in the village as a skinny stray with bleeding ears and a bolshy swagger and attitude, no doubt formed on the street. He took up residence on my doorstep at the start of the pandemic. I read him as a sign. Inextricably linked like a Tarot card to the pandemic.

My need to be needed answered by this skinny pup. He'd come down from the mountains during the first few days of the pandemic. A sign, a gift. He reminded me of my dad when he was young, full of everything and nothing but swag and more swag.

Every morning he waited for me to walk my other dogs, barking at the top of his lungs like a king announcing his needs. Like my dad. King of the village, king of the road, king of nowhere.

He made so much noise demanding that we walk at sunrise, as he, the little sun god, awoke and barked. A huge bark for such a tiny dog – he stands perhaps six inches tall (the length of an average cock according to men) and a foot long. The dimensions of a small chicken.

Underneath his waistcoated-bullfighter bravado, Pup isn't robust, he's like a Tudor child-king, sickly and skinny. Doomed to an early death if he hadn't met us.

His head is too slight to hold a crown.

There are dogs like Pup all over these mountains, broken by harsh country lives. Most are used for hunting, kept unfed, living on the edge of starvation in dark, discarded spaces. Tethered with old rusty chains. When I see them chained up, they remind me of the photograph of Brunel standing in front of the Great Eastern's anchor chains, and I wonder why men, it is men, feel the need to use such big chains on dogs with such slight necks.

They treat them appallingly and then, after a single season, often abandon them as they don't want to have to feed them through winter. Local myths abound of dogs having their legs broken, being left to die slow, painful deaths in mountain ravines. I've never seen that, so it could just be folklore, but I have found many skeletons of dogs that once chased down rabbits, not for the love of their masters, but because they were starved to death. They are like the lowest rung of workers, alongside the donkeys, doing until they can do no longer.

That's Pup's inheritance, that's the life he narrowly avoided by finding shelter on our doorstep. He's got such Cockney charm that I couldn't resist him. It's in my DNA: like my mum, I'm drawn to a chancer.

When I first moved here my sensibilities were acutely challenged by the treatment of animals in my village. A snake which had sneaked under a doorstep and eaten a bird was dragged out by its tail by a neighbour.

'Look at that,' he said, pointing to the shape of the bird, swallowed whole, midway down the snake's length. He proceeded to smash the snake's head open on the floor, swinging it like it was rope with a knot. 'Don't,' I screamed, 'please let it go.'

He laughed, handing it to me. A lifeless, bloody snake containing a bird that occasionally moved.

Later, I buried it in my garden, hugging my dogs close. I vowed that I'd save every creature I could, no matter how terrified I was of it.

I'd never seen a snake, or a scorpion, or a giant poisonous centipede in London, but I've found many of them here in my garden and occasionally in my bed. I've never killed one of them despite being utterly terrified of all of them. The giant poisonous centipede I captured, put into a jar, and tried to feed strawberries all day to change its carnivorous ways. It didn't like the strawberries; when I released it at dusk it shot out, looking for something blood-filled to munch.

When Pup turned up bursting with damaged Cockney charm, I knew I had to save him.

Both of my other dogs are affectionate and needy, they help to fill the cavity that loneliness has chiselled out of my childless being. My body couldn't materialise motherhood; I had all the emotional needs but no womb, no tubes, no chemicals, no female innards.

I stroke my dogs and they lick the moisturiser off my legs until my legs are dry and grey and need moisturising. They allow me mammalian touch. Warmth.

I know they are replacement children. Through my relationship with them I know I am an ageing mother, maybe even a grandmother now as I'm getting to that point where I'd rather stay in the warmth of my bed on winter mornings than march dogs up into the mountains to create bodily heat. My days of non-motherhood motherhood are almost done. That pain has almost seeped out of my bones.

Thus, Pup was a dog too far, he moved into the house of a grandmother on the cusp of settling her maternal business.

One very cold evening, Pup slunk into the house, climbed into the log basket, squished himself between the logs and never left.

In his mind though he's still a stray, the king of all strays. His personality a facade from who knows what early horrors: a boot, a kick, an escape from a cold, dark outbuilding, an impossibly weighty chain.

He loves the warmth, the food, the raw chicken, the almonds and raw eggs. He loves his adoptive canine siblings whom he snuggles deeply into.

But he hates human touch. Hates it. He runs from me like I'm a monster. At the vets it's embarrassing, I blame his shaking on them. 'It's you he's scared of. Poor thing.'

Occasionally he runs to me and kisses my nose with a flick of his cold tongue, but if I try to hold him or stroke him, his tiny bird-like body becomes as stiff as a board, his eyes freeze in whatever direction they are looking, too terrified to look at me. I sense him silently counting himself down through the uncomfortableness, the foreignness, the unpleasantness, the pain of my touch. I whisper in his ear, *I understand, Pup, I'm like you, I'm in the mountains avoiding the very same touch. I'm a stray, Pup, an old stray.*

Like Pup, I don't trust touch; I think that touch will always insist on prising me apart to search my insides. To finger my innards stuffed, like a turkey, with historical pain. I haven't retained any pleasant somatic memories of touch, though there must have been some.

Like Pup, when touched I feel like an empty rattling shell. Echoey.

Now that I've aged, my age creates actual distance between me and touch.

Far fewer people want to touch a body in its late fifties, whatever the anti-ageing ads proclaim with faded jeans, oversized white shirts and French-grey cashmere sweaters. I suspect even those Hollywood actresses, shoehorned by economic need into Canute-esque thirty-second slots about crow's feet and cellulite, get kissed far less. The anti-ageing industry is so facile, so terrifyingly dumb it beggars belief that we ever actually made it to the moon.

I like ageing, it keeps the world at bay.

Between me and Penge Railway Station are seven mountain ranges, including the Pyrenees, and over two thousand kilometres of differing terrain. That's how incapable of being touched I feel. I put continents between me and it.

One of the last times I had sex, it was with an adorable ~n in America who will remain nameless, a man who gave ⸀ of keys to his house and asked me to marry him. But during sex, when his skin touched mine, my skin burned. The physicality of sex, of touch, was so fraught with spiky, scaly emotions by that point that my body recoiled from contact, writhing in pain like a snake trapped by the burning sun on a tarmacked road. I see snakes like that here on the single road up into the mountains, their bodies writhing upwards away from the only surface that could propel them forwards to safety. They die, overheating, because of touch.

So deeply fucked up by my past was I that as he moved his beautiful body on top of mine, I slunk inside my mouth, down behind my tongue and waited for sex with my American man to finish. My body lifeless until he came, his droplets of spunk hit my skin like bullets.

After he came, I wriggled out of my mouth and back into my body again.

I was literally the worst fuck in the world. My mum's friend once told me she hated sex so much that whenever she did it, she acted like a dying sparrow, lying on her back, flapping her wings wildly until he'd finished.

I didn't even do that, I didn't even flap my wings, I just lay completely still, like Pup freezing when I try to pick him up. My only movements unnoticeable, imperceptible. When his spunk hit my skin, a millimetre of me would pull away, recoil as if disgusted, revolted, but I wasn't, not by him. I desperately wanted to be able to love him. To be in love, to wrap my legs and arms around him.

Crying afterwards, I tried to explain away my lifeless-ness. 'Your spunk felt like a hail of bullets,' I said to him, 'it's not you, you touched me lovingly, I could see it in your eyes, deep down, hidden behind my tongue, I could see your love.' I sounded like I was deranged. I tried to explain climbing inside of my body whenever I felt that touch was dangerous.

He said he was sorry that I was so damaged. I said I should go.

And I did, I left, and left the keys and the dream of my American man on the top of his marble kitchen counter. A countertop we'd chosen together.

I understand Pup more than I understand any living creature – human or dog.

Like mine, his skin, his surface, responds automatically and historically to the present. It recoils, reactions instantaneous. Memories inhabiting each and every cell.

I whisper in Pup's ear, *I'm not offended that you stiffen when I pick you up, I'll just hold you loosely and let you know that I'm here*. I think that's OK. I wish the American man had tried to encircle me in a way that allowed me to stay but also to know that I could escape.

I'm beyond touch but I dream incessantly about being touched, about being held. I dream of romantic things, of dumb romantic things and nuanced romantic things. I dream of someone catching me when I fall. I dream of shoulders that cradle my head. My skull.

A few years ago, I wrote an article about relationships and dating, the last line was, 'I'll always believe in love'.

It wasn't a lie, I will.

# Three

# Stuck Between Two Pandemics

This cold morning in January 2021, I was rudely awakened by a head-thumping text from the United Kingdom Government which told me that as I was *clinically extremely vulnerable*, I should shield from COVID-19 and not leave the house unless it was absolutely necessary. Not for anything or anyone, nor anywhere.

*Leave the house to go where?* I thought. I live in the middle of nowhere, I sought out this nowhere place as my place to live.

There's nowhere to go and I've gone everywhere that you could possibly go in this nowhere place of mine. My place, this place is like a beautiful but empty mind. At least it was before this past year. It was beautifully inert, but now I'm struggling to see the beauty.

Seeing the words 'clinically extremely vulnerable' made me freak out, silently freak out.

If you'd seen me looking at the text you might have only detected a tightening around my eyes and the corners of my mouth. I do that, my mouth tends to tighten like a cat's arse when I'm stressed. I've developed cat's-arse lines around my mouth as I've aged.

But that tightening would be the only reaction you'd see: nothing more, nothing dramatic.

My reaction to fear is part of my anatomy now, built in like a valve that pulls something scary or fearful deep inside. *Suck it in, Juno, swallow it down, hide your fears.* When no one's looking, open the valve, release the fear, spit it out, then close it again.

I realised long ago that there's no point in sharing fear or letting it show, it only makes you more scared. Occasionally I post something online about being HIV positive and people send me meaningful and earnest private messages telling me that they are here for me. I think, *that's nice but you're a complete stranger and I don't think I asked for support.*

It bothers me that people see me as needy.

I think that the fear I think I'm hiding must show through the written word, even in a throwaway tweet. A tweet becoming a cry for help. Maybe they are.

Even if I think I hide it, it must spill out. I must bleed out which is strange because I've spent the last thirty-or-so years trying to keep my viral blood and my dysfunctional feelings in.

Sometimes I wonder if I've been wallowing in the clinically vulnerable or taken refuge in the sadness of vulnerability because in truth I want to be hugged. Maybe when complete strangers tell me they have my back, they're trying to hug me and I freeze up. If I have wallowed, I don't think it's an active choice, which is another way of saying that on some level I'm too fucked up not to wallow.

Which is worse than just occasionally slipping in to wallowing because perhaps now it's my resting space, to reside in sadness. Wanting to be hugged but incapable of being hugged. Such a pointless dilemma I surely should have solved years ago in therapy. But I couldn't because even then I couldn't say I want to be held, intimately and safely held. Hugged. I've always pretended to be good at oneness, at aloneness.

Staring at the official text message, I couldn't decide whether to jump out of bed and try to exercise the vulnerable away; exercise equalling strength, strength equalling robustness, robustness equalling being alive and therefore the very opposite of vulnerable.

*Exercise?*

Or pull the covers up over my head, reach my hand down, insert my fingers into my stitched, finite cavern and try to wank the vulnerable away. Wanking in this pandemic, this airborne pandemic, feels like far too much effort. I can count on one hand, with the same few fingering fingers, how often I've tried to engage with sexual self-pleasure during this time. Spittle on fingers drying before the fingering begins.

I'm wallowing in gloomy viral familiarity and that's not a sexy or an erotic, wanking state of mind. But I'm needy.

I've always needed a hug, a hug not a kiss, not my fingers doused in spittle trying to cheer up my once-was-a-cock now reshaped into a clitoris. I just end up feeling after sex before sex, beyond sex before sex, like sex is already over for me, historical and dry. I'm dried out by this bonding new virus of ours. It is all of ours, not like AIDS or HIV which was so easily partitioned off from society by old white men in ill-fitting political suits. This pandemic coats us all.

Feeling beyond self-pleasure is clearly not helpful in the grand scheme of pandemics, I need to feel positive. But this feeling hums deep in me, it's familiar. I felt like this after AIDS in the late nineties and the early two thousands – unsexy, undesirable, too aware of the implications of my bodily fluids. I felt after pleasure, beyond pleasure. The day after pleasure had stopped.

Pleasure for me, done and dusted. But pandemics seem to recur.

Early mornings in the mountains are freezing at this time of the year as the January sun climbs slowly, sluggishly yawning its way up into an expectant sky. Like a lazy lover who takes a lifetime to get hard, an *I'm cold now, forget it, don't bother* waving in my face.

I don't wake up like I used to when I first arrived here in these Andalusian mountains, a fresh-faced, fifty-year-old explorer. I'm getting slovenlier as I age, I can cope with that, as I think I can cope without fingers exploring my cave. She's packed up for the season and gone off to somewhere without the pandemic; *good luck with that*, I whisper to her, *I think you'll find it's everywhere.*

It's the second time they've told me that I'm clinically extremely vulnerable; the first text, sent back in March 2020, bleakly stated that if I contracted COVID-19 I would likely become extremely ill and that I was at far greater risk of death. *Cheery bleeders*, I thought, *don't they know that I'm living my nuanced, working-class dream in these Andalusian mountains?* No one could be further from vulnerable. I'm here striking out as a lonesome prospector looking for love, intimacy and a family to call my own, and maybe a gold chain or two.

Send me flowers or a card that says, 'well done, you working-class queer, you made it all the way to the sunny uplands and out from our grasp'. Not an un-sex-text telling me that I'm likely to die because of a pandemic that's currently raging across the globe. Timing, people, timing. Turn me on, make me wet. If you're going to send unsolicited texts at least do the do.

'I fucking get it,' I say to myself aloud and slide the phone back onto the cold marble surface of my bedside table. I let my hand linger on the cold surface, I love the cold defiance of marble; it grounds me, especially in the wicked heat of summer.

I've lived with a virus, HIV, for most of my adult life. *I get it*.

I roll back under the covers, shielding my neck from the cold, shielding my body from the encroaching virus and my mind from unwanted governmental text-attacks. I feel peppered from all sides.

Around my fifties village, the number of cases is rising. For a time, it felt like the pandemic was being restrained, leashed over the other side of the mountains, but now it's slipped into the valley like a trickling glacial overrun, and into all of the toytown whitewashed villages around.

Mine is a minuscule toytown whitewashed village. It's a dot on the map that I've ended up living in. Even when my village is enlarged a hundred times onscreen it's still a dot, like the tiniest of ants, the kind which gather in my courtyard in great Romanic lines, ferrying the dead and the dying over their bodies, passing them back to their nests. It takes hundreds of them to dissect a wasp fallen in battle. That's the village I live in, a dot full of ants who clear up.

It's bizarre that I'm here, even in my life's bizarreness it ranks as being pretty strange.

COVID-19 has slipped into our village like a silent assassin. Like AIDS slipped into the saunas, bathhouses and consciousnesses in the early eighties. Silent, unannounced, prowling, hunting, stealing.

GRID, CAID, HTLV-III, AIDS, HIV, like COVID-19, were all utterly meaningless until they became meaningful.

This virus is deadly to many of the older people who linger lovingly in these villages. Occupants of a bygone age. Them and me, I moved into this village to squat in others' bygone ages.

According to the government, my HIV makes me high risk to COVID-19, one virus providing a leg up to the other. If both viruses blended inside me would they become a new thing, a marrying of viral particles with different interlocking arms and spikes. *HIV, meet COVID-19, they're new around town, quite dashing, perhaps a little overbearing, they'll take your breath away.* Too soon?

I snake out a hand from beneath the snowy accumulation of duvets and blankets that have gathered since the sun got lazy, and flick on the electric blanket, my trusty new lover. I'm hidden from everything if I stay like this. Safe, shielded, warm and alive.

I listen to the sound of my breathing; at best it's controlled and mediated panic. Managed.

I once went to the London Buddhist Centre to try and get better at breathing, but I ended up holding my breath because to breathe in silence felt too loud. I felt noticed, 'seen' is the word people use. I felt seen. Meditation only made me dizzy.

The dogs are curled up on the end of the bed waiting for me to get up and hit the mountain trails, but they know from experience and sheer canine grumpiness that the heat from the electric blanket means that they should settle down. That there's no point in trying to bully me to get up. The heat from the electric blanket eventually has a stupefying effect on us all. I curl up into a foetal ball; I must be scared, quite frankly I don't want to go back into any previous womb. The foetal ball is about me and the world.

I don't want the texts; I don't want to be this person. I want to be other than me. Other than vulnerable. I've spent my whole life running away from feeling vulnerable, always blindly and stupidly charging towards greater vulnerability.

Are these mountains my saviour, the womb, or the ending?

I was born into a house in which children were completely vulnerable because they weren't the issue, or the focus or even the reason for the apparent familial gathering. The children, we, weren't the reason for anything.

We were a by-product.

Other things were at play when we happened, historical and contemporary dysfunctions and violence, and a myriad of addictions and emotional contradictions. Class contradictions, people running from class. These things created us: don't talk like that, talk like this; don't stand like that, stand like this; don't talk like a girl, talk like this. The list endlessly shuffled us to and fro with gradations of swinging violence. The siblings, us, now live separately from each other in every way possible. Like distant stars in the night sky, we'll evaporate before we collide. I miss the idea of them; once I dreamt we might become a constellation.

The bed warms up, the drowsy legacy from the sleeping pill I'd taken the night before gently unfurls any lingering tensions from the governmental text, I uncurl my foetal tension. My feet try to stretch out, they push at the dogs, but they are immovable. The three of them collected, waifs and strays, curled on the end of the bed like the curled sleeping infants in Titian's *The Three Ages of Man*. They form a gently breathing mountain.

They cluster for warmth, the occasional grumble of a single canine dream making their whole form move as one, gently stirring in our collective utopia. It looks like a utopia. I'm good at that, my Andalusian Arcadia, my sanctuary. The place of pomegranate and fig trees.

I hate feeling vulnerable, and this pandemic has pushed me to the edges of the reservoir that allows me to live here. It's not easy living alone in the mountains even if it was easy to move here. Viral fear, pandemic fear, COVID-19 fear, AIDS fear have all made me childlike again. Not very grown-up at all. Do I need to be a child here or a grown-up?

Under the heavy blankets I fantasise about letting go of life. I'm not the suicidal type so letting go of life isn't a straightforward thing, but I am very tired of working at life. Is that a terrible thing to say?

I once read a book, I think it was fiction, about a woman who went to bed for a year. I think that's what I'll do, but I'm so uptight that I know that my hiding under the blankets will last only minutes before I force myself up. The internal chart of long-held domestic anxieties forcing my day to roll on forwards. Cleaning, dog walking, eating, dieting, writing words, deleting words, questioning whether or not I have the right to use long words and wondering if that's a question everyone has, hoovering, dusting, trying to relax, trying to write. Not relaxing, writing/not writing, taking paracetamol to deal with the headache from not relaxing. Feeling robotic, but that's no bad thing, it's kept one foot in front of the other all these years.

A lot of my life has felt painful but never painful enough to stop feeling the warmth of the sun on my face or the warmth from the electric blanket under my body. I still desire warmth, therefore life. The only part of death that truly scares me is the language of coldness, of a freezing body, an icy body which slows and disintegrates because it can no longer create warmth. Despite my wallowing and nightly pill popping, I must be optimistic. An optimist who fundamentally believes that it's better to be warm than cold. Is that not the absolute definition of being alive?

Soon I will get up to walk the dogs in the idyllic landscape that surrounds me. That's an optimistic gesture. To walk up into the mountains rather than stay under the covers. No one sees me so it wouldn't matter. I could post a photograph on Instagram from last year – who'd know, who's really looking?

I will get up and put one foot in front of the other and march up the mountain path, the dogs pulling me in three different directions – I never trained them because there's no one here to berate me for their thuggish behaviour. Only me and them, and I'm sure they know that they outnumber me, that our ratio of one fucked-up human to three reasonably happy dogs means that they're in charge. I don't mind, control is not something I've ever felt like owning. I'm shit with control, bad shit happens when I have control, people get hurt and I end up in bad places. I'm no team leader.

But I feel safe under the blankets, securely pinned down by the weight of the dogs, pressing my legs and feet flat to the mattress. I'm hiding from a virus in my bed, in a house in a country I'd never seen until I moved here. I didn't even know Andalusia existed, let alone this village in these mountains. This speck I inhabit.

It's a fucking mystery how all this happened. Like so much about anything in life, until it's here it's nowhere to be seen. COVID-19 would have been as meaningless in October 2019 as AIDS was to us in 1978 or 1980 even. I didn't even know when I was a kid that new diseases could rise up like an army and kill, almost at will. I'm a child of the post-illness era, post smallpox. A child raised on antibiotics and strong narratives of curative medicine. Of General Practitioners who knew everything that there was to know. I trusted life until I didn't trust life.

Until a GP told me I'd regret the risks I'd taken. That lodged in my throat.

I first heard the words 'gay cancer' in September 1983. I was lying on a single rickety bed in a boarding house in South Wales. Newport to be exact. The docks area of Newport to be even more exact. Rough as fuck, momentarily I felt at home and then realised it wasn't London and in 1983 London was the only place I wanted to be. My relationship with that place in Wales lasted only a few short months. But we are forever joined, me and that boarding room, by the words 'gay cancer'.

I was half-asleep, watching the news on a small black-and-white television set which sat on a stained, lace antimacassar. Aren't all antimacassars stained, isn't their sole purpose to capture and hold stains, Brylcreem from men's slicked back hair, pretty things made to be ruined? The history of gender as written by old white geezers summed up in a six-inch oval lace antimacassar.

The television was on a small bedside table which was next to an unmatched small walnut wardrobe. The furniture was possibly post war, but only just. It was a doll's house bedroom, just so, one piece of everything. A small wardrobe, a bedside cabinet with one drawer and a small cupboard. One round, hand-knotted, scuffed rag rug by the bed, a small single bed with one pillow. A single china ornament on the windowsill, a grey kitten sitting on its haunches wiping a tear away from its eye. On its head a sailor's cap. A sad sailor kitten heralding the age of AIDS.

It was a typical boarding house, the type that hadn't changed much since the fifties or sixties.

The landlady was in her eighties, *eighty-one*, she'd say, *you'd never believe it, would you?*

She'd leave the words 'believe it', hanging in the air expectantly, at one point in her life she must have got the response she needed. I know that line.

I know that line because sometimes when people ask me my age, I say, *fifty-seven, you'd never believe it, would you?* That line. *In the age of Botulinum Toxin type A, Juno, yes we would. You, frankly, look your age, which is something we don't do in 2021.*

The reporter said, 'A few homosexuals are in different hospitals dying from a cancer called Kaposi's sarcoma.' Cut away from the reporter to a crinkly black-and-white film of gay men walking arm in arm in New York and then to gay men dancing in a nightclub. More voiceover, 'these men's lifestyles seem to be putting them more at risk from this deadly cancer than anyone else in the community.' It was a revelation for me to see men proudly walking arm in arm, but the reporter was saying that these kind of arm-in-arm men were getting this cancer. Their lifestyle put forward as the cause.

Gayness, queerness, poofness, sissiness cause death.

In 1983 in that boarding house room, I pulled the single candlewick bedspread up and over my head, I felt sick. Somehow I knew, years before it would ever happen, I knew that it would happen. I'd been sucking men's dicks in public toilets since I was in my early teens. I wasn't exactly arm in arm, but I knew.

I knew that the lifestyle he was talking about, the one that attracted this gay cancer, seemingly magnetically, was akin to the lifestyle I was leading. He was talking about men having lots of sex with different men in bathhouses and I was sucking lots of strangers' cocks in public toilets. There was no difference in my naive mind. I would get the disease, it felt fated.

I did.

The government telling me in 2020 that I was extremely vulnerable wasn't news, just an affirmation of all that I'd ever felt. That's why I'd run my whole life from everything, from everywhere and from everyone. But mostly I'd run from myself because I blamed myself for all that had ever happened. Kids from difficult backgrounds do that, they internalise and blame themselves for everything that's happened and everything that hasn't happened because of everything that has happened. Who else are you going to blame, the only people you can call family, the ones you love?

I run from everything.

I ran and ended up here. Here is nowhere, but to a small group of people, the villagers, it's the only place that there's ever been. To me it was getting lost and hoping to be found. I arrived with the imprint of an adopt-me badge resplendent on my lapel.

Seven years ago, on my birthday, I travelled to this house in this village surrounded by these mountains. I ran from London to isolation. Maybe I was already isolated in London. Isolated but surrounded on all sides. I felt embarrassed about being alone in a city full of people, being alone in a city somehow highlighted my aloneness, although looking back no one was looking, no one saw or documented my aloneness, only me.

But I yearned for space and to feel lost, or at least to start again, to become a different version of me. New.

I left London before Brexit was a thing and before COVID-19 was a thing. I left thinking that the door to England was still open. I think I thought that I could go back if I wanted or needed to. Spain didn't instantly feel like home, it felt like being in a movie. My HIV care is in London, so I needed an open door, or at least a revolving door that didn't need constant greasing or cajoling. Brexit is that stupid greasing and cajoling.

I ran here trying to escape everything that I knew. The family dramas that never stop, factional infighting that barely lessens and the suffocating claustrophobic feeling that I'd never get away or be more than this. Not them, I wasn't judging them, but me. I was unhappy being me because I felt that I could be something else.

As random as it was, and as romantic and brave as people tell me it seems, it was really quite easy to up and move to the other side of Europe. As the crow flies, I'm closer here to North Africa than I am to Madrid. There are mountains all around me, I'm cupped by them. It might have taken someone else months or years to find or reject this house, but I told my mum, I'm going to buy a house here in the next two days and I did. I'm like that, for good or bad.

The simple facts about buying my house: I had a house in London bought through a key-worker scheme when I was a teacher. I became a teacher when I was running away from being a drug addict, a sex worker and working in the shadier parts of porn. Becoming a teacher rather than a drug addict who sold sex was a good move. At the time it seemed absurd but it worked. A classroom fixed my addictions and I adored teaching. A classroom to a working-class kid is the pinnacle of achievement. It was my moon landing.

So, the key-worker scheme, called Open Market HomeBuy, was brilliant because it gave key workers autonomy over where they lived. The scheme treated you like an adult, allowing you to pick a home that might have loomed large in your dreams. An old Victorian terrace or a new square-roomed starter with a postage-stamp slabbed garden. Each to their own; I'd spent a lifetime as a matchgirl, so big Victorian houses with shuttered windows were what I hankered after. *Please, sir, can I have a bigger window?*

The year after I used the scheme and bought my perfect Victorian house on the edge of Penge, the government scrapped it and replaced it with the ridiculous, punitive ball-and-chain scheme of new-build, part-buy which essentially meant that you had to live where the town planners had decided key workers should live. And you didn't own your home. Areas like Croydon, which apparently needed to be smartened up, gentrified, were packed full of cheaply thrown-up housing developments.

Small primary-colour-clad blocks of one- and two-bedroom key-worker flats around a smidgen of designed greenery. At first on this scheme, you could only own 25 per cent of your property. You'd have to pay rent and a mortgage, the total often much higher than a mortgage alone. The places were impossible to sell; who's going to buy 25 per cent of a flat, so it was a governmental way of repopulating areas with supposed professionals. Luckily for ex-addict me, I had my dad's sense of timing and chutzpah and avoided all of that regularity and conformity. I sneaked in under the fence.

If I'd applied a year later, I could never have been here in this vast landscape and expansive history. I'd be depressed, possibly an active drug user, planning shoddy lessons in a primary-clad box in Croydon.

My timing has always been lucky. I've always known when to arrive and when to leave.

I bought the upper floor of a big detached Victorian house

and owned all of it; when I sold it, every last penny of the profit was mine.

When I came to Spain for a week's holiday with my mum, not looking for a house but with money in the bank, deciding to buy a house was the easy bit. They were all beautiful and all the price of a garage-lockup in Penge. My last London abode was near to Penge. I like Penge. It's a great word, Penge.

I bought the house here outright because I sold a flat a London.

I did nothing remarkable, romantic, or brave, I just benefited from capitalism and that's a fact. I benefited from capitalism, made some money, so it could happen. Money gives you choices. Choices give you freedom and freedom gives you space inside your mind and inside your dreams to be fucked up, but also real space, actual space in the world that you can call your own to repair yourself in. I'm ensconced in three-foot-thick adobe walls, repairing myself. And sometimes also the bloody walls.

Money gives you security. You don't have to run any more. If we really wanted to improve the world, we would make all houses as cheap and accessible as they are here.

Owning this house allowed me to stop still.

I own every last speck of mud and brick and stone and pebble that my adobe house is made out of. When I think of it in mud terms, it was actually quite expensive, like buying a sandcastle a little way up from the sea. It's a constant battle to stop my house from returning to the soil, subterranean termites weave up through the adobe walls, ever weakening the structure. It is a mud house with art on the walls. But a mud house nonetheless. I like that, the earth owns it really, not me.

I'd never been to Spain before I bought a house here and had never had a desire to visit. I didn't therefore speak a single word of Spanish. I'd only ever been a tube ride away from the queer hub of Soho, which is also the square mile that contains my HIV care, for most of my life. There was nothing planned about this move, no preparation. No eating or praying.

But like Elizabeth Gilbert, I'd always been looking for love.

I was in Spain with my mum, who loved Spain because Spain. The Costas are one of the epicentres of working-class aspiration. A holiday villa, a timeshare, a communal pool next to an apartment, paella made with chicken and cheap sangria. That Spain is the antithesis of all that I needed, but it was all I knew about Spain. That and bullfighting, and even though I adore the lines on the Picasso lithographs, I hate the murderous sport. But I love Mum.

I woke up on the first morning of our week away, looked out of the apartment window and saw mountains and a person walking up into the mountains with a dog. It was 16 January and it was sunny and warm. The sky intensely and cleanly blue. I immediately told Mum, *I'm moving here; we've got two days for me to buy a house.*

Spain wasn't an active choice based on any lived experience beyond that morning, that morning was my Spain, a single glance. I knew I had to walk up into the mountains. This was the space I needed to run to. I'd never seen such huge skies, they made me and everything feel so small and easy. My past a speck. An ant.

I'm obsessed with Georgia O'Keeffe and her house in the desert, Ghost Ranch. Or rather I'm obsessed with films about her and her life in the desert because I don't know her or her house; she could have been a complete fucker for all I know. The film about the life of O'Keeffe, *By Myself*, is beautiful. Deluded me saw smatterings of myself in it. In her. I too can be a completely awkward cunt who's better away from people, a home in the mountains seemed perfect.

Her life and house are beautifully curated, pared back, monastic, contemplative. Silent. Painted still. For someone who grew up surrounded by angry, violent noise it seemed like the only kind of place in the world where I could be silent. Andalusia looks like New Mexico, so much so that many Westerns (and *Star Wars*) were filmed here because it's a cheaper location than America. It's a facsimile.

That morning, looking out at the person walking their dog up into the mountains, I thought I could be Georgia O'Keeffe, and within two days of looking I'd found a house that looked a little like Ghost Ranch. A little. My version of Ghost Ranch.

The second year I was here a heavy rainstorm washed away great swathes of soil alongside the mountain trail revealing a horse's skeleton. Both parts of the skull now hang in my courtyard in homage to Georgia. I took it as a sign that I was Georgia O'Keeffe reborn. I tried to paint and realised I was just deluded.

I've always had the capacity for great delusion. Thus Juno O'Keeffe, alongside many other aliases. This makes me laugh so I don't care about the instability of my delusions.

Being deeply delusional quite brilliantly means that I don't really perceive boundaries. I didn't think deeply or critically about moving here, I've thought more about buying a brand of jeans. Especially the jeans that include the word 'mum' in their marketing pitch. High-waisted mum jeans that frankly only look good on daughters.

My delusional side is a bit hit and miss though, which makes sense with delusion.

Sometimes I've ended up sucking old cock for a tenner and sometimes I've found a home that reminds me of Ghost Ranch. God love me, in for a penny in for a pound.

Over the years I've honed that skill to suck far less cock and to be more attuned to finding the sanctuary I need for me to exist within. Actually, since sucking cock for money I'm far less interested in cis cocks full stop. I lost the taste. Quite literally, the thought of sucking a cis cock makes me gag now. Cut or uncut, I don't care. Perfect or imperfect, I don't care. Big, thick, fat or small, I don't care. Finally, I developed a gag reflex when the world no longer cares if I gag, spit or swallow. It's the way of life. I often think that a successful life is one in which the protagonist feels able to claim their space without feeling a whole raft of conjoined emotions linked to other people's expectations, demands or wishes.

I come from a tough family with a deeply dysfunctional core, a family who I've been running from my whole life. Their dysfunction and mine – I am them and they are me – had me running into the arms of education, books, men, drugs, addiction, sex, teaching, and maybe lastly, here into the mountains, into a facsimile of a life as Georgia O'Keeffe. Or Julia Roberts in *Eat, Pray, Love* or Carrie Bradshaw, the fictional yet ever-so-real writer. Those three characters blended together, smoothed, define this moment and the possibility of this moment, deluding myself that I could be them carried me across borders that others might perceive as difficult or impossible. I didn't even consider the move as anything but normal. When I left my mum's house to move to Spain, I got in a taxi and said, *I'll call you later.*

I ran away and put thousands of miles and row after row of mountain ranges between me and my past. There was even a different language. Spanish. One I didn't speak a single word of. Not a single word ... *Hola?*

Over the past few years, as my family has aged, our dysfunctions have partially morphed into ill health which has felt and become overwhelming. The dysfunctions haven't disappeared, but they are often masked now by the emergence of ill health. My HIV has felt strangely manageable in comparison to the litany of serious conditions, illnesses and struggles they are experiencing, most of their lives being rounded off with bouts of poor physical and mental health. My mental health has always been poor and difficult, I've grown used to it. It's always been it and me.

So, I had money and delusion, and reasons to want to get away. I needed to get away from the truth of my family, from my roots. To start again, to reinvent, to renew. Or just to die in peace.

I was running away from the realities of the lives around me that stifled and depressed me. That constantly reminded me of who I was and who I could never be. I wanted to write with the ease of Carrie Bradshaw, who I'd first seen on the television while smoking crack in a dingy flat in east London, sitting on a sofa, the heart of which had long since gone. A sofa without stuffing is like a corpse. I sat on a corpse, smoked a rock, and saw Carrie zing in the window of a Brownstone.

I was running away from events in my past that had become like hills I had to climb every day in order to feel good enough to have the right to suck in oxygen. To breathe.

The time before my dad left, the time after he left that we thought would be calmer, the time before drug addiction and cock sucking for drug money, and the time, the beautiful time after I discovered philosophy. In the spaces between the climbs, I knew I was searching for something called love. I've always believed in love like a child believes in fairies at the bottom of a garden.

When I came here, I was running from somewhere, from some pandemics, AIDS, violence, a lack of love or under-standing about love. I had no idea that I was running towards new pandemics. That's the thing about pandemics, they happen to you, not you to them.

# Four

## (M)others

*A love letter is an expression of love in written form. However delivered, the letter may be anything from a short and simple message of love to a lengthy explanation and description of feelings.* Wikipedia

The text from the government about my vulnerability was the second text I had received from them this past year. Before then, they'd ignored me like an errant unwanted lover, not even noticing when I left the country. Like I'd never existed. All those years I waited and wanted them to hold me tenderly in their capitalist claws but no, nothing, nada. Only the taxi driver to Gatwick asked me where I was going. *Spain*, I said, *for how long*, he asked, *for ever*, I replied.

But now a blizzard of texts. Well, two, which after years of nothing feels like a blizzard.

Loving, caring letters in text form, signed 'Matt', from a man who obviously cared enough about me to be intimate and drop formalities. I wondered, *was he a trick I turned in the old days, was he a twenty-quid blow job?*

Two loving texts from Matt which seemed to want to protect me at all costs from dying, which is weird because in most of my thirty-odd years of living with HIV they didn't seem to give a fuck. I think to myself that I'll compose a short reply – *Dear Matt (and Boris), you can't even keep yourselves safe. Bugger off. Juno.* I didn't send it, it would be a waste of money and besides, because of Brexit, transoceanic texting is so slow now that they probably wouldn't get it until they are sleeping in the back row of the House of Lords. Boris with an even scruffier performance of hair. A wayward straggle which clearly defines privilege. Someone should write an essay about privilege and scruffy hair.

When I got the first text telling me I was clinically extremely vulnerable my mum was here, trapped for months in the mountains with me. The day after Mum flew back with me for a visit in early March, the country went into complete lockdown and all flights stopped. It was 16 March 2020. It was the strangest feeling to know that great swathes of the world had come to rest. Birds chirped loudly, lizards sang, rabbits hopped ... Mum despaired.

Bless her, after a week or so she was so fed up. She's a Londoner at heart, and although now she lives just to the west of the city, she's still surrounded by friends and life and noise.

Being trapped in the mountains with her spiky, complex, gender-everywhere child isn't easy for her, although she'd never admit it.

The first text made me so angry because it made me feel fragile.

I showed Mum the text and said, *who the fuck do they think they are, telling me I'm vulnerable, that I'm more at risk than anyone else, who the fuck? How dare they, Mum, how fucking dare they? I've done nothing but work hard to keep myself alive and invulnerable for thirty or so years, who the fuck do they think they are?* So many fucks were spat out even she couldn't keep up, and she's the queen of fucks. The word cunt has always loomed large around our tables; I try my best now not to let so many expletives roll off my tongue but it's genuinely a part of me.

The anger in me welled up like the great wave off Kanagawa. Momentarily it consumed me lock, stock and barrel. I can't capture that moment in vague description, although it was slightly akin to the very first moment of knowing that I had AIDS. A paralysing fear, not of death, but of vulnerability. Of being told that I was fragile, that a new fragility had to reside atop the layers of old fragilities. I felt my insides fluttering, my pulse, my heartbeat, it felt like they were rushing towards something, somewhere. A panic attack.

*Who can I call, Mum, to get my name taken off this list, who can I call?*

I can't stand pity or people thinking I need additional support – in many ways I've been able to kid myself that I've thrived with HIV because I largely ignore the virus inside of me, pretending it doesn't exist. I avoid almost all intimate contact with humans – thus my remote mountain home. My silent sanctuary.

I've largely ignored the very thing that's given me strength and succour, the portal to understanding the flimsiness of life. The understanding I garnered from an AIDS diagnosis enabled me always to know that I'd die. But I've largely ignored it. Some people marry the two together and become

AIDS activists or work in the fields around AIDS and HIV. I've simply plundered the AIDS orchard for all its worth yet ignored it. By ignore it I think I mean that I've lived a stigmatised life, full of self-stigma I'm ashamed to admit.

I looked over at Mum; we were sat outside in the warmth of spring, fortuitously she'd dozed off, saving herself from any more of my effing tirade. I sometimes forget that she's lived with the prospect of my dying for as many years as I've tried to ignore it. She couldn't ignore it, the thought of me dying before her has been ever-present since my diagnosis. I wonder what that's stolen from her.

She looks beautiful asleep, not that she doesn't awake, but asleep it's as if all of her troubles have floated away, vanished, and instead of being a tough, hard woman who's had an incredibly tough life with kids who bounced squarely from one drama to another, from one disaster to another, from one fight to the next, she seems serene and peaceful. Awake, she's never been serene. Always ready to fight, to protect, to lash out. Even in her eighties.

She may not have had the skills to parent brilliantly, but she's always loved us like a lioness, a child-like lioness. Brimming with love and utterly protective.

It must be impossibly hard to have children that you know you haven't done right by because you didn't know or have any different way to raise or parent them. But by not doing right by them, as you grow older you have to watch your whole brood making predictable mistake after predictable mistake. That's got to be tough. I escaped the repetition as my being a mother is as much a fantasy as my being Georgia O'Keeffe.

I looked at her sleeping in the sun, her head tilted back,

small snoring noises emerging, whispering out between thin lips, and flying up and away like bluebottles towards the sun. Her face is lined from years of smoking and sitting in every ray of sun that she could possibly suck up.

If there was no sun, then a sunbed would always do. Sometimes I think she likes sunbeds more than the sun. In her eighties she still has tanning sessions. I picture her settling down on a sunbed and puffing away on a fag before indoor smoking was banned.

She's such a woman. She has such forceful beauty.

A beauty that is so present when she's at ease and asleep.

She's always been present for us, she knows she had a hand in us becoming us, but she has never shirked her responsibility of trying to patch us up, again and again and again. Like a cornerman in a boxing ring.

Rehab after rehab, divorce after divorce, police cell after police cell, fight after fight. Always there, taking our side irrespective (often wrongly) of whatever the situation really was.

Even though the sun's rays were splayed across her, I worried that she might get nippy, she does now, she feels the cold. I went in to get her a blanket, put it across her lap and took the cigarette from between her fingers, dropping it in the ashtray bought specifically for her. The ash of her fag had burnt down into a splendidly long tower; it looked like Pisa leaning on the edge of the ceramic rim.

Even though she's dozing I still register my disgust at her smoking with a shake of my head and a look that she'd pay no attention to if she were awake. When I used to tell her to stop, she'd say, *not today, I'm too depressed, I've got too much shit going on to stop, the cigs help me to cope.* And possibly they did.

I don't even try to get her to stop any more, a fag is her comfort and joy. She told me the other day that if she got ill with COVID-19 she didn't want to go into hospital onto a ventilator. She said that she couldn't stand it. Looking at her I feel tears gathering. The thought of her, my most useless but wonderful of all mothers, not being here makes me cry. Like proper tears. I never cry, not because there's anything wrong with crying, but what's the point crying about things? I learnt that many years ago as a kid.

But the thought of losing my mum accesses the very deepest emotional parts of me that I cannot control. I adore my mum.

I sat on a chair next to her and watched her and wondered how different her life might have been if she hadn't had the childhood she'd had. Her childhood passed on from her mother's own messy childhood which was passed on to her from hers. Like a hand-me-down trench coat that might come into fashion in one generation out of four. A Burberry mac with grubby collar and cuffs. Tattier in each hand-me-down.

My mum was the youngest of three children, by at least ten years. Her sister, who died this year, was twenty years older than her. Her dearly departed brother was ten years older.

Gertie, my mum's mum, was a worker, a relentless worker, like an ant in my courtyard, born into a poor south London family. My mum's grandad, my maternal great-grandfather, was a blind beggar who played the accordion for pennies on Rye Lane. On census after census, he's listed as Joseph Reeves, a blind beggar, or a blind street musician on Rye Lane, just up the road from where his children went to school and where they lived.

Seeing him beg did something to Gertie, his very being made her want to run the fuck away, not from him, she loved him, but from poverty. Away from ever being that poor. She loved her dad, and when he was widowed he came to live with Gertie in a house that was bought, not rented. The only time he lived in a house that wasn't rented. His wife, Alice, had died many years before, and she was also blind from birth. What struggles they must have had raising a large family on the takings of his busking.

Married and widowed twice, my grandmother Gertie inherited a shop on Lordship Lane from a man who might have been a lover. She worked night and day, bought houses, drove cars, and palmed my mum off with a succession of carers and babysitters as soon as she was born. She thought was doing the best job possible by providing for her family. My mum had new dresses, a nice house, a Morrison table, not an outdoor shelter, which her mum said would ruin the garden, 'ruin her Salvias'. Gertie loved bright red Salvias. My mum hates red flowers with a vengeance. My grandmother was never really a mother, but in her eyes she was working relentlessly to be the best mother she could be, working to provide all the things that she never had. No childhood friend of her daughter would see her begging, no way, she worked and she worked and then she worked some more. Mum said that even when the bombs were dropping that she went to work as normal, marching down Lordship Lane, leaving my mum with a succession of lodgers as babysitters.

Mr M was one of a succession of men who were entrusted to look after my mum. Gertie's lodgers were always men.

He didn't look after her though, he abused her.

'He made me climb under the old Morrison table with him and then he'd push his fingers into my knickers and make me promise not to say anything, else he'd have to leave the house and Mum would be mad at me for causing money worries.'

The fear of poverty digs deep.

He only stopped the abuse because he lost his job at a department store in Paddington and had to return home to Cambridge. He abused Mum for years, becoming so confident in the silencing power of his abuse that he once bought my mum a gossamer, see-through blouse for her birthday. She was eight years old. He gave it direct to Gertie who apparently said nothing, just put it on the table and left for work as usual, like she did every day apart from Sunday when she'd work at home, spreading out her needlework over the Morrison table.

'He also gave me a tennis racquet,' Mum said. 'I thought Mum might think that was strange because I hated sport, but she didn't say anything, she didn't even seem to notice that it was a tennis racquet, like the see-through blouse she just didn't see.'

I was the first person that Mum talked to about the abuse by the lodger and about the abuse by the two grown-up brothers who lived next door who were also charged with looking after her if no one else was around.

'They were both as bad as each other,' Mum said. 'I think one of them had some mental health issues, he didn't really say anything, he just silently copied everything his brother did. By the time I was eleven and going to secondary school, I thought it must be something about me that made men do bad things to me.'

*

Mum wanted out, she wanted to be anywhere but her child-hood home, which was a dangerous place for her. At eleven my mum begged to be sent away – her mum never questioned why – and within a month she was enrolled at a Catholic boarding school on the south coast.

'I went there to get away from them,' she said, 'from the men and their hands.'

Gertie wasn't intentionally a bad mother, but an absent mother, who in the forties and the fifties was trying to provide like a father could. Her own father had shamed her to the core. Not because he, Joseph, was trying to; on the contrary, he was trying to scrape a living together by busking. Both great-grandparents blind, poor and blind, living in a succession of rented rooms, with nine kids to provide for. You do the maths. How many 'Roll Out the Barrel's would it take to feed nine kids?

My mum said that her aunts told her how kids in the street would make up rhymes about her blind beggar grandad. Gertie never saw the harm that came to Mum because she was looking the other way, towards work, towards money, away from poverty, away from the shame of poverty towards material salvation.

She was running away from her own childhood.

Mum was vulnerable and defenceless to abuse because her mother was out there trying to create a better life for her kids. Women's labour is never fully supported and working-class women are always judged harshly. I could demonise my gran, blame her for being a bad mother, but my mum doesn't, telling me that she would have been mortified if she'd known about Mr M and the boys next door. She would have beaten the living daylights out of them. All she wanted was for them to have the things that she never had.

'She didn't know,' Mum says sadly and wistfully.

*But what about the see-through blouse, Mum, didn't she think that was odd?*

'She didn't even have the time to notice, she probably gave it a brief glance, dropped it onto the table and went off to work; it stayed on the table for weeks, eventually being covered with scraps of fabric from her work as a seamstress, his rotten, cheap blouse hidden by yards of heavy expensive curtain fabric. In some way, Mum drowned him out.'

As soon as Mum could, she lashed out at the world by lashing out at herself. Her first boyfriend was aptly called Chopper Green, her next, apparently, was as bad. She told me, 'I was drawn to petty criminals who thought they'd grow up into proper gangsters.' Her mother, who wanted anything but that for her daughter, was horrified by her choices.

But she didn't know that her daughter had endured years of abuse and was now silently lashing out at the world and her mother; she really believed that bad men, boys pretending to be gangsters, might have the strength to protect her from *really* bad men. She was lashing out at Gertie for not being there, but Gertie had no idea she wasn't there, so never realised or understood Mum's intentions. My mum's experience of World War II wasn't with the Germans.

In the late fifties she met my dad, a boy called John or Johnny from the East End who now lived in Tooting, his family shipped out of run-down blocks in Bethnal Green to newly built council estates south of the river. He looked like a film star and had a reputation for being up to no good. He was charming, with olive skin. *He looked Italian*, Mum said, *tough and Italian*. A gangster, then.

They met at the Streatham Locarno. I have a photograph of them there in 1956, sitting on a bench, bottles of Coke on the table in front of them, my dad's arm around my mum, my mum looking emptily into the camera. Her eyes aren't registering anything – the camera, my dad's arm, the bottles of Coke. She's motionless and stiller than the captured image. Almost absent. I do that in photographs too.

My mum is sixteen in the photograph and quite possibly already pregnant. She doesn't show and she can't remember if she knew then, but by the time she was seventeen she'd married him, had her first child – my sister, and they'd moved into a rented flat. They had to get married, no choice in it.

My dad says that he was forced into the marriage by his mother Louise, or Lou as we all knew her, a strict Catholic who said that his behaviour was bloody shameful. Lou, who all too clearly remembered her own difficult past, wouldn't allow any shame to fall on the family.

My grandmother Lou was a brilliant character – small, tough, riotously outspoken – who ended up moving out of the East End to a new council place in Tooting. She looked after my dad's elder brother Vinnie, who'd had electric shock treatment after the war. Vinnie sat in the same chair all the time I knew him, in exactly the same position, right by the door so he could escape. He smoked a hundred fags a day, drank whisky and told stupid jokes. Really stupid jokes. You couldn't really see him for the clouds of smoke that swirled around him; his nervous twitchy fingers, stained a deep nicotine brown, occasionally peeked out from the smoke. The centre of his lips had a deep brown stain from holding cigarettes. His lips constantly looked pursed. Lou looked after him his whole life until she died in her nineties. A month or so after she died, he let go and died too. He had no one to tell jokes to any more. Bless her, she always laughed to make him happy. What a life.

*My mum held me down on the train all the way to bloody Camberwell*, Dad said, *I wanted to jump out of the window. I was seventeen and I wanted to be in a band with the lads, not saddled down with kids*, he said, quite openly talking about me and my siblings as if we were tumours that had grown on him, tumours that needed to be cut off. He did eventually cut us off when he left to inherit a new family, a new family he didn't seem to mind so much, a new wife (the also-called-Ann) with pre-existing kids. Ready-mades.

He became a much better dad for them – they call him Nobby – and a good husband to her, which doesn't make me completely unhappy because at least it means he's mended a little, but I do wonder if he was ever a dad to us or something else. What would be a better word, a more apt noun?

Once Mum and Dad had my sister, the next three followed in quick succession, born into a family tugging, pulling, pushing chaotically in different directions. I was the middle one of the 'next three', so not quite the middle child. After children, after us, Mum retreated into uppers and downers and Dad became consumed with anger, his legendary temper barely concealed – we all carry scars, emotional and literal. As Mum wilted into prescription addiction, his fists surfaced higher and harder, no middle ground, no greys, just black and white.

Punches to put you down on the deck.

We grew used to a level of violence in the home that defined the home as anything but a home – a battleground perhaps, a boxing ring, a crime scene, a bloody, bloody mess. We couldn't protect ourselves because we were kids, and this was the only version of home and love that we knew. The love we grew into and out from. The love that created our version of love. Our love-chrysalis.

Our formative years were striated by violence and sedation. Body chemicals – the adrenaline of violence and fear, and an ever-growing band of chemical prescription drugs that Mum took daily to alter her mood, the mood of the house, and thus our moods, thus us. We weren't born addicted, but we became so as youngsters. Drugs had real currency.

Both Mum and Dad had been running from their child-hoods when they met in the Locarno; out of their union they would only be able to create a space that their children would need to run from. Like for like. They taught us how to run, nothing more.

We were born into a space that we needed to flee, that was the deal, and we knew that as soon as we knew anything. They didn't mean any harm, they were kids, that's all most of us ever are, kids trying to be grown-ups.

My dad was running from poverty and violence and my mum was running from the fingering of men into her child-hood body. My mum wanted to be able to treat her kids better than she'd been treated, but didn't know how, and my dad didn't want kids, because they'd only make him poorer. *How could he be a poor king?* Kings weren't poor, even ducking and diving, Italian-looking kings. And he wanted to be the king of the street.

*All these kids*, my dad once told me, *all these kids came along, one after the other, and we had no money.*

'That's us you're talking about, Dad, those kids, that's me.'

He didn't hear me. He could never hear or see us. He never has. We were the kids that didn't fit in his life.

When I was diagnosed with full-blown AIDS, he didn't call for weeks and weeks and when he did, he said, *keep your pecker up.* That's all he said when he thought I was dying of AIDS.

Be cock-ready.

Between each of Mum's four, full-term pregnancies, there were others, the family that never was, the siblings that never were.

Dad pushed Mum to have one abortion after the other – four. An equal number gone to the number here. I'm not sure who were the lucky ones; isn't that a terrible thing to think? But my childhood still haunts and misshapes me and so often I've thought that not being here would have been easier.

There have been three different scenarios of children. Us as we are, the rejected demonised four; he tells us we're like our mother, mad, and that's why he rejects us. The eight that we could have been, who knows, just maybe, there might have been a more radical early tipping point and a different intervention. And lastly, the scenario that my dad has now, in which he has new children, ones that seem to make him a happy dad and grandad. He has no blood tie to them, so maybe that's it. No real connection, so a completely real connection.

The myth of blood ties, or blood being thicker than water, often such bullshit.

After each abortion, Mum went out and shoplifted. I always had a sense of this, not just because once I think I saw her nick something, but because there was a cupboard in the kitchen full of weird, brand-new stuff, like first-aid kits in plastic boxes, unopened and piled high. She nicked things that embodied her fears and desires, that explained motherhood – first-aid kits to keep us safe, steaks to feed us and Christmas tree decorations to make everything all right.

A 1970s well-done (burnt) steak was the height of fine dining. It was everything, steak and chips or scampi in a basket with chips.

You don't have to be Louise Bourgeois or Joseph Beuys to make sense of her collections. Between each happy full-term pregnancy lay pain. Men, and sometimes other women, tell women to have abortions as if it is a tooth extraction.

'Your dad once told me I should lie in a bath of quinine to get rid of one,' she said.

They destroyed her, the children who never became.

The last one was a late abortion, and she asked the doctor what it was: *a girl*, he said. A sister. Another sister. Three times after abortions she was caught shoplifting, the third time she had to go to court. Her secret pain had driven her to steal, and now court. She wanted to be punished, she wanted to be caught.

When she appeared in court, Mum wore an indigo-blue coat with a funnel neck that she kept pulled high and tight throughout the whole proceedings.

'I wanted it to swallow me whole,' she said, 'I was terrified that it would get in the papers, and that everyone would find out what I'd been doing. That you kids would find out.

I wanted the neck of that coat to engulf me like the freezing inky sea off Southend.'

She talked to no one about the abortions or the shoplifting, only her doctor, who gave her more pills, stronger pills.

By the time I'd grown up, she was buying speed from our dealers.

That she'd been caught shoplifting was horrifying to Mum; she was always tough but not criminal. Not really. She'd lie for us to the police or whoever or take in some snide goods behind the bar of the pub, but she wasn't a professional shoplifter. Far from it, she's grafted her whole life – working in pubs, cleaning people's houses, caring for people, wiping people's arses. But she had abortions which made her feel such acute pain that she wanted to be punished. So, she shoplifted. Her pain came from such a deep place, a place in which she was a child at risk wanting only to look after children. The abortions were antithetical to her most inner desire.

Like Mum, I'm a shit shoplifter. I always get caught. My sister Jack's always been brilliant: she can slip mascaras and other bits into her bag without even the flick of an eyelash. She's always been Thelma, Louise and whatever pretty boy Brad was called.

'I shoplifted because of the depression,' Mum told me. 'After every abortion I shoplifted because I had names planned out for each and every one and lives planned out for each and every one. In reality I might have been an awful mother, but I always felt so full of love. That always felt overflowing in me, maybe drowning me. Maybe love is the problem, but I loved being a mother. I know that's hard to hear because I probably haven't been a great one, but I've loved trying.'

I always tell her that she's the best mother, and that I wouldn't change her for the world.

I tell her that I've always wanted to be a mother and I'm sure, Mum, I'd have been as shit at it as you and as full of love for my kids as you are for us.

I think that's why I had genital surgery, to be able have children, even psychically, to become psychically ready for birth. To try.

*Children come out of a vagina, don't they? I needed one, an exit for my trapped children, Mum.*

She always looks at me like I'm deranged, maybe I am, but I did think that a vagina equalled mothering potential. I did back then when I had surgery.

Five days after surgery to construct a vagina out of the unloved cock and balls, the surgeon did his ward round, alongside a nurse carrying a tray of single use plastic speculums. Like a Jeff Koons piece ready to be installed in MoMA.

The surgeon pulled the curtain around my bed, a dramatic yet intimate gesture, then caringly he rolled up my mint-green hospital gown, concertinaed it up and over my rounded belly.

*Was I already with child, or was it wind?*

He snapped on his latex gloves, a ping on each finger on each hand. He put his right palm out and took out the speculum from the nurse. At the start of this pandemic, you had to wear latex gloves in the supermarkets here in Spain, and whenever I pinged one on, I thought about him, the first man who entered my cunt and made me realise that I'd always be childless. He became the father who didn't want kids.

While he readied himself for our moment, the nurse slathered my anxious, naive cunt with lashings of lube. *Wasn't this what I'd always wanted, to be fucked like this, to be greased up and entered?*

*Wasn't this about becoming and not about loss? For fuck's sake, Juno, stay in the moment,* I thought as he prepared to enter me.

He placed the tip of the cold plastic speculum on the new driveway and pushed slowly inside of me. There wasn't a debate; it didn't feel consensual. I didn't ask to know my depth. But that's what he was going to tell me, my depth. I didn't know that I could say no.

I'd never had a vagina before my legs were opened through misogyny. My history was already cemented in being silent in moments of doubt, I was passively ripe for misogyny.

It hurt, I'd refused morphine, terrified I'd leave the hospital with an opiate-addicted vagina. He pushed in deep and spread open the jaws of the speculum to assess my fuckability, my possibility, my depth.

Unknowingly, he couldn't have known, his actions felt like the actions of certain punters, pissed punters, lovers or fuck buddies, who are determined to do a particular thing and don't care when you say no.

They just close their eyes and ears to you, and push in. Kissing and biting your neck at first, as if a love bite will soften you up, then rolling you over, face down, still trying to be tender, then brute force. Pushing inwards, relentless, like a dog fucking a bitch on the side of the mountains.

I know you want it; you're resisting because you want it, playing hard to get, how dare you tease my cock,

Your word 'no' meaning 'now'.

Words never mean a single thing. Sadly. They should but they don't.

Once a word leaves your brain, your mouth, it becomes fair game for others' internalised readings and consumptions. *No don't fuck me* is me saying *there's no space for that to happen*. To him, to them, it indicated a landscape of openings and possibilities. However dry, however painful. They assume your word 'no' means that your cunt, arse, mouth are in fact open for business. For their pleasure.

I once worked in a paint factory which was next to a chicken abattoir. I was a heroin addict at the time and took any job that would have me, I wasn't career building. My periods of employment usually lasted until I didn't make it in, or was caught using drugs at work, or was caught nicking at work. Most jobs lasted a day or a week or maybe at a push, a month. Never more than that, even the truly shit ones on live sex lines. Which are almost impossible to be sacked from because there's always a kink you can satisfy. Always, even a shit lazy kink is a kink you can earn a few quid from.

One day, a chicken escaped certain death from the abattoir and ran screaming with the all the joys of freedom slap bang into our yard. One of my co-workers, a man with sexy gnarled hands, asked me if I liked chicken, I said *yes, I do, I love chicken*. He grabbed it, snapped its neck, and tried to hand it to me, its body violently shaking. I moved back, feeling sick. His hands didn't seem sexy any more. They were hands that had snapped the neck of a free chicken.

What I meant to say was, *yes, I love that the chicken has*

*escaped, not that I wanted you to snap its fucking neck.* But I realised that a single word from me, the word yes, had reached him with a completely different meaning because it wasn't clear, obviously.

My yes, meaning a plethora of different yeses and yes outcomes. I wasn't clear. I was a junkie taken in by his hands, it wasn't his fault or the chicken's. It was mine for being clumsy with words and smitten with hands.

I walked out of the yard, the chicken still shaking like James Brown on the paint-strewn floor.

I needed to score, to use drugs. I never returned.

I've never forgotten that a single word from me meant that the chicken who'd escaped and was momentarily free, clucking its joyous beak off, had its neck snapped.

*Yes,* I said and *no* I've said to different punters, who've heard *yes*.

The last punter I ever did was a man who picked me up in east London at three in the morning. We walked down a long alleyway near to a tube station and stopped when the lights from the street were barely visible. Mood lighting. Sex lighting.

The streets were empty.

That part of London is so beautiful when it's empty, when the noise of traffic or the hum of the street market is absent. Despite its historical reputation (I highly recommend Hallie Rubenhold's brilliant book *The Five: The Untold Lives of the Women Killed by Jack the Ripper*, which tells their stories, the women's stories), I've always felt safe in that part of London. Generations of my dad's family lived in and around Shoreditch, Whitechapel and Bethnal Green. I liked wandering there, especially when the streets were empty. I feel the ghosts.

Back to the man, the last ever punter. He never paid by the way, so possibly not a punter at all, just another man whose cock I sucked.

At the end of the alleyway, he said, 'I just want a quick blow job, suck my dick.'

I squatted down and unzipped his cock. It was soft, there was already a drip of pre-cum from his piss slit. I took his cock in my mouth and started to work. It was work, I wasn't turned on, I wasn't thinking about the quality of his dick, I was thinking about scoring drugs. That's all I ever thought about in those days. Getting drugs.

He started to get hard, he started murmuring things that I couldn't make out. The harder his cock the more definite his words became. They were angry words. I couldn't make them out, his body didn't feel angry, but he was, his words told me so.

I said before that words have a plethora of different meanings, they do, but tone definitely sets meaning, like hairspray sets hair. Whatever he was saying, he was getting angrier. Scarily, the words felt utterly detached from him. It was like his body, his cock, was one person and the words another. Duality. Internalised homophobia was a common customer.

He grabbed a handful of my hair, yanked my head back hard and spat in my face, telling me, you made me do this, you got me to come down here, I should beat the fucking life out of you. As he spat out his words his cock, now rigidly erect, was threatening to whack me in the face. Looming like an omnipotent demon.

I'd been in similar situations before. The man in the

top-floor flat who told me he'd been a professional boxer and that if I made a single sound during sex that he'd beat me black and blue, so I held my breath. The man in Kensington, it all seemed very straightforward at first, it was Kensington after all and I'm a matchgirl swayed by a big window, but when I got there, he had someone else with him who was a slave, someone he never mentioned. A twenty-four-seven slave who did everything, cooking, cleaning, paying, buying.

Fuck, the slave even drove me home after the shenanigans. He got his slave to tie me up and hold me down by kneeling on my shoulders, my arms pulled back. The client then inserted whatever large objects he could find into my arse while the slave stared down at me with insane eyes, honestly, fucking insane eyes. No kink shade, I've been there and enjoyed it. But they had intensely spiteful eyes, I understood that they'd be happy for me to be taken to an edge in this scene.

I needed the money so I tried to please the slave with my eyes, as Tyra Banks would say, I looked up and smized. I said, *this hurts*, with my eyes. The slave came in my fucking hair, I hated that. My hair is my thing, don't come in my hair.

These situations were edgy, maybe frightening, but I knew that they weren't life threatening, somehow I knew. I developed a set of strategies to get in and out of situations with the least possible friction. I was born into a violent home, you develop strategies.

But the man in the alleyway, his demonic cock slapping my face, droplets of his angry spit raining down on me, I thought that he might fuck me up good and proper. In one hand he pulled back my head and with the other he cupped my chin almost tenderly, both hands felt entirely different from one another, like two different men were holding my head, good cop, bad cop.

Then he snapped out of whatever, wherever, whoever.

Pulling my face up to look at him, he said, 'This is your lucky day, I'm going to let you go.' And he did. He zipped up his now rock-hard cock and walked away without looking at me or saying another word. Not a word. Not a glance. Nothing. It was over in a minute or two. I think it was the closest I've ever come to being hurt. Really hurt. Not slapped around hurt but really hurt.

I couldn't move. I couldn't stop thinking that he was two men and not one.

He said it was my lucky day, but I knew it wasn't because I'd always have the fear from that moment.

I smelt piss, it jolted me back. Of course I smelt piss, this wasn't some beauty spot on the green rim of London where lovers came to kiss, it was a place where people shat and pissed and people like me sucked cock or used drugs. It was a place I'd visited many times, like an alternative guide to London, all the places you can earn a tenner and inject without interruption or interference. It's the kind of place I'd now fearfully walk a mile to avoid.

I stayed there for an age, until a different picture was framed at the end of the alleyway. The light from the early morning, a Turner. I said to myself, *I'm never doing that again*, and I never did, I didn't have it in me any more. Not that.

The surgeon didn't ask about pushing the speculum inside me, because the action was all about his success at surgically creating cavities to look like vaginas, vulvic regions. If he'd just said, *do you want to know your depth,* or *this might feel uncomfortable,* or *I'm your first fuck, I'll be gentle, I'll whisper in your ear letting you know when I'm inside of you. I'll hum you a love song. I'll send you flowers. I'll be a good dad to our kids.*

But no, none of that, he just pushed the plastic inside of me and told me how much depth my cock and ball skin had provided for a cock to enter me.

He pushed the speculum in, sliding it over lubricated, moistened opening wounds, like a steel-grey battleship being launched over greased poles in a northern boat yard, he kept pushing it in until it hit the back wall, the back wall.

A back wall. A back wall. *A back wall?*

My brain repeated the words over again and over again. A back wall. There's a back wall. My children, my babies trapped inside behind a wall.

'You have a good six inches of depth,' he said.

I turned my head to one side and a tear emerged, rolling down onto the pillow. He touched my shoulder gently, my tear creating a soft response from him where before there'd only been perfunctory actions. He thought my tear was rolling because of uncontrollable emotions that I could take, manage, contain, hold, please a six-inch-cock. I was ready, I was real, I was six-inch-cock deep. How odd that anyone would think we'd go through all that just for a cock.

I wasn't thinking about anything or anyone penetrating me.

No, when I felt the speculum hit the back wall, I knew that I'd never be a mother. Right up until that moment, the moment when the speculum's tip touched that cis-stitched wall, I'd still dreamt I'd be a mother. I wasn't stupid or mad or driven to surgery by uncontained or controlled fantasies, but I did think that an opening down there between my legs would serve as a portal, an entrance to my need to be a mother. I thought it was the start of a conversation, not the last word.

I thought it was an orifice through which I would connect with my maternal need. When the cold tip of the plastic speculum met the newly constructed stud wall at the rear of my neo vagina I knew that even my dreams about motherhood would have to end.

In the singular movement of my head from left to right on the hospital pillow, I pulled down the shutter on my own cavity, closing the cave as if in a fairy tale, keeping the loss deep within and allowing the depth to close up naturally. I didn't need a cock to become a vagina for a cock, I needed it as a spectral birth canal birth for the children who could never be. My fantasy children. My family. The ones I could never grow old with.

# Five

## Mum

Mum eventually got a flight home on 16 July 2020. I drove her to the airport. She'd dressed up and looked beautiful in a denim-blue dress, necklace and earrings that matched and a lick of blue eyeliner. The airport was like a vast empty whale's belly, cavernous and echoey. Marble floors gleamed because they were roped off. There was a line you could walk, socially distanced, but there was only a handful of travellers, so distancing wasn't an issue. It felt so final, like a real goodbye, not see you later, not like when I'd left England to move to Spain, that had been a see you soon.

This felt different. My mum's health is slowly deteriorating, years of inhaled fag fumes clogging her veins, lungs and arteries. She moves slowly, painfully; I watched her walk the line to find someone, anyone, to ask about the flight. She looked grand but frail, the dress will outlive her, I thought. We hugged goodbye and in the safety of my car speeding down the motorway I cried.

The day after she leaves, Spain closes all of its borders, all travel in and out is suspended. I can't leave and no one can visit. Roadblocks go up on the outskirts of the nearest town, there are police everywhere and warnings about fines and imprisonment for breaking the various curfews. I don't have a Gender Recognition Certificate, here I'm still legally male. So I obey the curfews for fear of incarceration in a male facility. My fantasises about being impregnated by some felon or another are well and truly over.

The village is silent, the square empty. So silent that when one of my neighbours was whisked away to hospital by ambulance, I didn't hear a single thing. Even noises, sirens, coughs, birds, are silencing themselves to comply with this new normal. I didn't hear a thing.

These latest COVID-19 curfews have kept everyone hidden deep in their adobe bunkers. Usually, the noise of children whizzing around the square, making up games, laughing, shouting, fills the air, especially at weekends, but not now. The curfews bring a silence to already silent mountains. But I don't mind the silence.

It sounds awful to say, but the sound of happy children is always a bleak reminder of what I don't have, perhaps what I also never had as a child. A happy childhood. I grew up dreaming that I would make my own children happy and safe. I grew up dreaming of holidays we'd take in caravans and homework I'd help them do. Most of all I dreamt that my children would make my life better.

So the silence of the square isn't painful, it's a relief. I was going to say that I'm not bitter about being childless, but I am, I'm bitter and deeply envious of people who have and create families, people who have children who will grow up to have children, who become your grandchildren. There's a sinkhole in my belly hidden behind a stitched fleshy stud wall and it always yearns.

Unhappy children wanting to have their own children to mend their fences is one of the most natural pulls in the world, one of the purest and most innocent. When I hear people talk, specifically privileged people looking down on 'council-house girls' having babies to supposedly make their lives materially better, I think *you don't get it, they're not trying to make their lives better, they know that their lives are shit, but deep within them they have a pull. A pull and a push and a need to create a cleansed sliver of life that might be or might become better than them. That might become more than them. They want to be outgrown, perhaps even left behind.* You can see this in my own family's history over and over.

When I was a teacher I would meet single mothers, and very occasionally single fathers, who'd attend every single parents' evening, never missing one, desperate to know that their child or their children were making progress. They'd say to me, *I came to this school years ago and wasted my time, I don't want that for them.* They'd say, *I know that they can become more than me.* They'd look me in the eyes and say, *please do your bit for them, help them to become more than me.*

They were the most engaged, committed parents I ever met, yet they are constantly demonised in the news as feck-less, untrustworthy bad parents who need training, parents who want kids to be able to get social to give them a bigger flat and a great big widescreen. In my experience, nothing could be further from the truth.

All parents need training, not just the working class.

*

Teaching other people's children was the closest I've ever come to motherhood, every day it made me happy and sad. I adored teaching but went home alone thinking I'd swap anything and everything to become a mother.

Like Shelby, played by Julia Roberts, in *Steel Magnolias* swapping everything for a few moments of being a mother, to carry a child, to give birth and to raise them, just a little. I'd do a deal with the devil to make that so. Fuck me, I've made enough crappy deals and wasted enough time.

Not being a mother has always felt painful. Even with my phantasmagorical birth canal all but closed up, the pain still seeps out, glugs out between old stitches, between roughly hewn joins.

In my fifties it can still floor me. The sound of silence on the square feels kind; perhaps I came here to escape the sounds that hurt.

When I tell people about the pain, they say, *you don't know how lucky you are to not have the worries of parenthood.* I can't show them my emptiness. Over the years I tried to show them by filling the emptiness with drugs and self-harm and they only saw poetic needs fluttering and floating just above my surface, not bellowing, and howling in the cavity, the sinkhole, an empty space of gestation.

I knew I had to leave teaching when parents' evenings became too painful. I was the wrong side of the table, I used to speak but also hear my belly speak sadnesses about being this side of the table and not the other. The words of loss in my belly grew too loud to be effective as a teacher. Towards the end, I barely concealed the screams of childlessness.

*

All of my siblings have children; my two brothers have thirteen children between them. One has nine and the other a much more manageable four, perhaps in some odd way they felt the brokenness much more keenly. I think men do break more easily, more readily. Or perhaps they fucked around more.

My sister only had the one, but I think that her running away from home at a much earlier age, at fifteen, almost sixteen, made her want fewer children, or perhaps need fewer children. Or perhaps being dragged off by our dad to have an abortion at just sixteen broke her.

Her first child.

Bless her.

I've never seen it written down like that. She was just sixteen, a kid. I think she wanted to keep the child. Even at that age, the desire to make a better world than the one you're experiencing is strong. Her child, her hope snatched out from within her.

There was a fight on the day of the abortion, a fight for the right to control my sister's body. For some reason we were all taken over to stay in our cousin's paper shop. My dad, deeply racist, couldn't let a brown baby come into this world, not on his patch, not on his turf, not on his watch.

They dragged her off to the abortion clinic on Brixton Hill. While they were gone, I found a copy of *Playgirl* on the top shelf and looked at cocks, at Burt from Nevada posing, one booted foot up on the bumper of a Mustang and his flaccid cock resting in his outstretched palm.

My poor sister. She's never talked about anything painful in her life and it's almost destroying her now.

*

Growing up I blamed myself for having a shitty life, we all did, we all do. It's what you do. Especially working-class kids who are always told that they are the problem. We ingest our histories and constantly rewrite them and hide them in shame and denial. We try to talk around them, paper over them, hide them behind shiny trinkets, like magpies.

We believe that the buck stops with us, *with me*. Not only does the buck stop with us and our depressingly crumpling egos as we fail to make real, upward gains, but it's also difficult for us to take any responsibility for our failings because we perceive them as being held within the vessels we are given. Our bodies, our skins, our minds are at fault. As if a working-class form, a working-class body, is inherently dysfunctional. Perhaps in a class-ridden society it is.

Arbitrarily formed from broken, discarded bits. Bits that people are running from. Like a bag of broken biscuits from the pound shop, a working-class body is seen as an inherently broken one. Or as a body to *be* broken, reformed, reshaped, educated. Cultivated.

Like a trans body, like a queer body, lesser, disposable. A working-class body should absorb trauma without emitting any sound. Containment. That's a word that describes my childhood or my childhood body, a container with structural failings.

In capitalist terms, the closer we are to the ideals at the centre – tall, white, slim, heteronormative, cis-normative, rich, heterosexual, blue-eyed, blonde hair, female with vagina, male with cock – then the less broken the presumption of our form.

I childishly presumed that my clumsy body could be

changed by watching films and reading books and then imitating them, but somewhere deep inside I also must have believed that on a cellular level it would always remain the same inherently bad, broken body. If a crime is committed and the person is marginalised by their class or colour, or both, then that becomes the factor, the defining criminal factor.

The body commits the crime. Society operates by enforcing the notion that a marginalised body is a bad body. As kids it's difficult not to ingest that or inhabit that, when you come from one of those families. *You won't be here long*, people would say to me. *You're no better than the rest of them*. Waiting and watching for me to fall victim to my own body. And I did because the world said it was so.

If only we were taught about capitalism at school, we might understand how our lives and bodies are used as fodder to hold tight the purse strings of others. We might rise up.

But we aren't taught about capitalism, so I presumed that I would fuck up because inherently I was a fuck-up born of fuck-ups. That fucking up is in your bloodstream, your bloodline, your genes.

Rather than understanding that I was born into a queer, trans, working-class body devalued by a broken society. Nothing more, nothing less.

No one talked about education to me or with me, certainly not further education, I had to fight at sixteen to even get people to have a conversation with me about me staying on at school to do A levels. It was presumed that I would go out to work or commit crime.

By sixteen I was exhausted.

By the end of our teens, we were all exhausted, angry, despondent containers. Containers full of depression.

Of my siblings and I, three out of four have been addicts, two of us are registered heroin addicts. One has been in prison in America because of dealing. I dealt drugs and sold my ass and only escaped serious trouble by a needle's breadth.

We were raised in a language that structurally accepted insobriety as a means to dampen down the anger and to find comfort. *You'll need this, go on, try it, take it, pop it, put it in your mouth/arm/arse, it's going to be such a long, tiring life being in a body deemed throwaway by a society that throws so much away. You're gonna feel second best at best and at worst invisible in whatever you do.*

*Take a Valium*, Mum's always said, *pop a pill to make yourself feel better.* She's not being a cunt, she's had no time for yoga or therapy because she's had no time full stop. For her, popping a pill was pragmatic. It got her out the door, it allowed her to crack a smile.

The vast pandemic of strong painkiller addiction across the world is more often than not embedded in the poorest and the most dispossessed. A capitalist means to isolate and shame. They blame the breakdown of society upon drug users when in fact, prescription addiction, which sweeps many up and into the arms of heroin, is a structural device, a product range created in Russell Group labs to control certain groups of society.

I'm not blaming my mum's intake of prescription medication for mine or my siblings' addictions, but we learnt early that chemicals, legal chemicals, can alter the way you feel and make your life feel easier.

My mum would say to us, *I'm floating*, or *I've got no idea what I did yesterday*, or *I can't remember a thing*. To kids already in pain, that seemed like an easy solution. A chemical solution. A hug would have done it, a daily hug, or the words *I love you*, repeated over and over again until they became commonplace and not just ones used after violence.

No, instead we learnt that chemicals helped. By the age of eleven, I would guess that I was ready to be an addict. Drugs were always a part of our lives; I didn't have to go anywhere to find addiction, it was always at the table, or if not at the table – my mum rarely ate with us – then sat next to us on the sofa, or if not the sofa – my mum never sat down, except to sleep – then addiction was all around in the air we breathed, in the language we used.

In my wardrobe here in the mountains, there hangs a sheer white cotton jumper. It hangs, sits, waits, gathering dust.

It has a V-neck and long, perhaps over-long sleeves. It's a size sixteen. It's never been worn. It's like an un-kissed kiss. Like a ghost or a shroud, it reminds me of the almond blossom that engulfs the trees here in January. Great swathes of fluffy white and pale pink blossom descend on the trees overnight, like scented clouds they appear and cover the mountainsides the next morning, emerging out of the early morning mists. Heralding spring.

I've never worn the jumper.

Mum never wore the jumper. She brought it here the first time she visited, the first summer I was here. A few years ago.

She turned up with a case heaving with new bits and pieces from all over – tops from the market and a few 'better' pieces from Marks & Spencer, like the jumper. It's the kind of top she would have thrown on over a pair of leggings, probably white leggings teamed with sandals. She never listened to what society said women should or shouldn't wear at certain ages. She didn't care. She dressed to please herself. The hairs sprouting on my chin are a testament to this characteristic I inherited from Mum, although she's appalled at the hairs.

*Fuck it*, she once said to me on the phone, *I'm going to dye my hair pink before I die*. She did. She regretted it, but at seventy-eight she dyed her hair pink. Her friends were used to her doing this kind of thing. But I knew that the pink hair heralded a certain waft of sadness, like a breeze, a subtle pink grabbing at something that was whizzing by – time. She looked beautiful with pink hair.

She never threw the jumper on, the white summer top, because I live in the tiniest of villages in the dusty Andalusian mountains, like I said before, an ant of a village.

'Isn't there even a coffee shop?' she asked, sad that she couldn't get dressed up to parade.

It's a south London thing. Parading. When she ran a pub off the Walworth Road, she'd get dressed up to saunter through East Street Market. Everything always matched.

Maybe she never threw the jumper on because the white combo didn't work for her any more, like the pink hair, maybe the white outfit was something passing. The white jumper sits in the wardrobe, totemic. A sign, a warning, an art piece, a relic.

I dread the day when I look in the wardrobe, see the jumper and know that she is no longer here. It fills me with sadness that her life – a life lived as well as she could, is at the point where we talk of funerals and the bits and bobs that she wants people to have. The jumper is a totem to her ageing, but at one point it will become the sheerest of ghosts.

This morning I pull the jumper to me and dry-eye-cry like a baby because she's left and I'm scared this pandemic might not let me see her again. That's how it feels now, now that everywhere is locked down, stopped, almost as if time has stopped but our ageing continues apace.

Mum's whooshing towards an edge in a time when everything else stands still.

# Six

# A Person in the Middle of Nowhere Who Needs People

Early this morning the mountain peaks sitting under the moon were streaked with lavender and the palest primrose yellow. The range opposite, waking under the rising sun, was bathed in warm burgundy and red ochre. There is a moment in the year's cycle when the moon and the sun are equally high or low in the sky. I often forget about this magical moment.

When I first arrived here to these mountains, direct from London – city to mountain in one day, London to nowhere in one day, I was so amazed by the vastness of the landscape that almost the first thing I did was to walk across it for miles and miles, which became Spanish kilometres. I felt small and silently unimportant in a way that cities pretend to not allow you to do. The idea of a city is that you are constantly seen, although in a heaving metropolis like London, nothing could be further from the truth. People, however remarkable, aren't remarkable in a city. Maybe fleetingly we stand out under the network of ubiquitous and dumb surveillance cameras.

I felt lost in my old life because I was, and then I came here to become even more lost with some (romantic?) notion that I'd be found. I'll never understand that part of me that runs headlong into the unknown. Perhaps I'm more comfortable at an edge, like a traveller or an explorer, except that I'm exploring my emotional innards by pushing my life experiences towards edges – addiction, a different country, crime.

The first time I saw the sun and moon balanced on both sides of the valley's edge, I believed that there must be a god or a goddess, or at least some being bigger and cleverer than us. Someone or some divine power who could create such a moment of artistic and spiritual brilliance and balance.

The first time I saw the sun and moon balancing was the first time I'd ever encountered such vast, grand natural brilliance, completely unhindered by us. No buildings, no roads, no noise, no crowds, nothing but space – the mountains, the sky, the valley floor full of almond and olive trees, and the sun and moon wrestling each other with colour, shade and light.

Like two cock-waving artists, outdoing each other, pissing beautifully up the opposite sides of the earth. (Note: the most beautiful piss artwork was in fact not by a cock-waving male artist but the artist Helen Chadwick's *Piss Flowers* (1991–92), beautiful casts of the interior spaces left when she pissed warm urine into snow.)

If I climb to the highest point of the mountain and close my eyes in front of the rising sun and the waning moon, I've learnt that in this silent wonder, I can vibrate away my awkwardness, my clumsiness, my fears and my depression. I can feel the negativities and pessimism I've learnt to endure and perhaps cultivate, dissipate. I trust this strange, vast moment more than any human.

If this world is large enough to contain this beauty, then the feelings inside me, inside my head, inside my mind, can only be small. Mere fragments.

I feel beautifully insignificant. Pointless, light but connected to the landscape, to the healing power of the earth in a way that cities, or my city, London, had never allowed me to do.

For perhaps the past three or four years before coming here, I'd only felt negativity in London. Often feeling breathless and disconnected. I kept having anxiety and panic attacks. I developed social phobias around groups of more than one. That's hard to rectify in a city of millions of disconnected strangers who spend their days connecting and disconnecting. You have to be good at it, and it's a skill. Networking or even being casually social is a skill that I don't have. It zinged raw in London, the zinging only intensifying as I aged. My uncomfortableness zinged like an abrasion.

Despite family, friends and ingrained familiarity in London, I never felt connected to the ground, to the soil, to the planet. I always felt like I was stumbling. I felt fragile there and constantly silly for feeling fragile. *Pull yourself together, Juno*, I'd say, day in, day out. I'd pop pills to pull myself together, which is the least efficient method of stitching.

The vibration I feel here in front of the sun and moon is low and steady and not an actual noise. I don't shake or sing or chant, the vibration is the pent-up historical sound of me capturing and controlling my errant panicky breath. Years of constraining it. I visualise gently tying it down with silken threads like a low-slung decorative tourist Buddhist drum and then, one by one, loosening each thread until my breath is free.

It's the closest I've ever come to meditative quiet contemplation. Visualisation or mindfulness. Bollocks maybe, but my mood does change depending on which planet or star I face.

I think the sun's a star, I think the moon is a planet.

Bollocks or not, it's become a meaningful moment and the special place in my life. A daily anti-depressive pilgrimage. Maybe a moment steeped in a deep-seated religious or spiritual need. A need to feel peace and inner quiet.

Maybe a cure. The daily cure for my depression, which could oh-so-easily be yet another tranquilliser. Prozac probably. This view gives me respite from my disease of addiction, from my well-trodden landscape of chemicals. I still need and use those chemicals, but this is a substitute that works. It balances me.

Some mornings I stand with my eyes closed and face the sun rising eastwards, other mornings I turn and face west towards the sinking moon. One view warm, the other cool.

Sometimes the warmth from the sunrise feels too much and I crave the coolness that only the waning moon can offer.

The mountain view changes constantly. The placement and the trajectory of the sun, the brightness of the moon, at night the stars, the clarity of the night sky. The absence of light and the endlessness of the blackness. The change of the seasons and the changes in my erratic moods. I think, I don't know, having never been diagnosed, but I think I'm mildly bipolar and marginally autistic. My behaviour tells me so, I wish I were young enough to have been diagnosed, but realising that I need mountains and not skyscrapers feels like I'm managing a little. Servicing my needs. Caretaking me as a property.

Climbing to the highest point and turning three hundred and sixty degrees on the spot and saying 'thank you' has become a sign to me that I'm in a mess but that I'm seeking recovery. That I'm feeling my depression rising and I'm trying not to allow it to smother me.

If I've walked to that high point, then perhaps I've been struggling with increasing depression and anxiety for a couple of days. It seeps in like a lightbulb dims, subtle, like a new lover putting their best foot forward softly, inching it into your space.

The mountain view, the vastness, undoes my knots and eases my irrational fears, brightens the bulb.

The balancing sun and moon are magical. Like a scene from Luke Skywalker's home planet Tatooine, or the Greek myth about Helios and Selene vying for our attention with mystical powers. It's balance incarnate. It's more perfect than anything I've ever seen so it empties me completely.

This is the place in the world where I'd happily die; I want my ashes scattered here if there's anyone to scatter them, if not, I'll will them up here on the North African winds from the public crematorium which is down the southern coast. They'll burn me and throw my ashes out with all the other people who don't have people, but the winds will carry me up here to feed the almond trees, back home. This is my home.

This is my childhood dream, the view over the garden fence of another's perfection.

This morning I walk up towards this place because the feeling of nausea in my stomach tells me that a new bout of depression looms large. When I woke, my stomach churned, I felt like shitting before I'd eaten anything. Only depression makes that happen. I knew I needed to seek balance up the winding path, upwards to the point at which I believe in things bigger and better than me. A god, a goddess, spirituality, the sacredness of this landscape, the beauty and majesty of this planet. The unimportance of us.

The clusterfuck of COVID-19, Brexit, Trump, Johnson, living with HIV and dealing with the plethora of memories rising up and out of this story is making me scared, shit scared.

I rarely, if ever, say that aloud. But what I'm scared of exactly I don't know. It's not death.

Being scared is one thing, saying it aloud only makes me feel more scared. But emerging in dream after dream of mine are scenes of me being a fuck-up, fucking up and being fucked over. My dreams are exhausting at the moment, long gone are the easy breezy dreams about sucking a fat cock or earning enough money by writing a bestseller to be able to buy my mum a house.

I hate remembering my COVID-19/Brexit/Trump dreams because in them I'm frequently woken by someone stabbing me; I feel the tip of the knife push into my skin, just the tip. I think it's really a needle.

Men like Trump create shit in the world, and I get stabbed in my dreams. *What the actual fuck?*

I want simple bouncy-cock dreams back; I want to wake up smiling and laughing at my primitivism. I want my dreams back about helping my mum out, making her happy, clearing her debts, buying her great wodges of cigarettes and a comfy chair that reclines for her to smoke in. A smoking chair. Smoking makes her so happy. A cup of tea and a fag.

I want that simplicity back, not this terrifying cacophony of pandemic Brexit dreams.

Walking up the mountain path this morning I've tried to

walk away from the constant noise of COVID-19, Brexit, HIV, lifesaving medication, vaccines and tests. Walking away from the fear that I've fucked up by coming here on an *Eat, Pray, Love* whim. That I won't be able to access the NHS and my HIV medication. That I'll die prematurely, either through COVID-19 or AIDS.

I don't want to die before my time, although what does that mean?

Julia Roberts in *Eat, Pray, Love* didn't need combination therapy or daily hormones to maintain her immune system and feelings of womanhood. She was unconstrained. Free.

I tried to walk up and away from the absolute silence that has invaded the silence that I used to flourish in. A new silence which is fear, fear is silent noise. I'm walking away from my longstanding depressive fear that I'll always have skin that recoils from touch in a time when I really want, no need, to be held, hugged and caressed. I hate that more than anything, that I still fear touch more than this isolation and fear.

Like Pup, I freeze in the proximity of love.

I try to walk away from anger, an anger I don't yet fully understand. A new feeling that's directed towards my HIV medication, the very brilliant drugs that have kept me alive all these years. Kept me alive like a god. Like a benevolent god.

I'm stupidly angry at them, the drugs, because of what they do and what they don't do. Because of their capacity and their limitations.

They don't cure me of HIV, of having to bear a lifetime of stigma, rejection and discrimination, they just keep me alive to endure more.

Saving my life so I can endlessly endure the ill-formed views of idiots who think that my blood is immorally toxic. Two pills a day clasp me tight to the cusp of societal rejection, bigotry and discrimination. I live in the land of stigma, and anyone who says it's changed is allowing the stigmatisers to get off scot-free. I won't.

The discrimination and stigmatisation still happens everywhere and anywhere and often where you least expect it to happen.

I have a gap in my upper teeth. A big gap, a two-teeth gap. A space big enough that I can easily fit my tongue through. Like parking a car in a garage. When I'm stressed I slot my tongue through the gap like it is a mortise and tenon joint that fixes something. Me to my past, grounding me within the history I've endured as a person living in this world with HIV, diagnosed many years before with full-blown AIDS.

The gap, the missing teeth, fell out rotten and decayed. The cavities painful until the teeth hollowed out, eaten away by the anger I retained, and then they were painful no more.

For almost a decade, I couldn't get a dentist because of my virus and then when I could get one, they gave me the last appointment of the day and covered every surface in clingfilm as if I were an infectious alien that had to be kept separate from all things earthly. It was demeaning in a way that was so fundamental to my sense of humanness that I wanted to die.

I carry that scar tissue, that bulbous space where teeth once sat as a record of their inhumanity and cruelty. Don't tell me it's changed. I've lived with the stigma, misinformation and sometimes pure hatred my whole HIV life.

The man on Tinder who I told in confidence that I was HIV

positive because we'd been talking for a time and it felt safe. His final message, his angry retort, 'You're a filthy whore who's on here to infect people, if you don't get off this site, I'll tell everyone what a slag you are.'

The gap between my teeth reminds me of how hateful the world can be, men on Tinder and supposedly educated dentists.

The HIV hasn't gone from my body, it's simply undetectable. It cannot be found. It's hiding somewhere in minute amounts, in ones or twos, couples perhaps, linking protein spikes, sleeping, snoozing, trying to make sense of the density of the ingested words of Derrida and Butler. Pondering why their host can't read something simpler like a magazine about celebrities, Kim, Khloe, Kylie.

I personify my virus as being simple but lethal, like snoozing karate black belts, one eye open, ready to pounce.

One viral ear pricked up, waiting for me to stop taking my meds so that they can return to their day job of killing me. I'm angry that in under a year they can find a vaccine for COVID-19, and in thirty not find a vaccine for HIV. Some lives, as Judith Butler would say, are more disposable.

I was diagnosed with HIV in the early nineties, just before I started at university. When I told them that my then partner was almost dead, so I wasn't sure I'd be able to make it, they said that they weren't sure I could attend anyway. That maybe it wasn't such a good idea for a person with AIDS to be at university. *What for, for what?* they pondered. My life on the lip.

What would I do, they asked, if I accidently cut myself open in the studio?

I felt stupid. Dirty. Toxic.

I'll carry plasters with me, I told them, and some bandages, just in case. They asked me if I was OK with everyone on the course being told, as they had a right to know.

I wanted to cry. I felt toxic. Dirty. Damaged. Soiled.

I told them they couldn't tell everyone because the law said they couldn't. I didn't know if that was true, but it worked. They didn't tell. I made work, carried plasters, bandages, Dettol, plastic bags to cover the bandages and slowly I stopped making any work that you'd consider risky. I made risk-free conceptual artwork.

It was that kind of time. You can look back and glamorise it all you want. You can think that everyone was marching with ACT UP or protesting bravely on the streets, or fucking celebrities with abandon, but the real bravery happened in the everyday spaces that we fought to remain inside, part of. Fighting to remain in our lives as the world sought to dispatch us off to an island where we could die, separated from the good clean folk.

I've found a way to live at the edge of life on my life-saving drugs.

COVID-19 has brought so much clarity to me about the edge upon which I teeter. I can see that I've been locked down in my dangerous body for almost thirty years, waiting on the promise of a vaccine. Of a curative HIV wet wipe.

Waiting for years on life-saving medication, medication that has started to drain the life out of me. I feel guilty saying that because of the many who still die. But I've not had a simple, unhindered kiss since my diagnosis.

Maybe it's just me, maybe I alone swallowed whole the narrative that I have immoral toxic blood, maybe my background made me more susceptible to swallowing whole great wide tracts of self-stigma. But I didn't shape the stigma. Or invent it. Or hurl the abuse. Or write the headlines.

I'm not that stupid or weak that I think I should blame myself for self-stigmatising.

The stigma has been unrelenting, that's why every HIV campaign still says versions of, 'We can't pass it on, love us.' Still maintaining our cleanliness while asking to be accepted back into the fold.

I hate those campaigns. Those doffing cap campaigns. I'm tired of holding my blood in and apologising for being HIV positive.

I'm tired of wondering who I should tell, when I should tell, and if I should tell. Recently a friend said to me, 'It's always going to be hard for you to find someone, with your condition.'

*With your condition.* They weren't being spiteful, ignorant maybe, but that's still the pervading feeling towards people with HIV. It's roll-off-the-tongue spiteful. I hope COVID-19 teaches us something, but I doubt it will. I'm beginning to think that humans are incapable of generating enough decency to build a kinder world. A happier planet. A fair place. A true democracy.

At the top of the foothills, everything is as I expected it to be. It's magical, it's beautiful. I stop and breathe it in through long, deep, barely constrained breaths. Managed breaths. Turning around as I do, humming Sylvester's 'You Make Me Feel (Mighty Real)'. I love that Sylvester comes to me here, his disco genius.

I stand still, open my eyes, look at the moon and contemplate its surface. What are the darker areas, are they valleys or water or craters and what are the craters? Did something or some things hit the moon?

I feel dimmed by not knowing about the surface of the moon. I want to get to the moon or at least get to know it.

I'll be fifty-seven this year, three away from sixty, which in many countries is the age at which you retire; I think I've left it too late to learn about the moon's surface.

I panic because I'll never get to the moon and I have an overwhelming desire to be able to do so, and then I panic because that's stupid, I've never shown any interest in going to the moon. I think I'm losing my marbles but then I realise the panic isn't about me becoming an astronaut but about my time running down, running low, running out.

*Will I ever be kissed again?* Perhaps I'll pay a person to kiss me. I think I am losing my mind. A second ago I wanted to visit the moon and now I want to visit a sex worker to be kissed.

Still, at least it's a cheaper option than retraining to become an astronaut that no one asked for. No one ever said to me, *Juno, have you ever thought about walking on the moon?* No. But I once had a client who'd pay me to gently kiss his face and neck and ears.

I crumble, my breath raspy, I turn away from the troublesome moon to look at the sun, the warm sun emerging over the other side of the valley. The sun who I've always been able to rely on. That's my person. Its warm light splaying across the flatlands between the mountains, gently lighting the fields of almond and olive trees, the light catching citrus trees heavy with oranges, lemons, and grapefruits. *Is this Eden?* I think, *have I died and gone somewhere. Is this heaven?*

I try to breathe, to capture and hold the panic and the fear that's rising in this second pandemic of mine. There's a voice in my mind which says, I don't want to deal with another pandemic. I try to breathe that voice away because it's the voice of me as a child. Scared shitless about dying alone in pain. That was a very real thing that happened in the AIDS pandemic. I saw friends die in agony.

But instead of being able to breathe away the child I gasp, crumble and my breath flutters up and out of me faster than I can process it into life.

No matter how fast I marched up the path this morning to escape my depression, the indigo bird in my belly, which flutters and then falls exhausted for a few days before trying to escape again, is already here with me.

Like a budgie in a too-small cage. Like the songbirds they catch here, trapping them in cages so small that they cannot open their wings, so they sing manically. People hear song but in reality they are screaming for help. Like the murderous dawn chorus that we wilfully misinterpret as tinkling sonatas. We do that with nature, make it what we need it to be. I did, before I came here and saw how unimportant I am.

I'm having a panic attack. I can't breathe. *Is it COVID-19?* I wonder briefly and then remember that I had COVID-19 earlier in the pandemic and was not able to walk more than thirty yards from my house. The dogs pissing and shitting on the terrace for a month while I coughed and coughed as if the blue bird had got trapped in my windpipe and was passively hoping I'd cough it up. Its feathers, itchy, inky blue.

I know I have a visceral fear about the UK breaking away

from this place that I now call home. I feel cut off, unexpectedly terrified about being stranded here alone, even though I always knew I was alone and can only cope in the world by being alone.

I wanted this, but I didn't know about this new pandemic.

In my head the words, *you made your bed, you lie in it*, ring out like the great Bow Bells. Pealing, repeating, you did this thinking you could get away. Thinking you could have mountains and a poetic view. Thinking it would be a clean break.

*You made your bed, your mountainous bed, now you and your inky blue fluttering bird lie in it.*

Exactly the same words Gertie said to Mum when she got pregnant at sixteen and had to marry my dad at seventeen. My mum had a black eye when she asked if she could move back home.

Gertie replied, *you made your bed, you lie in it*.

Mum told me Gertie was the hardest woman she'd ever known. She'd cut you dead.

I think I'm like her, but I'm hard on myself rather than others. I blame myself for being me and being like me. I blame myself for not crying in therapy when I knew I should, when I had permission to cry. I held the tears in because the fucked-up me thought the therapist might use my tears to hurt me. Tears are a conduit for pain to escape, but also for pain to climb in.

Tears shared require trust and I don't know how to trust.

It sounds warped, but when you've learnt to absorb fear and perhaps even terror, you realise that tears can provide a way for bad people to wiggle in.

*Don't cry, I didn't mean to hurt you, don't sleep on it, let's make up, let me kiss your tears away, see, I'm the custodian of your tears, of your pain, you can trust me.* I kiss tears. I'm the tear kisser. But I can't share my tears.

The only time my dad said he loved us was after hitting us. Punching us. Cutting us open. Then pulling us to him and saying, *forgive me, I love you*; he'd let a tear or two trickle down into the silent gap.

If only people realised that the stuff children see or experience can't be unseen or undone. I am a product of that stuff and I blame myself for still feeling like a product of that stuff when the world tells me I should have repaired myself in therapy.

Like a clock or a sofa or a roof with loose tiles.

I blame myself for still being broken.

I try to breathe calmly, to breathe through the panic that stems from feeling scared. The raspy short breaths don't help, indigo wings already unfurled, trapped inside my belly, they try to force space, to create space by fluttering wildly. They want out, I want out.

I shout as loudly as my breath allows, shouting at the sun, *where the fuck are you, God?* to a god that I don't believe in unless I'm scared or overwhelmed by a beauty that feels beyond human capability and capacity.

A lover once told me that my problem was that I was scared of being heard, he told me that I needed to learn to shout. To learn to shout and not to care what anyone else in the world thinks about the noise I'm making and the space that I'm taking up making that noise. We were in Tunisia when he told me this essential, life-changing fact.

The nights there were beautiful, airless, silent, balmy. He

insisted that we walk to the edge of the hotel complex, face out towards the desert and the mountains and practise shouting into the night sky. A deep maroon sky.

'Go on then, shout at them, tell them, shout as loudly as you can,' he instructed.

'Tell them what?' I asked.

'Whatever you need,' he said, 'like this,' and he shouted as loudly as I've ever heard anyone shout, bellowed like a trumpet. Clear and punchy. Impressive. I thought, *let's have sex*.

But no, he carried on, shouting questions like the age-old, *who am I*, obscenities like, *who the fuck am I*, and booming pointless phrases like, *this is how you shout loudly*, just to show me how to shout loudly. He led by example, as if shouting were an easy act to replicate. As if shouting doesn't come from a deeply complex place within.

My quiet, almost silent response wasn't just a fear of being heard; I genuinely find noise invasive and scary. I moved here to live in the middle of silence.

My childhood home was wall-to-wall violent anger and its noise.

'I can't do it,' I said, because I couldn't.

The maroon sky seemed ominous, it made me panic. His instructions pushed me towards abject (in his eyes) failure and that made me panic, and when the panic set in, the indigo bird first emerged and fluttered in my belly, draining all of my air. Whooshing it out from the inside. That's what a panic attack does; it drains you inside out. Leaves you exhausted, dripping in sweat, gasping for miniscule amounts of air.

Fuck, I need people. I realise I do; I need someone.

# Seven

## Outgrowing Death

In my bedroom I have a small pair of ancient white shuttered doors that lead to a courtyard. When I say ancient, I mean they look old. I hate painting, especially woodwork, so the paint is flaking. I'm happy with the flaking but I doubt that ancient is the right word.

I have a pair of scruffy shuttered doors that lead out to my courtyard.

At the centre of the courtyard is an old, sexy, gnarled olive tree with beautifully sinewed limbs like an ageing stevedore carrying bales of olives down from the Mediterranean hillsides.

The tree is in a space I bought with my own money. No one gave me a penny's worth of help. Not now, not ever. So that's a strange concept to me, that somehow I did something right enough to own this beautiful space. It makes me realise that I must have taken some decent decisions. I've visualised this space, or a space like this space, my whole life, from nipper to now.

Years ago, I worked in the old East End docks. It was a new

museum project to catalogue all the leftovers and trinkets abandoned in the vast warehouses. We cleaned, catalogued, smoked dope, and then cleaned and catalogued some more. Most afternoons we were so stoned that we couldn't guarantee that the numbers on objects matched their descriptions, especially on warm, summer afternoons lounging on the docks, our feet dangling in the icy cold water.

The man who ran the project was an ex-docker with beautifully tattooed forearms and muscular fingers. Individual fingers that all worked out, beefed up, flexed, heaving bales of imported goods.

He came from a long line of dockers.

As he issued instructions for the day, I watched his arms bulge and tighten under his shirt sleeves. I became obsessed with the veins in his arms; his forearms became cocks that I watched plump and swell each morning. Imagining him fucking me behind one of the old cranes that stood like huge rusting wading birds waiting to snag a fish the size of a whale. At one point in my life, I was that simplistic. Arms have always been my things, arms and hands. I'm a sucker for a forearm.

In honour of his forearms, when I left I stole a Chromonica from the museum's collection. A Chromonica is a little like a harmonica but with more tonal options, if you can play it, which I can't. It sits in my bedside drawer between a pink vibrator and an even pinker clitoral stimulator, it gets used slightly more than either sexual option.

It's a noise that sends the dogs into a frenzy, they howl and I laugh. That's sex now, making the dogs howl and me laughing. Soon I'll be pissing myself and laughing at that. And that thought makes me smile. I know people might find that weird in this real-housewife, botoxed world of ours, but I'm enjoying every facet of ageing, the letting go, the new, the losses and the unexpected.

I love the olive tree, it's the thing I love most in my whole house.

A dear friend once gave me a nun's holding cross carved from olive wood. When I first arrived here I bound it to the olive tree in my courtyard with gold wire. Not real gold but gold coloured, which was the same thing to Ratners, the 1980s jewellers of choice. Gerald Ratner, the CEO, once said that his shops sold 'total crap'. Half of south London sighed with embarrassment and tossed their belcher chains and anklets into kitchen drawers then slammed them shut. That statement shamed so many people for whom the shiny stuff, gold, is the mainstay of family inheritance.

My mum has a gold chain, which I hope she leaves to me because it's *her* gold chain, she wears it every day and has worn it every day for as long as I can remember. It's all she'll have to leave, one object each – a brooch for my sister, a ceramic box painted with fishing flies for my younger brother, photos for the elder and the chain for me.

Seven years on, the tree has started to grow around the holding cross, taking it back into the olive family fold. Clasping it tight.

Olive wood is described as strong, as hard, but sensitive to environmental factors. It's expensive wood. I love seeing the two different olive woods becoming spliced together, the gold thread disappearing under a thickening ridge of bark, a consummated marriage.

*

This morning, I woke up and instantly wondered if I would have moved here if I'd known that I'd have to live through another pandemic, alone in the mountains. I couldn't decide.

Looking out at the old olive tree through the old shuttered doors, I know that the tree is the most beautiful thing I've ever owned. If I hadn't moved here I'd never have owned an old olive tree. Olive trees can live to 1,500 years, most average five hundred years, the oldest olive tree in the world is the Olive tree of Vouves in Crete. It's over 2,000 years old and still produces fruit. I imagine my tree laughing at the idea that I own it rather than it me.

I get up to open the ancient, nay tatty, doors to let fresh air in to help clear my muzzy Valium head. I curl up on my bed and stare out at the tree. I think I'm in love with the tree, I wish it could talk. It would tell me to shut up whining.

It's the kind of tree that I used to dream about having, about hiding under, or climbing into. It represents safety. It feels magical to have been able to buy a house with this tree. A tree privilege. The tree is more important than me, I think, or anything I might do with my life, apart from perhaps writing about the tree, immortalising it.

One day, years after I've moved, or perhaps after I've died here in this bed, someone will run their hand over the tree and find the smooth embedded cross and think it's a miracle. Perhaps it will become a place people visit, a shrine, a Catholic shrine. I'm very much my errant father's lapsed Catholic offspring, forever caught up in signs, symbols and meanings.

The tree of life.

I pull the duvet up over me this morning as the air is cold. I listen to the *Today* programme. I can manage about ten minutes of news before it overwhelms me. It automatically wakes me; my alarm is the *Today* programme, which is terrifyingly like sleeping and waking up with posh folk. I don't think I've slept romantically with a proper posh person; I've had sex with many. They sound nice in the morning; I must change my dating profile to include the word plummy.

All talk is of COVID-19, lockdowns and vaccines. I can't stand it, my anxiety levels are sky high, waves of anxiety ripple through my sleep which isn't sleep, its hours are fitful and disturbed. I keep waking with numb hands and numb feet from tension, feeling more exhausted by the action of non-sleep than by any daytime activity. I dread nights, I feel destroyed by them.

I turn the radio off and scroll through my texts, seeing one I've missed from the government about a letter they will be sending me about how to be *clinically extremely vulnerable, but safe*, which sounds oxymoronic. Then I notice an older text from my HIV clinic telling me that my syphilis test was clear. *No shit, Sherlock*, I think, wondering why they keep testing me for syphilis. I've told them that I'm far too complicated for quick sex now, but they think I'm trying to be funny. I'm not. I wish I could have easy breezy fucking, sucking, licking sex, but like sleep it's become far too complex. Rough terrain. Impossible terrain.

I've had syphilis before, maybe like other viruses it can remain dormant and re-emerge years later, maybe that's why they keep testing me despite my protestations.

I make a mental note to research syphilis, because that won't add to my anxiety, will it?

I stare at the olive tree and imagine what it would be like

if it could reach into the bedroom and put its arms around me and cuddle me. I'd like to rest my head in the crook of its branch.

Syphilis seems like another lifetime; it was, I suppose. I was the same person but a completely different person. I've been different people my whole life, it makes my personal history very fragmented.

I caught syphilis from a lover (not the lover who tried to teach me to shout) who wouldn't stop buying me shoes, shoes that never fitted because he never asked me my size and I didn't want to hurt him by telling him after the first wrong pair. I was always silent, silent with men who told me I should shout and men who told me I had syphilis. After my AIDS diagnosis when everyone told me I should be angry I couldn't find any anger, just resignation that this would be addressed in silence. I've sometimes wished to join a silent order of nuns.

*They're lovely*, I said, squeezing my trotters into extremely tiny, pointy toes.

I thought that maybe, one day, a pair might fit and that would mean that we were right together. A weird, convoluted Cinderella complex. None fitted but he gave me the clap, so something worked.

Some of the shoes were so small it was like my toes had been bound, and others so big that I'd have to grip the insoles with my toes like I was trying to hold on to our love. It wasn't love. It was sexual and very dirty. I ended up getting a text from him telling me that I needed to visit the clap clinic and get tested for syphilis. He was mortified, I could tell from the text, and, to be frank, so was I.

I wish the olive tree could reach in and hold me to take away these memories.

I was once given crabs by a French porn star who didn't speak a word of English. I speak hardly any useable French, despite my ancient Huguenot roots. Certainly, nothing as intimate as the sharing of news about pubic lice. The relationship felt very romantic and international, so one day when he indicated that he had something *très important* to tell me I asked my flatmate, who was fluent in French, to translate. I thought he was going to ask me to move to Paris with him, I actually started to pack and dream of a life making Super 8 black-and-white porn films. So romantic. *Juno in Paris.*

It turns out that he'd given me crabs and had brought some crab lotion from the chemist for me to apply to my genital area and his, not a word of a lie, as he fucked me. All of these medicinal details translated by my horrified flatmate.

Mortifying. I do wish the olive tree could hold me now and take away these memories.

My flatmate, who acted as translator, gave me notice to leave the flat as she was worried that the crabs might become a flat infestation. Just me and my lonesome crabs homeless out on the street for a couple of months until we found a squat and in perfect symbiosis, I squatted a house while the crabs squatted me.

A group of us – bikers, models, drag queens, pretend artists and my oldest friend who is the greatest painter I've ever known – squatted a Crown property in Regent's Park. It was a property that belonged to Prince Charles. It had no running water, scant electricity, a mud floor in the basement (the servants' quarters) and noble floor-to-ceiling windows that allowed light to flood in. The windows were taller than any person. Grand windows. I saw nothing but the windows.

We painted the walls of the basement pink because we found a tin of pink paint outside the old pet shop in Camden Parkway. The pet shop used to have a sign that said *monkeys and talking parrots*. The paint was bubble-gum pink, a cold pink if pinks can ever be cold. We thought it was Floridian meets old English chic.

The floor remained mud and after painting the walls pink, we never visited the basement again because we convinced ourselves that it was haunted by the dead servants.

We were so poor that we made porridge by dissolving cheap biscuits into a cup of tea, but the windows made me feel like the matchgirl who'd brought the outside in. My last memory of the house is having sex with a man for ten pounds who put his underpants over my face explaining that he wanted to kiss me through his arsehole and that this was the most practical way of achieving that kind of kiss. I do feel privileged by the kinks that have come my way.

Lying on my bed looking out into the courtyard I listen to birdsong and laugh about the man wanting me to kiss him through his underpants. Such sweet memories.

I don't want to get up yet, so I switch the radio back on, changing the station, looking for something lighter. I settle on a man talking on a radio phone-in, talking through his tears about losing his mum to the virus after she'd gone into hospital for a completely unrelated simple everyday procedure. It's not lighter, but it's about mums, which always grabs me. His mum caught COVID-19 on the ward and died three weeks later. Never leaving the hospital, she, and they, imagined would only be a temporary residence.

*We'd done everything we could to keep her safe, everything, had cups of tea with her through the window and sent food parcels round rather than even knocking on her door. When she was in ICU, I could only tell her that I loved her through the nurse's iPad, she was already ventilated, the nurse held it near to her face, but I could see that she wasn't there any more.*

By this point he was crying uncontrollably, crying his heart out on a daytime radio phone-in. His tears shifting, moving, distorting the airwaves in great waves of sobs. His tears all our tears. All our thoughts with him.

*Can you hear when you're ventilated?* I wondered as the radio host told the man, 'You've got to know that she loved you', which seemed like an obvious thing to say considering the man's tears, but in these dystopian times the word 'love' in any context seems vital. The man's love for his mum was overwhelmingly obvious.

I started crying because a human was crying and the sound of a human crying makes humans want to cry unless they're a sadist. I once knew a man who'd ejaculate if he made you cry. He was a sadist.

I started crying because I'm in the mountains and my mum is a thousand miles away on the outskirts of west London, I picture me telling her I love her via my iPhone. She's at that age where death, from COVID-19 or otherwise, becomes ever-present.

I want to keep her alive, to stop her from ageing; I remember her much younger than me, all the years since have been hard for her. Brutal. She's always struggled financially, more often than not on benefits, always on Valium. She'd always gone without and would go without to help any one of us, she'd give us her last fiver.

Part of my buying this house was to give her an easier time, to keep her alive longer in the sun she so loves and maybe, just maybe, to make her happier. I think the Spanish dream was always hers. Not this dream in the mountains but an easier, beachside dream.

I thought that she could visit for long stretches, sit in the sun, get a tan, and smoke cheaper Spanish fags. She did for the first few years of my being here; she'd visit, we'd drive down to the coast, eat scampi and chips, and she'd sit, her beautiful face tilted up to the sun, roasting until she was a dark leathery tan. Coughing constantly but happy. Or happier. Or perhaps a cough seems more palatable in the sun over scampi.

I'd always get angry at her coughing and beg her to stop smoking even though I know it's her only real pleasure in life. That and sitting in the sun getting angry at the Tories, swearing at them. Calling Boris every cunt under the sun, her word not mine. She's always hated the Tories, she loved Jeremy Corbyn, she thinks Keir Starmer is slimy, she says, *never trust a man with that much product in his hair.* As a rule of thumb, it's not a bad life lesson, if a little harsh on men who like hair products.

But I also bought this house to run away from my responsibility of trying to keep her connected to life and trying to make her happy. It felt like my role to keep her alive, to try to ward off the suicidal ideation, the actual attempts, and the sweeping manic-depressive falls. The attempts at self-destruction – the walls she'd knock down with a sledgehammer in her rented bungalow, leaving piles of rubble and angry landlords, mystified at her reckless behaviour. Physically she was always so strong, she'd knock down walls and dig up trees, I miss her epic feats: age has stolen her wall-destroying capabilities.

My mum, so angry at life that she attacks the very building around her, then relents, tires, sits down, smokes and says she's sorry. And she is sorry, constantly surrounded by one form of rubble or another, frequently us kids.

The nihilism. The anger. The fatalism that her life is shit, that life on earth is hell and then you might go to a better place. I ran away from that, wanting to disappear, to change my number, my email address and my identity, but I couldn't because my love for her is gigantic, is mountainous, is as big, if not bigger, than the mountains that surround me. My love for her is everything. I know the intricacies of her life; I am the closest person to her and she to me.

Because she's never been happy to be alive, my work to try to make her happy in this shared lifetime has never been done. My attempts to make her happy have only scratched at the surface of her pain. So entwined is my need to make her happy with my own happiness that I sometimes feel I'll never be free. Even after she dies I'll know she died unhappy. All I can do is to help her financially, with her bills, treats, hairdos, clothes, trips out to see me and, when she could, trips to other places. But then she had a terrible fall in Egypt, so trips to other places stopped.

I've asked her to come and live here with me in the sun,

but she loves her radio, her kitchen table and being able to smoke indoors; I can't compete with indoor smoking, however much love there is.

I've paid for her funeral so that we don't end up squabbling over burial costs. I know we would, and she'd end up having the contemporary version of a pauper's burial. I know that no one else would or even could help to pay for it, they all struggle to make ends meet. I'm the most comfortably off, the queer, trans, HIV positive one with a shilling or two.

I paid for it because I couldn't stand the thought of us bickering over anything on the day, or days after she dies. I want her to have everything. Flowers, a beautiful casket, a lovely service, sausage rolls and a headstone in the Camberwell cemetery where she'll be buried with her mum, dad and sister who died as a toddler. She loves sausage rolls. Her friend Betty, who died just before the pandemic, used to make the best sausage rolls. Mum would say, *get Betty to make them if she's still around.* But she's not.

In the coffin she wants a spray tan or if she can, she wants her corpse to have sunbed sessions. We've often laughed about that. I love that she imagines her corpse could be carried and laid to rest on a sunbed somewhere in a salon in Uxbridge. *They wouldn't need to limit the exposure time, I'd be dead anyway*, she laughs.

I tell her that's where we'll all come to pay our respects, each of us with our strange sunbed googles on, watching her frazzle. She'll lie in state like the queen of the tanning salon.

She wants her upper lip waxed and her eyebrows done. She always waxes her facial hair, even in her eighties. She scolds me for not shaving my legs and waxing my chin.

*How could you*, she says, *you look like an old goat.*

*Thanks, Mum,* I say, thinking I am like a goat up here in the mountains.

After she goes, I always shave, it's a guilt leg-shave straight out of the seventies when English women imagined that all German women were covered in hair. *You don't want to be like one of those Continental women*, my mum would say. She always shaved everywhere, completely; she was Brazilian long before Brazil became linked to vaginal bush plucking. Before Carrie Bradshaw was even a jot on a pad, my mum was as smooth as a baby's arse. We grew up without pubic hair.

Obviously, I have a resplendent bush as a protest, and in comradeship with my EU sisters, who are now my siblings. I'm also far too lazy to do the minutiae of personal haircare.

We've bickered in these strange ways for years, especially since I transitioned. She preferred sons: that's not a guess, she's told me many times. *Daughters are too much hard work*, she says to me, me never being having been hard work.

I know her past and understand that her anger towards women is really anger at herself. I once tried to tell her that's what I thought, and she said I was fucking mad and that I should keep my therapeutic babble to myself. I do, out of love for her. I know she adored the son I was and that to her I probably still am, still that son all these years later. She calls me Juno but sees him. I can live with that if it gives her peace of mind, she's had a hard enough life without Juno coming in and stealing her son away.

She wants to be buried in matching bra and knickers, of course, and a simple shroud. She wants Frank Sinatra's 'My Way', which is odd because it's never been her way. Or maybe this is her way, her only way, her only choice. She was born into such trauma, a dead dad, who might not be her dad – rumours abound – and a mother running from poverty. And sexual abuse.

Maybe 'My Way' is an acknowledgement that she is at peace with it being her only way, but she seems so unhappy with it all.

In *The Body Keeps the Score*, the neuroscientist Bessel van der Kolk says that children who've been abused or molested, sexually or violently, have to summon up immense energy to keep functioning through life while carrying the memory of terror and the shame of utter vulnerability, that in feeling completely out of control, survivors of trauma often begin to fear that they are damaged to the core and beyond redemption.

I've always told Mum that if I die before her she's not to cry or waste any money because I'm not scared of death. I've had many years beyond diagnosis that have become a rich, long life. I have no fear of death, of my own death. Living with an AIDS diagnosis and then HIV all these years has emptied me of that fear. It helps Mum to feel easier about my dying as she knows I'm not scared; I've spent so much of my life at the edge, where life meets death.

Maybe 'My Way' is a truism about our life and death, a Holzer truism.

I plan a bench for Mum with the words 'MY WAY' in full caps surrounded by the emojis that populate her texts.

# Eight

# Hello Again

In the nineties, an old friend was told that I'd died. We haven't been in contact since because apparently I was dead. In a way I have been, I did shut up shop.

Them being told this almost, well, completely incorrect fact, perfectly illustrates the expected trajectory of my life. Throughout my twenties and thirties, it felt like the whole world constantly shook its head in disappointment at me.

A fucked-up, drug-addled trajectory going nowhere but down.

So after the greatly exaggerated rumours of my death, we lost contact, reconnecting by email the morning after the news about the new COVID-19 mutation, the Kent strain. How very British. The morning of the Kent strain.

I also thought he was dead; someone told me he'd died of AIDS in the mid-nineties. I never believed it because I still felt his energy, but I never thought we'd reconnect because of the messiness and unruliness of my drug years. I was too messy for almost everyone I'd known before Drugs Proper.

He'd written a book which is now out of print. I know because I kept trying to buy it over the years as a reminder, a trinket of our friendship. In a way a book being out of print is like a death. If you search and it says *out of print*, it feels beyond or in the grave.

We reconnected by email the morning after the news about the pandemic's new mutation. I found an email address on LinkedIn. I'd spent years wondering what happened to them, where had they gone, if they had died, where were they buried if they had. The only thing I've ever found on LinkedIn was the existence of them so I sent a single email to a work address. This pandemic made me reach out.

I'm not sure how to document this pandemic, it's so alive and bleak. I'm not sure I should even try.

Every day a new speck of bleakness or fearfulness arrives in our new normal and then spreads with the kind of speed only possible in viral infections. The ages of people dying, the types of people dying, the youngest to die, the oldest to survive. The numbers in Brazil, the numbers in California. The numbers in India.

Data peppered with horrifying images of ventilators, people intubated, people trying to warn us from behind masks, from their hospital beds. It is without doubt the most intense period of anxiety I've ever experienced, and I was an HIV positive addict for over ten years; I get fear and an edgy existence, but this is everyone, everywhere, all scared, all unknowing. This is finally us.

Christmases everywhere are being cancelled because of the Kent strain which is much more transmissible than the last.

At the time of editing, this strain has been superseded by at least two others, both more transmissible.

Poor Kent, previously known for apples and hop-picking, now forever known as the birthplace of the mutated strain B.1.1.7.

I wonder if there'll eventually be a tour of the places and cities out of which new strains have emerged, plaques perhaps. One day, in tens of years' time, this will have been normalised down into whatever pop culture is then. It's too soon to contemplate a creative response to COVID-19, but in a few generations the horror of this will, hopefully, have become nothing more than a history that no one alive experienced. But I'm writing this book now and it seeps in of its own accord.

One day the Kent strain will be a film and a book and a play, perhaps even a joke. But not now. Not yet. Not while the dying are still dying and the living are still too scared to hug.

I understand viruses because my life has been altered, shaped and defined by one. I know how they mutate to avoid and dodge us. I know that effective drugs can stop working. It's like dancing with someone with razors on their toes, following a routine, learning to avoid the razors, then the record changes and you have to learn a new routine while avoiding razors. You get cut, you bleed, but then you learn the new steps and avoid their razor toes.

I lived through the experimental stages that defined the response to the early years of the AIDS pandemic. At least one of the drugs I'm still on was one of the first drugs to be manufactured in the mid-nineties. In 1996. I've never stopped taking it.

It's worked for me; it's been superseded many times over by better, more effective treatments but I can't let go, I'm an AIDS ol' timer.

I'm ridiculously superstitious, a creature who finds great comfort in aged habitualness. I'm sure it comes from those early years of AIDS fragility. I'm the kind of person who can move to the wilderness but once I'm there I never go beyond the one or two places I know. I need to know every part of a route. I hate driving, I'm terrified by speed.

I get bogged down by superstitious thoughts and illogical thought patterns.

The clock in my car doesn't work but I never want it mended, as I'm sure if my car finds out the right time, they'll know how old they are, know that they are an old banger and stop working. I know the absurdity of that personification but whenever I take it for a service I say to the mechanics, *don't mend the clock please, just leave it as it is.* It's the first thing I check when I get in the car.

I'm terrified that if I stop my original HIV drug then the AIDS-laden sky will fall in.

It's my saviour. If there is a god or goddess, it's the mountains and nevirapine. One begets the other, one allowed me to dream of the other. They link my life.

Hearing that the Kent variant had made different mutations in one jump is terrifying because we are only presuming and forecasting everything using data as it arises. We are involved in the construction of a completely new block of history. It will become a unit of work in lessons years from now. Usually new history is within our control, new technology, new places to visit – planets, new materials and ideas about equality.

But then we had Trump, Brexit and COVID-19. And then we had the Kent strain, which in the briefest of moments defeated Christmas and us. Albeit temporarily. Cross fingers.

We are in a race.

In the early days of AIDS, people would keep at least a couple of feet away from me because they thought that I was terribly infectious, that my infected corporeality could dissipate into the air and drift across the space between me and the cleanliness of them.

There was no *us* then.

No one knew otherwise, so people behaved atrociously.

They'd throw away any bed linen I slept in; cups I drank out of. They gave me my own special mug for my toothbrush, which sat as far away from their toothbrush mug as possible. It wasn't special, just lonely.

I became a walled-off city, an island, a thing within a thing but separated from that thing. It's always felt like that. Red crosses appeared on my medical and dental notes and the words 'highly infectious' and 'high risk' became adjectives that followed my name or hospital number or more exactingly, my blood.

Juno, five foot six, grey haired, highly infectious, risky, loves trees, wants to write a book and save the planet.

From the early days, we knew that HIV could swiftly take lives; we saw it happening in appallingly brutal and disfiguring ways.

We are born scared of death, of painful deaths, and we watched as the virus killed painfully.

It was a nightmare to live through, already people talk

about PTSD in relation to this pandemic, but no one has addressed the trauma that long-term survivors of HIV and AIDS endured.

The emergence of the Kent variant takes me back to those early days of HIV, when a great proportion of my time was spent making sure that I kept my body in check, sealed. My blood and fluids kept within, away from the world. I feel like Kent, a pariah county, somewhere to lock down. Reinforce the borders.

The night after the cancellation of our collective Christmases (we were *us* again), I couldn't sleep for thinking about the hideous potential of viral mutations. A single virus can spawn billions of copies in a single day. The chance for change is vast. Much vaster and more rapid than anything we can contemplate. It's not a Darwinian clip-clopping time-scale, it's overnight, it's in the blink of an eye.

So fast it's unseen. Chances are, we will never witness the birth of a mutation, the very thing that might wipe us out. Not like a volcano erupting, or even a swift tsunami. The birth of a deadly strain happens deep within a body somewhere on the planet, an act of creation so small that its beyond our searching. Viruses are, ironically and malevolently, smaller but far, far bigger than anything we can comprehend.

God-like, really. As much the God-particle as the Higgs boson. Perhaps more so, considering our obsession with our death. The Higgs boson deals in creation, viruses deal with sublimation and destruction.

The virus doesn't see us or perceive us as good, bad, rich, poor, ugly or beautiful, it doesn't care. We are not an enemy or a foe. It infiltrates prisons and million-dollar Malibu mansions.

Those are our narratives of protection – a high wall, a security gate, a morning a week on the treadmill.

In Russell T Davies's *It's a Sin*, a central character shouts, *I'm going to live*. The language of battling. Of having a say. A choice with death. He dies.

If I run out of my HIV medication, I can battle all I want, I could perform endless battles until the performativity of my battling pops up as a dance move on TikTok, but inside me the virus will nonchalantly clock on and multiply.

Viruses don't consider us worthy or unworthy of life. We are merely hosts and as hosts it's helpful if we're alive. We are houses, rooms, hilltops, mountain ridges, streams, rivers, seas. We are all the places they need to inhabit to thrive. Around HIV was developed a moral narrative; society – moral, religious society – decided to assign the viral pandemic to the existing pandemics of hatred, discrimination, racism and homophobia. That overlaid pandemic, stigma and discrimination and shame, has killed thousands.

I'll never forgive the world for those deaths.

Why we haven't evolved as a species to worship viruses, or at least pay them due respect by preparedness, seems absurd, as we experience their power and devastation literally in a way that we don't with our absent conceptual gods. We believe in the power of one through the written and spoken word, and one wreaks actual havoc. Viruses write their own scripts and biographies on our skins, our lives. Viruses bring us to our knees and we pray. I've prayed during this pandemic for the people I love to be kept safe. Who I'm praying to fuck only knows. *A viral god?*

It's taken a single year for the world to be brought to its knees: capitalism, luxury, celebrity, the outdoors, safety, consumerism, healthcare, leisure, exercise, family. We are a broken us, a scared us; I don't rejoice in that, I just hope that people better understand the fear we as people with HIV experience, as you shun us.

Every aspect of our world has been halted and opened and halted some more. There is no new normal because our understanding of normal is a concept that worked with the old world. Not this one. In this world your family can be the unwitting enemy, the viral spreader, the super spreader. The barbecue. We have to keep distance from them.

That's antithetical to thousands of years of history in which touch, from those you love, often takes you directly, instantaneously to the safest of places, to love.

To give someone COVID-19 is anything but loving. When people refuse to wear masks I think, *it's you that you hate principally, it's your safety you don't hold dear, people hurt people often because they are happy with or accepting of hurting themselves*.

When AIDS happened, everything changed. For everyone, even if they didn't admit it. Even if they pretended that AIDS was happening over there to junkies, hookers and homosexuals. Sex changed. The term safe sex became part of our lexicon, even if we chose to ignore it, we ignored safety and welcomed risk.

Sex had never been dangerous before. Not lethal.

Princess Diana held a hand and that was seen as a watershed

moment. That's how dangerous our bodies were made by the application of morality to a virus. The moral pandemic rides the AIDS pandemic and a princess's hand cuts through. Fuck me if we aren't condemned by our emotional simplicity, which is innocently our emotional need to be close to each other. We think that a hug solves all.

The term 'high risk' became part of the sexual lexicon. Morality became embedded in the mainstream's understanding of those communities who seemed more high risk. They should have safe sex, if sex at all. These were the already marginalised. I fell into that category. I was queer, sold sex and injected drugs. I was high risk, obviously immoral and obviously incapable of safe sex. I didn't know sex had to be safe, none of us did. That was the point. We were all innocent before the words 'safe sex'.

Why did you separate us and treat us so badly?

*Ship them off to an island,* the eighties headline screamed. I sat on the London Underground, reading over his shoulder, and thought, *ship me where?*

The concocted link, the created pandemic, between the white, Christian, angry God and AIDS was made ever more explicit. This was God's work; these people hadn't been rounded up and finished off in Sodom and Gomorrah like they should have been. This dangerous, murderous narrative allowed many thousands to die, often alone.

People balled and chained HIV to God's work. COVID-19 they've tried to link to Chinese food markets, to the pace of Chinese capitalist growth. We have allowed viruses to become part of our colonial diatribes, polemics about them and us. Always seeking to create and separate the them and us, to find someone who can be blamed.

In headlines, in the comment section, on the letters pages, written and delivered in sermons, debated in parliaments and other places of political discussion, they decided to pretend that AIDS was sent by God to destroy all those who posed a risk to the purity of the normative, centralised, nuclear, apparently capitalist-efficient family.

A dad, a mum and their cluster of innocent kids who'll never grow up to be poofters or druggies but hopefully bankers and hairdressers.

This was only a few years after the murderer, the Yorkshire Ripper, had killed prostitutes and innocent women. Or so they said. I remember watching news coverage where conversations, which should have been about the horror of women being murdered, being bludgeoned to death, morphed into debates about prostitutes spoiling nice streets full of young families. We as a species utilise horror to our own ends when it suits. I wonder how they'll frame the Kent strain in years to come, no doubt they'll find a black or brown skin to park the narrative within. Perhaps in a post-gendered landscape they'll blame a trans person, fuck, they blame us for everything.

AIDS killed indiscriminately; it didn't care who the person was fucking as long as it could gain access to your bloodstream. It didn't care if you were Rock Hudson, Gia, or my many dear dead friends, forever in their twenties. Held in divine memorial stasis in outfits popularised by Wham!, their bodies peppered with Kaposi's sarcoma.

Viruses simply find the easiest way into our bodies and then do what they need to do. Like squatters, really successful squatters deftly opening doors, cranking electricity supplies and moving friends in before sunrise.

The evangelical, right-wing Christians who said that AIDS was God's work had no comprehension of how empty their spiteful conversations with their version of God were. Many of them died from their own smiting, lifting up their cassocks after their sermons to fuck the marginalised, the people they condemned. I blame the evangelists, the extremists, for almost all of the ills of our time. They create risk by their claims that somehow this world should be demarcated by moral certainties and hard lines over which different groups of people should exist – the right and the wrong, the good and the bad.

Now we have mask refuseniks who say that God will protect them, only to die a month later with their lungs so packed full of virus that they cannot pray. They have been led to believe that they are untouchable and safe from harm, that they are on the right side of morality, by the extremists and their ill-informed followers who now populate the internet.

Sadly, some political leaders are now the extremists. Surely we understand one simple fact: if there were indeed a god, it is not one we can harness, or control, or call on to do our spiteful biding. No god would exist to do any but their own bidding.

We may try to turn viral nightmares into battles we can understand, we may seek to personify a virus, to battle it in our own conflicting moralities, but they don't care, they exist simply to transfer their being, their DNA, into our cells. That's it.

We may bang our Churchillian fists on wooden tables, but

the viruses aren't listening; they're sleeping or reproducing gazillions of copies. It happened to Boris as he thumped the air. The virus sighed, shook its head, giggled and reproduced, and he ended up on oxygen. You can only pretend to be Churchill if you're battling other Churchills on beaches. Viruses don't give a flying fuck about all that Churchillian bullshit, nor should we.

Boris with his fist waving is such a wanker, Hancock sending me texts signed *Matt* is such a wanker. We're doomed with this bunch; they are a pandemic.

A pandemic of upper-class immoral wankers. I'm glad I said that; I can die happier now.


COVID-19 has dragged me back to the time when I was told to prepare myself for my premature death or at best a shortened life. I was young; I was diagnosed just before starting at university. But it was more complex and less binary than being struck down in my prime; I was an addict, I was already trying to leave my body, and did for periods of time every day. I didn't want to die but I was tired of trying to live like other people. I cannot claim the fertile grounds of a prime life being snatched away, I need that to be clear. I need clarity. I was a mess; a diagnosis of premature death was added to a pile of other things that I should deal with.

What happened?

My boyfriend, T, had started to get extremely ill a year or so before. T was at first a lazy shortening of his name but then it stuck and blossomed with its own sexual energy. T.

Coincidentally, we were at that very point on the cusp of splitting up. We'd been together since the start of the nineties, our relationship held together and levered apart by constant drug use. It was chaotic at best, only very occasionally loving. His illness had nothing to do with our drifting apart; I wanted to change my life to stop drugs, I wanted away from that lifestyle.

I've carried a terrible guilt, but at the time I thought he was trying to make me stay by feigning illness. But his illness intensified, T started to disappear in front of my eyes. Without knowing it, he was dying, how would I have known, how does an untrained eye recognise the process of dying? Especially in your twenties when your sights are firmly on the potential of living.

I'd also been ignoring a whole cabal of infections and illnesses that were wreaking havoc on my own body over the previous couple of years. I knew somewhere in my psyche that something was happening, but I didn't know what. I kept getting bouts of oral thrush that we put down to my addiction. The thrush made it painful to eat, to swallow.

I started to lose weight through days of painful thrush, awful diarrhoea, and weeks of night sweats. But when you're a heroin addict, no doctor wants to get too close to you; maybe it's changed now, but when I visited the doctor for anything other than methadone, I'd be kept at arm's length. Outside of the surgery if they could, literally on the doorstep.

I'd been ill for a long time, but no one, me included, had joined up any of the dots.

One day T collapsed on Brighton beach. It was a beautiful warm Sussex day, breezy but warm. Somehow, one step at a time over the pebbles, I got him home and laid him on the bed. His body was emaciated but still a dead weight. He was a whisper of a body, papery skin and frail bones. On the bed I could clearly see his lungs rattling under his ribcage. *Why hadn't I noticed?*

I wasn't a complete cunt, I don't think I was. I might have been, but we'd been on drugs for so long that our intimacy was with the crack pipe, the needle, the spoon or the chased line on the foil, that's where our bodies met. Our gaze. Our bodies had become distant, almost useless. Like old coats that cover you without any warmth or protection, threadbare, worn thin. He was on the cusp of life. I panicked, cried, T was after all my partner in crime, we'd ridden every shitty dangerous highway on our drug escapades for years by then. I did love him.

*Don't fucking die*, I whispered. His eyes closed, *please don't die, keep your eyes open*. I shook him, I pleaded, *I need you; I can't be alone like this, no one will ever love me like you have*. I think I meant it. I was distraught.

I jumped up and called his GP, they came out, and after the briefest of minutes said, *can I use your phone? Yes*, I said, *it's there*, and pointed to the phone table in the hallway. They called for an ambulance and in my earshot said, *he has full-blown AIDS, it's an emergency, get here as quickly as you can, I don't expect him to last the night*.

At this point I knew nothing about AIDS other than it emptied nightclubs and pubs and queer venues of young people. I'd visited friends in hospital but it terrified me, it only ever seemed to kill.

*What*, my ears pricked up, *what did they say? What? What the fuck?*

I collapsed inwards. If you'd seen me, you would only have

seen my shoulders slump and my eyes glaze over. Truthfully, I wanted, no needed, to smoke crack, to use heroin, to stop the world. But you wouldn't have seen any of that. I was so disconnected from my body that I wanted to run. He couldn't die, the snippets of love we'd shared, even those through drugs, were intimate moments. He was the only intimacy I'd ever known.

I knew, I just knew; he was me and I was he. We were an *us*. Swallowing spunk had been commonplace, fucking constantly without condoms and him coming inside me was sure as the day ending with darkness. I knew. I just knew. That call, *I don't expect him to make it through the night*, was coming for me too.

I'd shared needles, not with him, he'd have been appalled at me, my addiction slipping faster and deeper than his. But I'd frequently thrown the threat of sex work at him and the risky dalliances I'd shared with other addicts and dealers. I just knew and I wanted to run, but not from him any more, from me.

T was rushed into hospital; they wouldn't let me in the ambulance, probably scared I'd try to steal drugs – I would have cast an eye around – so I ran after them, trying to chase down the ever-decreasing siren. It became a white dot over the crest of a hill. I slowed down to a jog, then a walk, then a stumble. Dusk. I sat on the edge of the pavement and realised I was sobbing, sobbing in front of people. I had no frame of reference for sobbing in public. I held back my tears, on the day of FULL-BLOWN AIDS I retracted my tears.

By the time I got to the hospital, I'd packed away every single tear neatly in the glass jars that sit on the shelf just inside my lower eyelids. Labelled glass jars.

I was taken into a side room and a nurse asked me if I wanted to speak to someone, anyone religious, they asked. I said *he's not a believer, so no*, they said, *we meant for you*. It hadn't clicked, but I was also a patient now, as well as a visitor and carer and lover and drug-using companion. I was a patient. A person with AIDS. A person expected to die. A person who might want to make peace with their maker.

*Crank up Whitney or Brandy*, I thought, I don't need a priest, I need to get stoned, smashed and listen to them sing my pain away.

I left the hospital, I ran, and ran, down to the beach, to the sea and called the waves useless. The shells useless, the sunset useless, poetry useless, my body useless. Me of course, useless. I stayed on the beach until the darkness was heavy, velvety, concealing. I thought about going to the cruising grounds further down the beach. In that moment I thought about my body as a sexual thing. I wanted sex more than ever, but something about sex, about intimacy, about touch had changed, or that night, that velvety angry night was changing. My body morphed into a risky vessel. I trudged back up the beach trying to tread silently on pebbles intent on percussion.

At home I smoked crack, ingested heroin, and played Randy Crawford's 'You Bring the Sun Out' on repeat until the sun rose like the words of the song, and then I walked back to the hospital, heroin dulling the pain, each step light. Absent. Absent. Absent. Gone.

That walk to and from the hospital was like the walks I made to school as a kid, keeping secrets in, feeling alone, separated from the rest of the world, the keeping of secrets inside making me feel more alone.

I didn't have a traditional family that could support me through AIDS, it was a tough time for Mum and it was almost impossible to bring AIDS into conversations with the people at university without scaring the shit out of them and eliciting tears. I felt very alone. It's impossible to explain what carrying AIDS around was like then. I carried hateful headlines around in compliant, beaten silence.

I didn't get a diagnosis for weeks because the focus was rightly on T, even though my world had begun to shift, to change, and to move towards a presumption of premature death. That annoyed me, how the world meekly, politely accepted my fate without ever consulting me. People advised me not to put myself through the stress of university, to leave, to stop learning because learning was for people with lives. Not people living with death.

*Fuck you all.* I pushed a needle into a vein, tied my hair back and thought if I'm going to die, I'll die with a degree. *Now leave me alone, I'm gonna die clever, with books and words coming out of every orifice, riding high on the waves of my watery shit, surfing my toxic expulsions. Expulsions of explosive brain power. I'm worthy of learning, so fuck right off with all your dying shit.* I put my foot down like a boss with rights. Like a person with a right to life. That was the first time I'd ever demanded anything in life.

I think something slipped that day in my already fractured sense of self and sense of reality, that enabled me to study, to really concentrate on studying at that moment in time.

I studied philosophy and art, art movements, conceptualism, neo conceptualism and the impending death of conceptualism and the shallowness or grittiness of what might follow in a post-everything world.

I was happy diving into concepts which required absolutely no emotional investment from me, at first everything was just investigation. Foraging. Prodding something I consider to be lifeless.

I measured my prospects, my potential, and the parameters of my life by reaching the last day of each university term. Half terms at first, then full terms – the spring, the summer, the autumn. I'd of course celebrate completing a term by binging drugs. As you do.

I made it through autumn, relishing the cornucopia of rusting, spent leaves. I kicked through them making a point about my presence. I was overjoyed to still be alive when the freezing winter winds arrived and the sea in Brighton became monumental, crashing, stark. I'd freeze watching storms batter the wreckage of the old Victorian pier. It reminded me of a dinosaur's skeleton rising up out of the waves, the Kraken. My mum remembers coming down from London for the day and dancing on the pier with her friends when she was young. I stood and imagined my mum being a teenager dancing on the pier. I wanted to dance for longer, my brain told me that I was not ready to go. I gripped life.

Spring arrived and carpeted every space between the tarmac with new blades of perfect grass and tiny crocuses; I wanted to stay for ever in spring. I thought if I die, let it be in spring. Let my ashes become food for new growth. A tulip bed perhaps. Flaming orange tulips fed by my corpse, now there's an installation. Flaming AIDS tulips.

But I survived spring of that first year and felt the warmth of summer spread, little by little across my skin. It held me. I'd sit wrapped tight in layers of jumpers on the beach between the university and the hospital where T lay, his body slowly repairing, oscillating between here and there. I'd close my eyes, look up at the sun and then open them, staring straight at the fiery ball, daring it to do its worst, wanting the heat to brand my retinas with that moment.

The monumental winter waves were replaced by a gentle rhythmic hiss as the waves lapped across the pebbles. I'd count waves, I'd collect pebbles, for a time I placed those by T's bed, but then the pebbles became too much, I ran out of space for them. I could see there was no room left for grapes and cards, but I wanted all the space and I resented other people's cards and well wishes; I crammed their cards into the small locker. I wanted the space by his bed to be ours and ours only. I wanted him all to myself, I wanted this intimacy. So, the pebbles stayed and spilled onto the floor.

Why did I want to own the bedside, fuck knows, we'd been on the cusp of splitting up but years of addiction had bound us together tight like Bonnie and Clyde.

We'd met in our twenties, him his early twenties, me my mid-twenties. We met dancing in a darkened club in Shoreditch, high on Es we kissed and then fucked in a back room. We left that first night convinced it was love and didn't leave each other's sides until it ended ten-odd years later. An awful lot of drugs were needed to cement our narrative of love. Our drug intake increased to maintain the illusion of love and because we had great sex when we were high.

I wanted the world to go away and let my superstitious collection of pebbles and shells repair him, not just the drugs they intravenously pumped into his veins. I stupidly and childishly felt in competition with the drugs, I wanted to be able to save him, to be able to save someone.

Were the pebbles and shells about me?

I become obsessed, there and then, at the side of T's hospital bed, with Beuys and Bourgeois, thinking that my objects could be transformative and perhaps even shamanic.

My pebbles and shells.

Pebbles or shells that fitted together sculpturally felt meaningful, I created an interlocking piece on the Formica cabinet top. A map, a jigsaw, a trying to make sense of what was happening.

Were we falling deeper into the abyss or climbing out?

For weeks, T lay in hospital, his congested, mucky lungs mechanically assisted to open and close until they started to open and close without mechanics. Breathing easier. Less sticky. At dusk I laid my head on his chest and listened to the inner machinations of his pneumonic lungs. The addition of the drug Septrin started to clear his lungs of infection.

Sticky, wheezing, faltering, repairing, clearer.

I listened to his lungs fail, then grow steady, labouring back to breathe, to reinflate, deflate and reinflate. The most intimate of all my journeys; the side of my head, my ear resting on his ribcage, listening to the sound of him coming back to life. His body was covered in painful outbreaks of folliculitis and psoriasis, great swathes of skin coming away even if I touched him tenderly. For a time, he was more corpse-like than alive, almost an artefact. A body that had once fucked me hard and used me in sadistic top and bottom scenes.

A body that had fallen below life and was now fighting to clamour back up.

I obsessed with how I could note or record dying and not dying. I measured the success of my life by the acquisition of philosophical thoughts and new critical frames of analysis and reference around death. I wrote everything down, filled notebooks with ideas and concepts and thoughts about living and dying. I wrote terrible poems about his ribs, his chest, his skin.

My days expansive – ideas, artefacts, concepts, philosophers and philosophies, reduced every evening to noting the rhythmic sounds of his laboured breathing. His belly like an old clock. His ribcage, like a filigree bangle crafted from filaments of silver thread, felt like it would collapse under the weight of all that I was learning and accumulating. I accumulated facts and images and words and concepts. It felt as if my learning could kill him, or at least kill us. I felt guilty for acquiring more as he lay there acquiring less.

It created a distance between us even as I laid my head on his chest, skin on skin.

Books ended us, not AIDS, and not for a few years yet. AIDS cleanly created two separate entities, perhaps a fear of death does that, inevitably you know or think you are being cut away from the world. Death is singular, even mass death isn't a single event but a mass of single deaths. In retrospect, the AIDS diagnosis was probably the most liberating thing that had ever happened to both of us, prisoners to our upbringings and nothing else. Prisoners of our pasts. The violence of an AIDS diagnosis shook us free. We were both apples that had never fallen from our trees; we remained stapled on a branch where we met and did drugs.

Despite his fragile ribcage and faltering lungs, T survived. Bless him, he survived. That still fills me with joy. He was my great love affair with the idea of love, we still had a few years of adventures before us and many hours wasted taking drugs; in the end, AIDS didn't kill us.

Before studying, I never knew that you could view anything from a different point of view or consider that something could have a different context depending on where you were standing. I knew nothing of different gazes. Not male, not receptive, not proactive, nor trans or working class. Not even the queer gaze. I was as scantily educated as I was usually dressed.

My experience of living beside death changed everything about my need to find a different gaze. Life was indeed, as my mum had foretold, shit – but was it?

If I could look at a work of conceptual art, an oblique work, and develop an understanding of its abstract or layered purpose or lack of purpose, its resonance within the world as an object, then perhaps I could also make sense of my life and AIDS.

I was on the cusp of new understandings. Perhaps I'll die, but I'm not dying yet, not this term, maybe next, but this term I'm finding out about something new, something that didn't exist in my brain or in my life before. If I keep putting new stuff in my brain, facts and ideas and questions, then maybe when I die, I'll die differently. It won't have been about the dole or fucking or getting smashed. It won't have been just about cocks, punters or dealers, or dealers' cocks, it will be about concepts and ideas. Emerging questions that force me along, giving my life new momentum. I'll die a thinker.

Term-time philosophy saved me. I set philosophical goals. Philosophical milestones.

I read texts, some bleak, some too dense for me to understand, Blanchot's descriptions of the night, Baudrillard's takes on the Gulf War. I got it but I didn't. Questions started to fill my cavity, my belly. I felt scared of dying but also calm about dying, I rationalised that no one had ever said to me that I'd live a long life. No one had ever made that promise, certainly not me to me. I was a shoot-up junkie, philosophy enabled me to gain a critical context of what I might be able to do as a junkie in the space of art. Art as breath, as life. Art, I rationalised, might save me in the short term. A fix.

Maybe that's the purpose of creativity: to save the maker.

I stopped making work that looked like work because my work that looked like work was shit anyway, and started to carpet the rooms that other people's work sat in. If they were OK about that. I used the same oatmeal-coloured carpet, rush matting or coir. It mattered that I was there, but not there. That the rooms were spaces I could occupy; the newspaper headlines wanted me shipped off, so I became invisible.

The carpets were always about legacy in a strange way. If I died, then for a time the carpets would remain. I imagined the conversations about taking them up and throwing them away, I wanted the world to know or to acknowledge how hard it had been to get to a university from my background. The carpets were me; they would at least linger.

The carpets were also cushioned floors. I lived every day with the fear of falling and cutting myself open, and the carpets were there to lessen the falls, to soak up the blood. If it happened, if I fell, then I alone would roll up and dispose of the bloodied carpet. The carpets meant so much, possibly too much in that I could never explain or talk about them, so no one really understood. How could I talk to a room full of wide-eyed hope about demise or the fragility of life? Sadly, they were consigned to being unimpressive artworks, forgetful, someone said, which poetically was the very opposite of what I needed at that point in my life.

The carpets did have a very real, practical, unintended consequence as I started to syphon off some of my drug money into buying carpet. Nothing had ever come before drug money. My drug money was ringfenced with razor wire. But carpeting people's spaces as an artistic statement briefly felt more important than heroin, just occasionally important enough to loosen its grip on my purse.

I started to ease off drugs, just a little.

I visited my doctor and persuaded him to give me methadone, first divided out by daily doses in millilitres swigged in front of him or the pharmacist, then weekly doses by the litre, and finally we arrived at an agreement in which I could be trusted to take six weeks' worth of methadone at a time. I seemed trustworthy and I backed up this by saying I didn't want the other students to find out. One methadone trip was one too many, if you know what I mean, doc.

I felt guilty about abusing his trust, but it was my route to becoming fixed to something other than drugs and addiction. I became fixed to art. To art and language.

I sold some of the methadone for heroin and the rest for carpet. I became a carpet fitter.

Through nine terms of learning, I fought back using not the language of battles but the language of art. I acquired a new context for me. I got a degree and it changed me for ever, separating me from all that had gone before. By the end of the nineties, just after a millennium party at which, high as kites, we bizarrely publicly proposed undying love to each other, I walked away from T and he from me. We both realised that together we liked the crack pipe more than life and that would always stop us from living.

Almost thirty years on, I'm still very much alive and kicking in the mountains of Andalusia, maddeningly, for the first time running out of my HIV medication. To get it, I need to get to London, but to get to London I need to be vaccinated to make sure I'm safe and not vulnerable, which I can't do here yet, because here I'm not seen as high risk unless I become high risk here by telling them that in the UK I'm high risk. If I tell them I'm high risk, that's all I'll ever be. That's such a mouthful, but essentially people's views around HIV are largely unchanged. People think you've done something in your life that connects you to a completely different place from most people, to those headlines – *ship 'em off, shoot 'em*.

I'm in a conceptual quandary. My body is a site of different risks in different countries, my healthcare needs addressed differently.

I did a Google search for *how long will I live for if I stop taking my HIV meds?*

The Google answer (which is shit by the way) –

*If you stop taking your HIV medication you will, within three months, go back to the place you were at when you started to take your medication.*

Fuck that's harsh, I thought, that can't be true. Does that mean I'd go back to the nineties, does that mean I'll detransition, my upcycled genitals once again revealing themselves, turning themselves inside out again, like a flower seeking the sun? I once had a nightmare that my cock grew back; I woke up feeling utterly desolate, immediately reached down, and sighed as my hand felt the cosy plumpness of my upcycled genitalia. My middle-aged cunt. It would be a nightmare to have a cock again. That's a fact of my life, a cock and me never matched. With my quilted cunt, like a vintage Chanel bag, I do.

From day one we were our own original moment. We bonded over lube.

Because of the way they crafted my genitals, too many stitches in time, a row too tight, flesh puckered and created a fatty hood above my cave; it was only ever middle aged. I remember feeling saved from the idea of a perfectly created pussy by its fatness.

People either love or hate the word pussy; I think I like it.

If you look on the private gender surgery websites in Bangkok they always display perfectly crafted vulvas, thirsty, youthful, glistening, dripping like sushi twirling around on a conveyor belt. Look at me, look at me, buy me, buy me.

Luckily (desperately annoyingly at the time) all the private clinics turned me away because of my HIV status, else I'd have had a pussy twenty years younger than me, shouting at me from between my thighs, demanding decent waxing and better sex, rather than the occasional blast from my fuchsia clitoral stimulator which, when cranked up to its highest setting, plays techno music at ridiculous beats-per-minute. I hate techno. If it played old school R&B I might wank some more.

I was sent a text from my doctors in the UK telling me that as I'm highly vulnerable and self-isolating that I will be in Group 4 for the vaccine and I should be vaccinated by March. But I'm not in the UK, and COVID-19 and Brexit have tag teamed to make it almost impossible to move freely between countries and thus to manage vaccines and viruses and personal borders. I really think it's time to reassess borders.

Ironically, I've discovered that I'm back in a very risky place.

Hard borders between countries violate our bodies. They do. Mine is torn asunder, one risk here and no risk there but the risk is still the risk.

I asked my mum to photograph all the vaccine letters and email them to me. She did, I've printed them out, letters that stake out my claim for vulnerability. Those letters and my broken Spanish would later enable me to gain access to the priority group in Spain, Grupo 7, the group with additional needs.

Like a claim on land, rights to fragility. Who'd have thought that in chasing my dreams I'd end up feeling so fragile.

I'm tired.

I've been on life-extending medication for almost thirty years, tied to a hospital, often a room in a clap clinic, *why a clap clinic still?* Tied to a consultant, a pharmacy, appointments, and blood tests. I've had blood work done for years. I could have made a thousand Marc Quinn blood heads.

People moan about temporary COVID-19 lockdowns but

HIV has locked me in my body for years because of stigma. Rejected by a world that deems my blood risky.

Untouchable.

I made this unknowingly risky bed here in the mountains, I need to breathe through this.

I get scared that I might die, because of my stupidity at not perceiving risk, with unwritten words, blank pages. That's all that matters to me now, getting words down, finding out why I need to get words down; what am I looking for?

Like those people we lost in the last pandemic – Nick with lashes that looked like inky black gossamer wings, tall Paul who always said of himself, *I might not be the best looking but I've got the sharpest tongue*, and Steve who announced he was off to travel around South America but never made it beyond the AIDS ward in Middlesex Hospital.

A list of unfinished stories, stories of so many who didn't make it. This time, I'm telling mine.

# Nine

## Simon

Ahh Simon, beautiful Simon, my namesake Simon, I've thought about him almost every day since he died. About his laugh, his wit, his creative genius, his skin, his lips, his eyes, the rubbery head of his cock and his velvety, voluptuous foreskin that could completely cover my mouth: it stretched like a balloon. I often think about him when I'm in my courtyard doing nothing but sitting and thinking about where my life has brought me and where and when his ended. He'd have loved the sun here.

We'll get to Simon, but first, his ever-growing community of crabs.

I met him in the last year of sixth form. He was as openly gay as anyone could be back then. He wafted in like smoke from a Gitanes: cool, camp, edgy, European. We bonded through our shared desires for sex with men, fashion, smoking dope and experimentation. We had a romantic friendship which fast became sexual.

Casual sex with him fitted more than anything else ever had in my life, I adored playing around with him, the exploration felt safe and nourishing. I grew up through our touch. I loved our furtive meet-ups, often in public places – pub toilets, behind bike sheds or in his bed if his parents, who were older, were out. His dad was already in his late sixties and wore the uniform of that time, place and age. A moth-eaten grey or tweed suit, a white or perhaps a pale blue shirt, and always a dour tie. Always a tie unless he was mowing the grass or doing the car, in which case he'd loosen the top button, carry on, then stop, wipe his brow, and then remove the tie, folding it neatly and putting it in his pocket.

So incongruent next to his louche, espadrilled, experimental son. I don't think they had any idea about him because they didn't have any idea about the world, which was changing faster than they could keep up. I understand that now, at fifty-seven. My hair is my version of a moth-eaten tweed suit, comfortable and protective.

Simon was a godsend, but he really annoyingly gave me crabs, not once, but twice. A double dosing of crabs, which means that in truthfully telling the story of our young and beautiful queer fumbles I also have to tell my emerging history with pubic lice, which foretold my future with all manner of sexually transmitted stuff. Crabs were the spiky gateway.

Before Simon I hadn't had meaningful sex, just uncomfortable furtive fumbles with men and cocks in dimly lit places. Often a row of men standing at a urinal, who'd direct your gaze to their cocks. Either they, or you, would head to a cubicle and then you would kneel on the floor, if it wasn't too dirty and covered in piss or shit, or sit on the seat and suck them off. The seat was often just as filthy.

Once you were planted there a succession of cocks would be presented to you as if you were a debutante at a passing out ball. Either you would open your mouth or close the door. It's where I first learnt to charge, for the cocks I didn't really want to suck. *A fiver upfront please, before you come in.* More lucrative than a Saturday job in a supermarket.

It was a sexual act in which my mouth was open and present, but which didn't involve the rest of me in any pleasurable sense. My mouth almost detached from me, a separate entity. I wanted to explore men, to taste their bodies, but the rest of me wasn't there, the rest of me was already busily planning motherhood and a farmhouse kitchen. *An Aga!*

No one was ever allowed to touch my genitals, I quickly attracted only those men who'd read that. People did then, people were quick and savvy in those dangerous spaces, they didn't need signs or symbols or endless rambling, exacting online profiles. When the sexual act between men was still punitively and sometimes coercively policed in public spaces, people's sexual radars were acutely tuned to what they wanted and what they needed to enable them to come, to ejaculate. Pronto. There was often a family at home.

People still married, then, stayed in deep, expansive closets. It was a different time in which we lived under the shadow of criminality, then just as we thought were getting somewhere after decriminalisation, AIDS hit and gave Thatcher the excuse to roll out Section 28 into every school. Cunt. Section 28, banning the promotion of homosexuality as normal, all sprang from a single book about two loving dads.

Cottaging had nothing in common with country cottages, even though in my already lost to Hollywood romance mind,

I was constantly looking for a saviour, for someone to father my children.

Cottages were about ejaculation and spunk, not wedding bands.

That's not to say I didn't enjoy sucking cocks in toilets, I did and I stand by that.

I idolised Simon, so sex with him meant the world to me. He was popular, easy-going and fluid. I was clumsy. He was proudly queer and I was closeted-trans before I knew what transgender meant.

Despite the frequent and anonymous sex I was already engaged in, I'd never caught any sexually transmitted disease, or sexually transmissible critters before.

The first time I caught crabs it was shocking; the second time even more shocking and repulsive because I'd already looked at them clinging to my skin under a magnifying glass the first time I had them. The second time, my brain ran riot imagining their pointy legs digging in, gripping on, their sheer pulsating bodies and mouthparts greedily sucking my blood.

I found the very first crab, the original crab, in my pubic hair sitting on the toilet before school. I'd been itching all night and couldn't understand what was making me itch. I thought it was a light sprinkling of subtle punishment from God for sucking cock. Like a torture that might intensify if I continued to suck cock. It did intensify, the itching became unbearable and it had sweet fuck all to do with any god.

Your skin itches and despite itching furiously you can't quell the itch; you can't see anything because juvenile crabs are little more than specks. Juvenile crabs are romantically called nymphs. The nymphs swanned around my bush.

I couldn't sleep for itching so I got up before sunrise and sat on the toilet staring down at itchy skin through blonde pubes. That's not me claiming to be a natural blonde by the way, I bleached for years but my pubes were always Scandinavian, always doing their own thing.

Staring through my pubes I started to make out small indistinct shapes, half-buried, like slightly raised pinhead-sized moles, on my skin. Maybe even smaller than a pinhead, I was young and I had great eyesight, now without glasses I couldn't see a kitten if it was nestled in my not-so-blonde, grey-tinged pubes.

Occasionally they seemed to shuffle around like a sleeping dog seeking warmth on a rug. When they shuffled my skin itched right where they shuffled. Minuscule movements. I watched, waiting for any sign of movement, waiting to connect a shuffle to an itch and an itch to a shuffle. Like a bird watcher, a twitcher, I held my breath and stared at my bush, looking for movement.

I itched one of the crabs and unwittingly reached up and scratched my eye, unknowingly shifting a single pubic louse into my eyebrow where it went on to develop a small high-rise community. A *favela*. Eventually its family outgrew the single brow and spread out over both eyebrows, perhaps journeying between the haired spaces like cousins living next door to each other on a street in south London, like we did as kids, shouting over the fence making plans to play knock down ginger, or to throw dog shit at the windows of people we didn't like. Kids and crabs are so similar, always up to no good.

Eyebrow overcrowding happened in a nanosecond.

Having creatures live and feed on you is repulsive – they literally made my skin crawl – but over the next few days I became hypnotised by staring at them through a magnifying glass, amazed at their life cycle and the speed of their population growth. I could have created a biology project right there and then. But I failed biology five times with five Us; that should please the radical feminists who claim we don't understand simple biology.

Apparently – I'm not claiming to be an expert, a female louse can lay six eggs a day, a hundred and eighty in their thirty-day lifetime. Let's say you have a pride or a herd of ten crabs, that's one thousand eight hundred pride or herd members.

The eggs are called nits. Nits which become nymphs and then crabs; there's a poem here.

Hundreds of nits in an area as small as my pubic-hair-land, which sounds a little like the film *La La Land* but possibly more interesting. They roam to other places, setting off in great explorations to armpits, eyebrows, lashes and your arsehole, should it be hairy. That's a lot of eggs being incubated in small warm spaces. An eyebrow soon becomes an overcrowded tenement prompting a need for better housing. Lucky for my tenants I'm a socialist at heart and open to negotiate fair rents and decent housing. Move here, I beckoned, shining a torch at my arse, it's dead hairy.

When I was a teacher, one of my pupils had such a rampant community of head lice that they would drop off into her workbooks, sit a while, and then plot their journey to the neighbouring child's hair. Shuffling over terribly drawn irregular shapes. Her head was overflowing with lice.

That first morning, sitting on the toilet before school, I only realised that the dots were living when I pulled one away from the skin between my pubes and watched as a small blob of blood bubbled up and replaced the space of its ravenous body.

Fresh blood, warm, drinkable blood, my blood food. I'd become food.

We always imagine that we'll be torn in two by a great white shark, and here I was being eaten alive by dots with mouths and pointy feet. It's a little like our fears about war and the destructive power of tanks and bombs, and not a virus. We always imagined that COVID-19 would be a film with an ageing Dustin Hoffman chasing both the virus and a woman half his age. Hollywood: fuck knows why I've allowed it to shape so much of my life.

I held the struggling, minuscule vampire tightly between my fingernails and then pressed it into a single sheet of toilet paper. Don't ever waste toilet paper; one for piss, two for shit. One for crabs. For a second the crab on the sheet reminded me of the handmade paper we'd made in an art lesson; my paper had fallen apart because I'd tried to incorporate whole sunflower seeds, I always tried too hard. A single sheet of arctic-white loo roll, my mum's OCD never allowed coloured loo paper in the house, with a small brown dot in the middle giving me a filthy look.

Surely that can't be alive, my brain whizzed and whirled.

The tiniest dot inducing panic in me.

I saw small but definite leg movements. Pointed crab-like legs and small mouthparts that I could just about make out. I may have imagined seeing the mouthparts with my naked eye, but I knew they needed mouthparts; I knew if they were crabs they'd be feeding on me. I kept thinking about Ellen Ripley and the Xenomorph XX121.

I left the bathroom and went downstairs to the set of drawers where I knew there was a magnifying glass, although I never knew *why* we had a magnifying glass. Perhaps like fathers in tweed suits and ties they were just more common then?

My pyjama trousers weren't tied up properly and started to fall down, grabbing them and the magnifying glass I tumbled back up to the bathroom and the freezing toilet seat. Sitting down I opened the folded sheet of toilet paper, trying not to shake the seething dot off. I looked at it through the magnifying glass. It was moving, I could see it crawling, sloth-like, across the sheet, a single crab, smaller than a pin head. My hand moved and it rolled onto its back, its legs in the air moving, grasping, like it was calling me to tickle its belly. Its blood-engorged, swollen belly. *Don't think I'm gonna pet you, love*, I said.

It repulsed me and sent a cloud of warming shame up and over my skin. I watched its legs move, seemingly independent of each other, each leg with a pointed toe-tip like a climber's rock hammer. Seen through a magnifying glass, pubic lice are almost translucent. I watched its brownish liquid centre pulse and slosh and then realised it was my blood pulsing and sloshing. I crumpled the single sheet of toilet paper and dropped it between my legs into the toilet bowl.

*Drown, you fucker, the battle starts now.* In my head I sounded like Ripley. But I wasn't Ripley.

I grabbed the bottle of bleach, opened it, and poured it over my cock and balls.

*Please die.*

I had no idea that every time I itched or rubbed between my legs and then touched another part of my body that chances were, I'd move them around, like a beekeeper tending and relocating their buzzing hives. Eyebrows, armpits and arse hair. I didn't think to wipe bleach on those areas, only pouring it over my genitals, which started to sting and burn.

Over the next couple of days my genital skin reddened and blistered. Between the weeping bleach sores, I could see many more crabs emerging to feed on my blood. On closer inspection under the magnifying lens, I could see clusters of eggs welded tight to my pubes like bunches of coconuts waiting to ripen and fall. It looked like a farm.

The bleach had made it much worse, creating a 1914–18 trench environment in which the crabs thrived in a soup of sore skin and itchy pubes.

They seemed impervious to the bleach. Years later I found out that a suggested home remedy for killing lice is oil – olive, coconut etc. It suffocates them, as opposed to bleach which they surfed in and merely burnt me. The bleach had removed the top layer of skin, giving them easier access to their food source, my blood. I was a takeaway with a help yourself-to-all-you-want blood bar.

From my very dear friend, who I adored and constantly tried to emulate, I'd inherited a community of microscopic blood-sucking parasites with imperceptible movements but a monumental capacity to breed, a process sustained by thimble-sized tumblers, sherry glasses, of my blood.

They were thriving in the communal space between my legs, a space already so disowned by my feelings of dysphoria that I was torn between ignoring them and hoping that they'd leave of their own accord, like tourists do, or alternatively applying more bleach in an attempt to burn the fuckers off at the expense of my skin. Even then I was self-harming without realising it was harm. The pain was helping, I convinced myself.

Scroll forwards a couple of itch-filled days and I was back in the toilet at home again, not knowing what to do. The itching had become unbearable. I started to cry in pain, I put my hand over my mouth to muffle the sound. At home tears were likely to result in you being called weak, a poof, a sissy, a pansy by those around you, especially your dad.

I thought about dousing the crabs in a mixture of vinegar and bleach, perhaps white spirit, and bleach, or just more bleach, but before I could, my mum heard my muffled cries and, talking softly to me through the door, she asked to know why I was hiding my tears.

Exhausted, I unlocked the door and pulled it open with my foot. I looked down at my crotch in shame and self-loathing. She knew, she could tell. She's always been canny and street smart, savvy. Empathic, maybe it's because no one heard her cries when she was a kid that she is so alert to answering the cries of others. She's done that our whole lives, been there when we needed her – drama after drama.

She wasn't shocked by the state of my genital area, or if she was, she hid it. In that moment she'd snapped into perfect motherhood, like a lioness with retracted claws.

Without judgement and without asking any embarrassing questions about who or where or why, she told me that she would go to the chemist's to get me some lotion that would kill them. She told me to go back to bed and wait and not to worry about school. I instantly felt safe, like she was the warrior queen, Ripley, who'd kill off the miniature beasts and not me.

When she returned she gave me instructions about how to use the crab lotion, Quellada. It's banned in the UK now because its active ingredient, malathion, has been linked to cancer and respiratory diseases, but it's still used by farmers in the US. Very Trumpian: too toxic for pubic lice but OK for salad bowls.

She washed my bed linen and any clothes I'd worn while hosting the lice, then we sat in silence having fish-paste sandwiches and cups of tea.

She never mentioned it to anyone in the family.

It's a moment that defines the nature of my relationship with Mum. Whatever else was going on, however intense the madness of those years, and they were mad, she would always be present for me, if her mental health allowed her to be. Even if it didn't, somehow the thought that she *might* be present could be enough.

She's always been that powerful as a mother in a drama, out of our dramas she falls into her own glooms. I suspect that our dramas were a distraction, a tiring distraction.

Crabs round one resolved, sex with Simon recommenced.

It wasn't really love but a romantic crush which allowed us to play and explore. Despite the crabs, he was a great introduction to proper sex, sex with kissing and hugging and an occasional trip to the chemist. I knew that I found men or masculinity sexually and romantically attractive, and my friend was an attractive man and a generous, kind teacher, but we were never each other's ideals.

Way out of the closet, he was already on the club scene, a regular at clubs like Cha-Cha and Heaven. It was the beginning of the eighties; casual sex was easy to find. It was the age of the bathhouses in New York and San Francisco and saunas, cottages and dark rooms right across London and other major cities.

An easy, carefree time, just before the whispers about a 'gay plague'.

Really I should have seen the writing on the crabs. I should have read them like runes, but I didn't, not for many years to come.

I had no sense of keeping myself safe. None. Not ever. Only now, in my late fifties, do I have mechanisms and safety valves that I have a modicum of control over, sadly I still have to occasionally use prescription chemicals to assist in opening and closing the valves.

The crabs should have been a lesson, a sign, piercing my skin with their razor-sharp mouths, but because I didn't fully inhabit my body because of my gender dysphoria or discordance – discord rings truer – I didn't stop and stoop to collect the imprint of the crabs. The pinpricked Braille stabbings a foreboding map of a bleaker time to come. I saw them and their blood-sucking work as part and parcel of a life that I was destined to lead, like heroin addiction or sex work. I sometimes wonder if we troublesome kids have been like crabs on Mum's skin; I'm sure she never wanted eighty years of kid-strife, even if she helped to create us in her image. I've always tried to lessen the burden of me on her.

In some bizarre, cinematic way, I saw the crabs as characters in my story, characters that made perfect sense. I accepted the bad stuff, the uncomfortable stuff, and the painful stuff as being part of my destiny. Maybe my mum always saying that life was shit, hell on earth and then you die, set me up to look for negative companionship?

Maybe I saw our shared crabs as elements in some gloomy Genet love affair. He dressed a little like a sailor, it was the fashion then, he was very Blitz, very Steve Strange.

He was the most beautiful and brave person I've ever known, even to this day. Most days I talk to him, just chit chat, and the 1980s version of him, eyeliner, orange mohair jumper, torn Levi's and faded striped espadrilles, talks back. He still makes me smile and laugh and feel that I have the capacity to be beautiful.

In bed he was a dirty, dominant femme top, sliding inside of me while smudging his eyeliner for demonic effect. He was gender non-conforming before we'd exited from the word 'homosexual'. He was the epitome of cool, blending punk-New-Romantic with a Californian aesthetic before Kate Moss was Kate Moss.

He had one blue eye, one brown, which made him look a bit like Bowie. He danced like Grace Jones.

We loved 'Pull Up to The Bumper', it was our go-to song when we needed to dance, or to fuck, or to get ready to go out, which we did in a small, tightknit circle of friends who'd all fit into a Renault 5. In our own ways we were all queer, despite the strict 1980s binary expectations placed on the young. Punk had only slightly dented the surface of laddishness, in many ways it simply reenforced it, whereas the New Romantics truly hammered holes with sharpened eyeliners through the facades of masculinity and machismo.

Punk did allow some women to smash holes in the expectations laid out for them. Women could at least be seen to be angry at the world and not just as compliant typists, which even in the eighties was still a huge sweeping Pitman wave of expectation: the actual typist, and the typist as a metaphor for comedic and passive placement within patriarchal economic and social structures. The woman as assistant, as support to an important man.

My sister was kicked out of school for throwing a bible at the religious education teacher's head, but not before she learnt to touch type eighty words a minute. I was so impressed by both of these skills, neither of which I developed. My sister was so kick-ass cool.

My friend and erstwhile lover Simon often talked in great detail about how he would live his life on his own terms and not to please anyone else. He'd travel to New York, work in fashion or music, he'd live in a loft with a succession of handsome lovers. He'd never settle down with one person, not like his parents, he'd say. I suppose in his own way, even in the orange mohair, he was running.

He understood me and I began to understand him and then me through him. He allowed gender to start to make some sense to me. He started to deconstruct the taut, thick ropes of masculinity that my dad had tied so tightly around all of us to make us fighting lads, fucking, and fighting lads. *Don't ever come home telling me someone's beaten you up expecting any sympathy. No, never. Learn to punch, sissy.*

I once heard my dad at a party say to a group of men, *what would you feel like if that was your kid?* They all turned to look at me.

I idolised my friend like he idolised Bowie. He embraced femininity through his masculinity in a way that made me realise that the feelings I had around my internal femaleness were different from his. He found a comfortable place within gayness in a way that I never did. It would take me years to even find the word transgender, the only words back then were sex change or sex swap, it would be years before I'd find my comfort in the word trans. I was rubbish at being gay, gay men always told me, and they were right.

His femininity was never a weakness; he never had a chink in his armour, which in those days was an indication of his sheer brilliance and rarity. He never needed to repel homophobia because he didn't care, he never noticed, even if some of us did. He'd brush off comments that lingered in front of my eyes, hoovering like spiteful bluebottles.

I dreaded the slings and arrows that had been thrown at me my whole life. About my femininity being a weakness, never a strength. My femininity felt less accessible than his, shut off from me. I can see how and why mine became weaponised and then internalised as something with which I could bash myself.

If my friend did care about the insults, he never showed it, he'd swipe on a line of electric blue eyeliner and move on. While I'd be left full of shame about the depth of the femaleness that was rising up inside of me every morning when I woke with a cock and balls and not a space to make babies.

He'd tell me stories about going to dark rooms, about being fucked and fucking different men. He'd explain the different men in great detail, the shape of their backs, their skin, the size and plumpness of their cocks, the dirtiness of his cock after fucking a shitty arse. He went into such detail that in school the next day as I tried to paint an enlarged section of a red pepper, my mind and hand would wander off the page and instinctively draw cartoon erections and open mouths on the desk. The teacher demanded to know who'd drawn the cock on the table. *It wasn't me*, I said, my pencil still touching the edge of the engorged piss slit.

He taught me about fisting and piss play.

I'm sure his stories were exaggerated, but our repeated bouts of crabs were proof of his sexual exploits. He never bullshitted; he didn't need to.

He once told me a story about being given a lift home in the early hours of the morning on the back of a motorbike, holding on, his hands gripping the cock in front. *I didn't move my hands*, he said, *I just let the movement, the bumps, the swerves and the abrupt braking make him come, and when he did I cupped all of his spunk in my hand and then flung it back into the wind like sticky, viscous snow.* That story made me come without a single touch, just the thought of something so sexual and free.

The crabs, our crabs, our children, our queer brood, forever bonded us in furtive sexual secrecy at a time when the innocence of those around us was being lost or given up in much subtler, rosier ways. Fingerings behind the bike shed accompanying teenage declarations of love. The film *Grease* had come out a few years earlier and had impregnated school playgrounds with such sunny, Hollywood notions of teenage love that everyone imagined themselves a part of that narrative.

A narrative that was three parts innocence and one part male and female sluttery. It became commonplace to transition, like Sandy, from girl to women over a white ham sandwich or perhaps a Spam fritter. Both boys and girls did that transition. Motorbike leather jackets became a symbol that marked a point.

Fingering or being fingered was the pivotal act of change.

But my friend already had crabs from expertly wanking off bikers. We went way past Betty Rizzo and Kenickie. The beautiful, rough-skinned Jeff Conaway, who played Kenickie in *Grease* and Bobby in the series *Taxi*, had a life beset with substance abuse and depression. I always thought he was the one I'd fuck in *Grease*.

I was psychically drawn to damage.

As those around me winked and passed notes in assembly I itched my way through the Lord's Prayer. *Amen*.

His was the first cock that I joyfully played with, and he was the first person I told that I didn't feel like I was a boy or a man. He listened to me, smiled, and used it as an opportunity to practise Ziggy-esque make-up looks, which, at that point, just increased my feelings of clumsiness, as the make-up connected with my internal, shunned sense of womanhood that was fighting to rise up in every moment of every day.

He playfully made fun of my shyness and clumsiness, but in a way that allowed me to feel safe and to build my confidence. He allowed the make-up that he artfully placed on my skin to connect with something so deep and fundamental within me that the Ziggy-esque looks became early therapy, art therapy, somatic therapy. In those moments I'd close my eyes and internally I breathed easy.

He'd sit astride me on the bed, naked, his cock resting just under my chin so I could smell it and kiss it, he'd convince me to let go and give in to experimentation. As he applied kohl to my eyes, his crabs must have made the short shuffle from one host to another. I wouldn't have changed a thing. I got so much more than just crabs.

I never told him about the crabs, scared that in some way his far cooler self would've been mortified, embarrassed. Perhaps he would have denied it and then he would have had to reject our friendship. Somehow I knew I had to swallow them. I couldn't have lived without him at that point. We never talked about our ever-growing family of little mites, our silent queer co-parenting.

After the sun-filled days of our youthful experimentation, we went our separate ways. I went to art college and he started working in a clothes shop on the Portobello Road. It was so him, he was in his element, the first step to New York and a loft full of handsome men.

I didn't see him again for a few years until one night in the late eighties, in a club in the West End, when I saw him standing the other side of the large central bar. His face and body had been ravaged by the virus that the world had punitively named the 'gay plague' or GRID (Gay Related Immune Disorder).

His body had been ravaged by the virus that people said was 'God's work'. Newspapers said it, politicians said it, police-cunt-staples said it. That one in Manchester, James Anderton, who said that homosexuals, drug addicts and prostitutes were 'swirling in a human cesspit of their own making'. Cunt.

He was alone, gaunt, nervous and jittery.

His beauty and confidence had all but gone. His sheen pallid, papery, powdery and taut.

He seemed dusty and old and at the edge of a quite different place. He looked like a slender piece of broken chalk at the bottom of a blackboard. Like an old man in his late twenties.

His beautiful, blond, asymmetric wedge had thinned and was pushed over to one side to accumulate in a hillock of light frizz.

I'll never forgive the cunts who said it was our fault, or myself for how I felt in that first moment of seeing him and registering the virus so cockily resplendent upon his surface.

I tried to hide.

Once, late on a Friday before we went out to the Camden Palace, he had intricate steps shaved into one side of his hair. Each step was then bleached a different gradation of blond – honey-blond to platinum. I'd never seen anything as beautiful as that side of his hair, it was like a perfect wave off the Malibu coast. Years later, when I made atrocious art installations, I'd silkscreen skateboards with his blond fade and hang them in impossibly near-death positions, high off the walls and ceilings, calling them, *After You 1*, *After You 2*, *After You 3*. I never explained to fellow students what they were about, how could I? By then the very same virus inhabited me, I'd re-joined my teenage lover. The work was about us both.

Across the bar, his beautiful bi-coloured eyes had sunk down behind razor-sharp cheekbones. He reminded me of a cat in the rain, all ears, eyes, cheekbones, skeletal, shivering.

AIDS terrified us then, it was a killer. Not many people survived. Many hid it from family and friends for fear of rejection and stigmatisation. Everyone that I'd known who'd caught the virus had disappeared into hospital and not come out again.

They died, we went to their funerals and then we stopped going to funerals because it was depressing. Being gay, being other, being queer then was as tough as fuck, funerals added to the tough-as-fuck side. We wanted to be free to do what we wanted, to be free to take risks if that's what we wanted to do.

They were the freedom years, the unconstrained years. The risky years in which you learn about life from taking risks. AIDS was a deathly risk that sneaked up upon us.

Young gay people coming out in those first years of the AIDS pandemic had to grapple with intense homophobia which was often violent and brutal, but then AIDS came along and we had to grapple with the very real fear of dying. Many thousands did. They died before they'd had a chance to be beautifully risky.

Let's not denounce risk-taking or moralise risk-taking, let's always try to create a world in which the young can take risks with a modicum of advice and support from their elders.

I looked at him across the bar, aware that he hadn't seen me yet and might not recognise me anyway. I'd changed enormously, growing in confidence through a diet of drugs, experimentation and an exploration of my gender.

Glancing over at him I felt angry. Not sad, but angry.

He was my idol, he'd disappeared and I imagined that he was somewhere in New York or San Francisco living a fabulous life, beautifully on the edge. Swaying through bathhouse after gay bookshop after gay pier, employed in some arthouse cinema or vintage fashion shop, ending each day lying naked on the waterfront or on a Fire Island beach.

But he wasn't, he was here alone, in front of me, wasting

away. The man who'd given me the gift of sexual and gender exploration when we were teenagers was dying because of a virus they called a plague. *A plague on his house*, they'd say, but he deserved everything good from this world, he was a genius, deft, artful, creative, bold, beautiful and kind. So kind.

I wish I'd kept one crab from him, however stupid that sounds. Not on me, but in a glass jar on a shelf with the other knick-knacks that summarise my life. The McDonald's toys from the seventies, the handmade camel from the kids in Egypt, the evil eye I found cast off in the mountains, a print of the portrait of me by the artist Sarah Jane Moon in which you can tell that I'm struggling with being looked at. I have all these things but not a single thing from him. Not even a photograph.

Across the bar he looked closer to death than to life. In a place like that, someone who looked like death unsettled other people and vibrated a low frequency out and across the darkened space, a frequency that made people want to turn away and ignore the person until they stopped coming out. Until they dropped and died.

It was fear.

Uncontrolled and uncontrollable fear.

There was a deafening sound to AIDS, that hid in the pretence of the silence around it. ACT UP picked up on this with their SILENCE=DEATH motto, originally created by a six-person New York collective. The metaphors of this illness, of AIDS, were so loaded that a body could never be silent, even in the process of death, it was a body ravaged by a plague, a moralistic plague. A body dying with AIDS screamed to the rafters, *why are you treating me so terribly?*

*

My beautiful teenage friend had wasted away to skin and bone, cheekbones once flashed and envied merely served to highlight the absence of blood pumping and plumped flesh.

People died so quickly, in weeks or months. He was dying in front of me on the other side of a bar in a club, the kind of which he used to tell me about when we were younger. This night-time world had already taken him, and now spat him out, rejecting him for taking pleasure and contracting the plague.

He stood alone, eyes fogged, glancing around, I knew him, he'd want someone to be intimate with. He adored sex and cuddling, kissing, stroking, body on body, skin on skin, he adored touch and the intimate feel of breath and scent. Sweat, he loved the smell of sweat and armpits.

He stood alone, looking around.

I wanted him to remain beautiful in my mind. I wanted us to be back on his bed with unknown futures ahead of us, crabs clambering playfully between us. I wanted to feel his body, his skin, his cock. To bathe in his all-American slash Hazel O'Connor glow. I wanted him to remain as he was in our teenage years. I'd travel back with him if he wanted. I'd never leave. We'd marry and raise our crab brood in a house on a river. We'd send each crab out into the world on a single leaf that floated downstream to an unsuspecting crotch. We'd wave them goodbye, make a cup of tea and a fish-paste sandwich.

He saw me, recognised me, smiled and wandered over. Closer, his eyes shimmered. I felt panic, AIDS was walking around the bar towards me in the body of the first person I'd ever trusted and loved.

AIDS was truly terrifying then.

*Fuck you, AIDS*, I screamed silently behind eyes which held gallons of tears.

Rounding the bar, I noticed his jeans cinched tight around his now doll-like waist. His clothes hanging off him. As he walked towards me his smile completely lit up his face and without any fear of crabs or the virus we hugged, we kissed and we cried. Tears and saliva mingling.

Tongues reaching deep, trying to interlock, to hold on, both of us trying to hold on to the other. Right there, in a club full of people dancing and having sex, we cried and we kissed.

I knew that people were looking, I understood why, we all did; why would anyone risk catching this disease by being this close to the disease. But we kept hold of each other as the song played out its beat. I tried to encircle him a thousand times to keep him safe and warm, and here, but he felt icy.

His scent was the same, the virus hadn't taken that. I sniffed the pit of his neck, the place behind his ears and then rested my head on his shoulder. His shoulders always held my head.

I don't know if he did, but I spiralled back to that time of playful innocence on his bed, us experimenting with kohl and gender on spunk-stained sheets.

As we parted, he whispered in my ear, 'It was worth it.'

I replied, 'Not if I lose you.'

Rest, as always, in creativity and brilliance, my dear friend.

# Ten

# Our Love Language is Valium

It's November 2020, it's early, it's still dark, the phone's ringing, it can only be Mum.

I get up to answer it and then roll back onto the bed, pushing my feet deep under the covers. I'm refusing to get up today; it's cold and I'm tired. The silence is tiring, I haven't seen anyone since Mum left back in July; months on my own, listening to my surreally stupid brain concoct endless pandemic dystopian outcomes is driving me a bit mad. The dogs push open the bedroom door, sit in a loose row and look up at me.

'Stop looking at me,' I tell them.

'Pardon?' Mum says.

'Nothing, not you, Mum, I'm talking to the dogs, telling them to stop staring at me.'

I tell her that I'm in bed and not getting up. 'Good for you,' she says, 'are you comfortable?'

'Yes, why?'

She clears her throat, lights a fag, I hear her take a deep, throaty drag, she blows out the smoke in a succession of mini coughs. She sounds like a cold car engine struggling to ignite, her drag is the dramatic build-up.

First she fills me in with the background palaver.

My sister had apparently bragged about buying an *I'm exempt from wearing a facemask* lanyard from Amazon. 'It was only a quid-fifty,' she told Mum cockily.

My sister's response to her own deep trauma is to veer towards being a controlling bully. She doesn't mean it; she has a good heart but she blames Mum for almost everything, even for being anti-racist. In some way she thinks that if my mum had also been racist then my sister's relationship with my racist dad might have been easier. It wouldn't have been.

'What can I do?' Mum asks. 'She believes the vaccine is a way for powerful people with money to get a microchip under her skin so that the powerful people can track her and make her do what they need her to do. She's told me not to have the vaccine because it's not really a vaccine.'

'What should I do?' she says. 'You know I love my kids.'

I attempt to be calm and rational but fail miserably, I'm not in the mood for family dilemmas a thousand miles away.

I say, 'Who the fuck is going to track her movements, Mum, when she hardly leaves the sofa, what fucking information are they going to derive from her inaction? She's such a fuck-ing dumbass.'

I get angry and swear far too much for rationality. My sister's not a dumbass, far from it, but like many people she absorbs a certain stream of news on Facebook which begets a stream of misaligned truths and untruths.

'You need to protect yourself, Mum, tell her you can't see

her if she's not going to keep herself safe, tell her she's being irresponsible.'

On many levels, Mum's never cared about her own protection or safety, that's why she was always drawn to dating minor gangsters, or men she'd visit in Wormwood Scrubs serving time for small-time cocaine offences. Ditto me and my dating past.

'We can't all be as hard as you,' she says, snapping at me like a cobra, 'some of us need family.'

'We', 'can't' and 'you' stick in my head. The words 'we', 'can't' and 'you'.

She snaps at me with words she thinks will hurt me, by distancing me from them. She's right. The use of *we* and *you* reiterating something I've heard my whole life. This morning it stabs. I feel alone, completely.

I've never felt this feeling before, it feels like a premonition of a time to come when I'll be older and she'll be gone. A time when it's harder to get around, to leave the mountains, to drive, to travel. That's what the lockdown has done, allowed me a vision of my future, and it's terrifyingly silent.

I feel needy, I gesture for the dogs to get up on the bed, they snuggle around me, I'm less alone, but it's still a silent world. I watched a news item years ago about older people feeling lonely, they interviewed a woman who said she'd not spoken to anyone for weeks. At the time I thought, *that's impossible, how could you not speak to anyone?*

'I'm not hard or perfect, Mum,' I say quietly, 'I'm tired.'

'Tired of what?' she says, her voice getting louder. 'I'm the one who has to deal with her ideas about Bill Fucking Gates, not you.'

She says his name like it is his real name, like he's a punk band who had a moment of success in 1977.

*Bill (bleeped out) Gates are at number twelve with their hit, (bleeped out) Knows Why!*

She carries on, 'I'm the one dealing with the mess, worrying about your nephew's heart attack (he's only thirty-eight) and his weed habit, about the girl who's bugging him and the police that are knocking on his door. I'm the one who worries about you and your disease, worries about your brothers and your sister, not you. I'm the one who has all the worries; you don't have kids, you'll never understand what it is to be a mother.'

I'm angry now, ready to lash out. And I didn't keep myself alive through a thousand crack houses without any weapons. I'm ready with something nasty. I go to say, *you'll never know what it is to really be a mother either*, but I don't.

'That's enough fucking emotional blackmail, Mum, enough.'

I shout so loudly that I look to make sure that my back door is closed for fear someone in my empty village hears my angry outpouring. Worrying about noise is hardwired even in this concrete silence.

'Don't you fucking dare bring up my lack of family, my lack of kids. I'm already feeling completely alone in this pandemic.'

I continue, 'I'm so fucking tired of trying to keep you happy and alive, Mum, trying to make you realise you're worth much more than all this stupid childish reckless drama. Tired of trying to make you realise that you don't have to make up for the stuff that happened or didn't happen when we were kids. It's gone. It's done. It's meaningless. It's over. You've done your best, you're worthy of happiness and safety. I don't want you to get COVID-19 and die, Mum. Just tell her to fuck off.'

Calmer, 'You're the best mum anyone could have, Mum, I swear you are.'

Which is true, if you think about it rationally, but my emotional response isn't the ball she'd lined up, so she hits back, almost ignoring my niceties completely.

'We can't all be as fucking perfect as you,' she screams down the phone, 'some of us fuck up.' She continues, 'I fuck up, your sister fucks up sometimes, we all do, but not you, no you never fuck up, do you, with your paid-for house, your pension, your books and your perfect life in the sun. We can't all be like you, we've never been like you. You telling me I have to be happy is no good for my mental health. You putting pressure on me to be perfect when I can't, it just makes everything worse.'

I can see it does, that's become patently clear to me over these past few years. Her sitting with my sister, with my sister's problems and conspiracies, and their shared humongous ashtray, must be an easier life than me banging on about therapy and her mental wellbeing. Little does she realise how much pain I'm in or know about the pills I pop to get to live my oh-so-perfect life.

She's going to slam the phone down, I can tell, so I snap back quickly, allowing her no space.

'Don't you fucking dare put down the phone, Mum, not this time, if you do I'll change my number and we'll never speak or see each other again. I don't give a shit that it's nearly Christmas; fuck Christmas and fuck you.'

Quiet. She inhales deeply, then with dramatic pause and

weight blows out the smoke, weaponry; she's hoping I'll bite and mention her smoking. I don't. *Fuck it, smoke all you want.*

She stays on the phone.

She doesn't slam it down.

I say, 'Mum, I'm exhausted, it's been this way for as long as I can remember. You telling us that life is shit and not worth the struggle, you telling me you feel like ending it all, you trying to end it all. You telling me that things are pushing you over the edge, me worrying about the precariousness of the edges around you. Me wanting to cushion your every fall, even as I'm falling myself.'

I tell her, 'Jack not taking this virus seriously is just an indication that she's unhappy, that she thinks her life is shit as well, Mum. We all got that from you, we inherited that bleak outlook about the lack of potential of life. Every day we all fight that, every fucking day we fight that feeling of despondence at being alive.

'It's exhausting, Mum.

'I know you didn't mean it, but it's like we were all born under a heavy blackout curtain that each and every day we all struggle to pull aside to see if there is a brighter world that exists outside of us. I'm exhausted, Mum, I want to close my eyes and make you all go away. That's my lanyard, Mum, that's what it would say, *exempt from COVID-19 due to exhaustion.*

'I wanted to protect you from Dad when I was a kid, pro-tect you from your own shitty memories; I know what you went through, I know you've every reason to hate life, Mum, but all these years we've been living this drama with you, this fucked-up drama.

'I admit it, Mum, I've run out of steam. I've failed to last your entire lifetime. I've fallen down a few years too early, I wanted to keep being here for you until your last breath, but I can't go on trying to keep you alive if you still think life is shit. Because I want to believe it can be more than that, Mum. I want to be happier; I don't want to sit in this beautiful house in these mountains feeling sad all the time.'

I stop. Tears gathering at the back of my eyes start to flow forwards, amassing inside my lower eyelids, threatening to breach the bank, to overflow.

Silence. My words become much softer in the quietness.

Quietly, 'Mum, I've tried my whole life to make you be happy to be alive and I've failed at that. So often I feel useless because I haven't made you happier. I hate saying it, Mum, but your dislike of being alive has been really fucking selfish. I know you never meant it to happen, but it's spread to all of us. It's taken the air out of our lives, out of our lungs. Any sense of happiness always has to compete with a deeply etched view that life is pointless and hard.

'I don't have the capacity for real joy, Mum, because you told us life was shit. I did drugs to make it less shit. I did punters because they made me feel needed, desired, wanted. Can you imagine how that feels, Mum, that a stranger with his unwashed cock in my mouth, looks down and tells me, you're doing good, and I feel needed by the world? Can you imagine how that made me feel?'

I realise I've said, 'a stranger's unwashed cock in my mouth'. We seldom, if ever, have talked about the work I did to maintain my drug habit.

My voice soft.

My head awash with tears that I'll never put on her. Tears

that slosh about behind my eyes. Hidden, retained, retrained, redirected to become sweat or piss.

'If you're still unhappy about being alive, Mum, please keep it to yourself. I can't hear it any more, I'm almost sixty, Mum, sixty, can you fucking believe it?'

'You're almost fifty-seven,' she says, 'nowhere near sixty.'

'Not far off, Mum, all these issues make me feel like I'm a hundred and sixty.'

'None of us could feel that old,' she points out.

A slight laugh on the word 'none' gives us both respite. A ledge. A turned corner on a page.

'Mum, some days I'm so tired of this life, of our version of life, that I feel like lying down, falling asleep and never waking up. I've never told you that, I keep it hidden like I kept my shitty drug habit and my fucked-up lifestyle hidden from you.

'Hidden behind a closed door, I sometimes think that's why I always moved away to protect you like a mother would protect a child. I always felt like the parent.

'However tough it was, I kept it behind the closed door, however awful it was, you never knew a thing. Remember the number of times you'd knock and I wouldn't let you in?'

Silence.

Silent silence. Then, 'You sold my puppy, so I knew something was up with you, I knew that you were no angel.'

And with that, I'm back in 1990. She'd gone away to Spain for a week with her sometime bricklaying, sometime cocaine-dealing boyfriend, to a fishing village on the coast, coincidentally not far from where I am now. She asked me to look after her new puppy for the week. Within a couple of days, I'd sold her. She replaced my arse for a single day, I've never forgiven myself. A puppy for a day's drugs.

She loved that dog; she was a small Spaniel with beautiful reddish-brown silky fur. Irresistible, an easy sell. Far easier to sell than my awkward, lairy, spotty arse that imagined it belonged to Kate Moss.

'I'm so sorry for what I did, Mum, I was such a cunt.'

'No, you weren't a cunt, just a junkie,' she replied.

When I close my eyes I replay that moment, that morning, the couple picking up the dog, handing over a hundred quid when she was worth three times that amount, me hurrying them out the door. *Fuck off then, you've got the puppy*, I whispered under my breath, *I need to score.*

'I'm so sorry, Mum.'

I can still see the joy in the couple's eyes as I faked tears, saying I couldn't afford to keep the dog as I'd lost my job. 'My job, Mum, can you believe I was capable of talking such shit?'

Silence.

The sale is equally painful for both of us, although at the time I barely noticed Mum's tears as using heroin every day allowed no time or capacity for emotional input or output.

Silence, then, 'Do you want me to send you some Valium?' she asked. *Our language of love.*

Silence.

'Please do, Mum. Please.' I feel like such a weak cunt.

'I'll pop them in a card like before and put some cardboard either side. Sorry, I've only got a wedding anniversary card that was for my friend, but she died so the anniversary didn't happen. I'll write congratulations on the envelope to make it believable.'

She's always been great at smuggling; she has skin in the game. She once met me in Faro airport with a great wrap of speed. She's had boyfriends in the nick, who I'm sure asked her for contraband.

These past few months I've struggled to get my HIV medication here from the UK, my supplies were running low, at one point I only had one month's supply of my life-saving medication. My mum, in her eighties, managed to smuggle one month's supply to me at a time. Even the Home Office said this was both illegal and impossible.

I told Mum that and she laughed, saying, as she always does now, *no one's going to put an eighty-year-old in prison*.

She concealed my medication in a variety of cards: birthdays, anniversaries, driving tests, congratulations. Always wrapping cardboard and silver foil around the drugs to disguise them before placing them in the greetings card and sellotaping the sides shut. She'd write on the envelope, *Happy birthday* or *Congratulations on your special day!*

She tells me that thinking about getting my HIV drugs to me wakes her up during the night with new ideas. I cannot imagine how it's been for her to know I was here running out of my drugs. Drugs that keep me alive.

The next day she calls me to tell me she's popped some Valium in the post, 'inside your Ugg boots,' she says.

'I'd forgotten they were there, Mum.'

'I'd have kept them,' she says laughing, 'but they were too big for my skinny ankles. I'm only kidding,' she says. She's not but I don't mind. I ask her if she needs a pair.

'I love you, Mum,' I say.

'I know you do and I'm sorry I've put all this on you, Juno.'

Valium and other prescription medication have become like love to us. We struggle to communicate deep feelings, but in the smuggling of pills that might allow easier sleep or less anxious days there is love, in its own form of abundance. She's always been there ready to dole out medication, legal or not. It's a language we understand, I might rail against it, but when the Valium turn up nestled deeply in overpriced sheepskin, I know that it comes from a good place, a deeply caring place in my somewhat still broken mum.

# Eleven

# Waking up under a Burning Duvet

I first smoked heroin, chasing lines of it across torn squares of tinfoil, in my early twenties in the 1980s.

I imagined it was recreational, but it's not possible to smoke heroin recreationally, to think so is verging on oxymoronic, certainly self-deceiving. If are you're using heroin, even that very first time, some of your being, your psyche, doesn't want to be alive.

You want to depart from this place but perhaps you're not the instantaneous suicidal type. There's a physical and mental exhaustion that precedes heroin addiction; I wanted to lie down and sleep without nightmares, and at first heroin obliged. I became obsessed with the paraphernalia and rituals of drug taking, they made me feel purposeful and in control.

In the early days of drug-delusion I'd spend hours cutting out exact squares of foil to chase the heroin on. I'd roll neat tubes of foil to capture the vapours, others would use flashy notes, a tenner, or a twenty-pound note but I always saw that as a stupidity, as the vapours, the smoke from the burning heroin resin, would hit the foil pipe and a minuscule amount would collect for me to chase later. Chasing an ever-decreasing line of smack.

Heroin isn't at all recreational, it's a drug that enables you to remain in the world while gently falling out of the world into the space that exists just below the surface, in the shady underbelly. You could fall lightly into that place and exist in the same but vastly different timeline. It's comfort that the facts of my life had never allowed.

Your matrimonial life with heroin starts with pure clean hits, soaring silent highs and soft loving lows, everything falling away like the leaves off a tree in a still-warm autumn breeze. It's relief. Simply.

Heroin soon becomes your increasingly errant, spitefully tinged lover. A lover who says, *put your head in my lap and let me stroke your hair while I watch porn.*

Heroin's intent is twisted, it hides its true nature behind a warm, loving embrace.

But by its deception I'd already shifted from being in pain to being pain free. I needed it. I was hooked, addicted. Taken to the space below.

Addiction allowed me to let go of fear, to feel confident for the first time ever; such a freeing feeling. Addiction isn't fail-safe, isn't perfect, isn't the answer, but addiction addicts, steals your time, your focus, your energy. Takes you to a different space which seems, at first, to be curative.

We shouldn't kid ourselves otherwise. If people are doing drugs, look around them for the problems, not at them.

I can spot the bolshy cockerel walk of a newly crowned junkie from a thousand paces, a walk that advertises a sense of new occupation and freedom that more often than not has been eternally lacking in their lives. Addiction enables (or perhaps forces) layers of historical discomfort to fall away.

I'm not recommending heroin as a treatment, just keeping it real; the first dates do go supremely well. It feels like marriage is on the cards. I bought a dress like Carrie Bradshaw's then sold it, along with the ring, which I pawned in East Ham. I lived in West Ham at the time in a council flat I shared with T. We were always there on drugs and borrowed time, addiction demands a higher place in the queue than rent or utility bills.

We didn't care about rent, as every shitty memory was boxed up and consigned to a part of my brain where I could forget them. Addiction doing the legwork. After boxing them up I stopped thinking about thinking about the painful things. I forgot or at least I momentarily lost the toughest parts of my childhood. My dad punching me, punching straight through my borders, my boundaries. He was Dad, I loved him, my boundaries mustn't matter else he'd have respected them. His punch like a needle full of heroin. I let go of boundaries and started to inject.

Heroin empties you.

I've chased that feeling of emptiness my whole life. Heroin ended years ago, but if I take a single sleeping tablet, my addiction wakes, just stirs; if I take two or three then I'm nudged by that same addictive feeling and an encroaching warmth fills the emptiness. It's like running a warm bath into a cold tub.

Opiates, benzodiazepines and Valium all warm up empty spaces. Like a fire in a freezing winter woody glade.

The sleeping pills I take – mainly Valium and temazepam,

open that warming valve ever so slightly. I prefer feeling warm alone here in the mountains. My nightmares have always chilled me. The bones and the blood in my hands and feet perpetually frozen by fearful dreams in which I'm chased down, hunted. My hands and feet – my toes tense from trying to curl inwards and hide.

I take pills, close my eyes, push my head, my chin upwards, my shoulders back, and I can feel at ease. I can find a place where I can surrender. Quietly, my fucks-ups and fears shuffle out in an orderly line, one by one I wave them off, they exit my head through my now open mouth. I need that occasionally, therefore I'm still an addict. I shouldn't claim otherwise but there's shame at realising in my fifties that I'm still there, that I'm still my mum.

My mum, with books, an agent and no mortgage, but still my mum.

I take pills and I fall into a deep, velvety benzo-sleep.

I dream about pushing a pram with my husband who makes stupid jokes that I always laugh at because I want to, there's nothing complicated, it's light and breezy. Laughter happens. I look at my child sleeping in the pram that I'm merrily, almost absent-mindedly pushing – it's the old-fashioned pram my mum had, it seems big and unwieldy but I'm light-footed, skipping. In my dream it's like I've pushed a pram since the dawn of time.

My child is snuggled deep in luxurious blankets that I know I've dream-knitted. In my benzo-dreams my crafting skills are a given, that the swaddling comes from me is a given, I'm a producer, I'm productive, I make babies. I make the swaddling like a spider spins thread.

Another child, an older child, a toddler holding on to the pram, looks up at me and says, 'You laugh funny, Mum.' Just then a teenager playfully flicks the back of my head, but it hurts. 'Ouch,' I say, 'that hurt.'

'Leave your mother alone,' my benzo-husband says. His hair is greying at the temples, it makes me feel safe and loved, he looks like the olive tree in my courtyard. His hair, like a stevedore, symbolises long-term safety. A man who doesn't flip, or crash or burn. A man without his fist trained on me.

'Mum,' the young woman walking towards me calls out, 'what's the exhibition again?'

She's my benzo-eldest, off to university this year to study art history. She's brilliant, beautiful, well-read, and savvy. I named her Betty after my benzo-mum, who dream-died last year. But I'm not unbearably sad, because I have my own family. In my dream the pills protect me from the sadnesses which are yet to happen.

We arrive at Tate Modern and eat sandwiches in the dappled shade of the silver birches. Every time we come here my dream-husband says we should plant silver birches at the end of the garden. Our beautiful skinny long garden that snakes out from our Victorian semi in Balham.

And then I wake, just as we are about to plant trees. The single sleeping pill only takes me to this point. If I want to plant the trees, I need more pills. I need to put another foot into addiction.

I think it was James Baldwin who said something like, *we're trapped in history and history is trapped in us.*

My life and my history are far kinder in benzo dreams, far easier to inhabit, far easier to be trapped in. I have a husband with greying temples and children ludicrously spaced out as if in my dreams I'll always be a mother. A baby, a toddler, a teenager. I realise a day after writing this that I've done exactly this with dogs: one old, one middle aged and one puppy.

The first thing I did when I moved to Spain was plant trees and then wait. In doing so I must have believed in my dreams about family. It's a recurrent dream, I know my benzo-family well enough to understand their foibles. If trees are an outcome of my addicted mind, I can live with it. I have trees. The trees are beautiful. They are the embodiment of my pill-induced dreams. They are family, safety and perhaps even ambition. I want nothing other than them.

I think it took me three months to become an addict who used more than once every day and then I used every day for over ten years. Always with T. We fell, climbed back up, travelled to far-flung places like Stoke Newington and Hackney Central, we ran, and fought on and over drugs for over ten years.

I'd grown up around such intense violence and dysfunction that the drugs, the addiction, did distract. Throughout my childhood and teenage years, I'd seen blood, cuts, stitches, gashes, punches, kicks, bites, handfuls of hair pulled out, people dragged off, family members dragged off by other people and by our own. I saw my sister dragged off by a man with a knife and a bottle of acid. I was fourteen, it was four in the morning, we were on an estate in Tulse Hill coming home from a club in Wardour Mews, I forget the name.

He, the acid-man, had beef with my sister's then boyfriend and my sister innocently became caught up in their violence. Unwittingly, he got a lift with us back to my sister's flat, forcing the car to stop on the way by brandishing a knife. He squirted acid at us from a washing-up bottle. I remember thinking how innocent it looked until it started to fizz. He made her sit next to him on a wall, putting his arm around her and then dragging her off into the night, saying if I called the police he'd kill her.

It was cold, so I walked towards a phone box to keep warm. He threw acid at me, it burnt my sweatshirt, my bottle-green Levi's sweatshirt that I'd worn to see Bob Marley with Mum, the one that made me feel grown-up. It was grown-up now, it was defaced. He kidnapped my sister for a night and a day, and while she was away I sat shaking, shivering, clutching a ten-inch carving knife, on the floor beside her bed. If he'd have come through the door there is no doubt in my mind that I would have killed him for hurting my sister, whom I adored.

I have a hundred of those memories in labelled compartments in my brain, which I can't forget. You never forget seeing your sister dragged off at knifepoint. She was tough, she was a fighter, but she must have been terrified. A day later, after he let her go, she just hugged me in her Cato Road flat; I dropped the carving knife to the floor and we never talked about it again. I went into school two days later and called the history teacher a cunt when he told me to sit down and shut up.

Children raised in violence become almost immune to the noise of violence, often wandering into its embrace unknowingly, or unwittingly, or perhaps because we're drawn to its familiarity.

Its shape, its smell, its lustre is familiar, familial. By my teens I understood the pace and patterns of violence. I was impossible, every lover rejected me because I was impossible. I felt I pushed everyone to be violent towards me, even if they weren't violent, even if they didn't have a violent bone in their bodies. Although I guess they did . . .

Life as an addict is simple: do drugs and forget.

Chase the highs and the pure moments that exist at the start of your addictive trek. Like the impossibility of trying to keep white trainers white. Find impossible amounts of money to buy drugs to chase those perfect first hits.

In the early days of addiction, you start to fray.

You have to use drugs at work, and do drugs in the John Lewis toilets on a Saturday on Oxford Street when you're still pretending that you can still shop like a normal shopper. Doing drugs in any shady nook and cranny you can find in the Underground. Subterranean. Anywhere and everywhere becomes a place that you said you'd never do drugs in, but you do. You slip and you slip, you become bottomless. *I'd never do that*, but you do, you will. You suck a cock in a phone box in daylight and you know that people are watching but your only thoughts are, please come you fucker, yes, shoot in my mouth, anywhere, I don't care, I need to score.

You seem to still have the sheen of an ordinary life, but your skin's a little greyer, your eyes a little sunken, your pupils constantly pinned to attention or the size of dinner plates. Staring intensely at the world from the smallest of black dots that expand, like the aperture of a 35mm camera, wildly trying to focus.

The pain of injection becomes a fixation, your focus.

Crack cocaine entered my life after heroin, and it is an entirely different drug.

If it provides any respite to your pain it is so short lived that you see it opening the back door even before the front door is shut. They dash in, shout and leg it, laughing. Only the first rock, the first pipe gives you the high that makes you feel like you are Bianca Jagger in a tailored white suit, no bra, trousers down, being fucked from behind by a young Marlon Brando.

The first high is so high that it's actually beyond physical sex, its pure pleasure. You burn the rock on a bed of ash and foil and breathe in the fumes; by the time they've reached your mind you are fucked. The fumes rush from the pipe to your brain.

In the seconds that follow every scene you've ever imagined in which you are beautiful, free, sexual and sexy flickers into life behind your closed eyes. You are a sequin which seeks the slip dress, which becomes the palace in which the dress is shucked. I'd never felt so present in my body; that first pipe showed me who I could be. It was the dawn of my transition. I said to T, *fuck me in the pussy*, he said, *you haven't got one*. I said, *I do now*.

Crack demands a level of financial input that is beyond comprehension. It is unrelenting. As a concept, or a lifestyle it is impossible. Never satiated, it demands more and more until you are on your knees sucking cock after cock, stealing wallet after wallet. Selling every square inch of your life and your flesh until you start to think about selling your inner-most organs.

Crack forced us deeper into dealing. Our flat became a place in which deals were made, strangers used and slept, a place in which I wandered the edges, looking for somewhere to use and fall into my dreams about husbands with greying temples and birch tree plans.

The smell of ammonia from cooking powder into rocks was intense; it drifted into my dreams, stole them from me. I never had a moment's peace in all the years on crack cocaine.

One morning, let's say, for context, four or five years into our addiction, we woke up to find the bed smouldering. Not from sex.

Tiny flickering flames rose up from the duvet, plumes of smoke whispered up into the air from the charred embers. Like a planetary landscape. The duvet, the kind of cheap duvet that's filled with chips of combustible foam, had been reduced to scarred flesh.

'Fuck,' I said, yanking it off and throwing it out of the window. It was a tough estate, no one took any notice of a burning duvet whistling down from the top floor like a humongous flying squirrel. There were cars, bikes and fridges strewn throughout the estate. The gardens more like rubbish tips. No one noticed. At least three out of the other six flats in our block were drug flats. A burning duvet wasn't even a moment.

We'd wake violently ill, needing to use heroin at around four or five in the morning, wanting to throw up, shiver-ing and sweating. When you start to withdraw, your skin contracts, your nerve endings try to fire up like a long-dead boiler, your skin can't cope and you shiver, you feel like a turkey waiting on a cold kitchen slab. You glimpse your old life, your pains, fears. Your thoughts start to run like a river which has broken its banks and is being funnelled down a narrow Cornish street. Your thoughts become a stream of fear, and panic ebbs towards diarrhoea.

Every morning we'd wake up sick in our flat, long before dawn. We'd wake, we'd use, we'd light a fag and a joint, share both, and fall back to sleep.

The sleep often dragged us back to cosy dreamy never-worlds before we had the chance to extinguish either blunt or fag. We'd often wake with burns on the bed or ourselves. But this was the first time the duvet had ignited.

*Fuck this*, I said, *we've got to get away, we've got to get out of this life. I can't do this any more. Us not being burnt to a crisp is a sign that we've got to stop. It's a sign. A miracle, a gift.*

T said, *no, it's a cheap duvet.*

By this point the drug is your life. There is nothing else, no sex, no laughter, no television, no books, no rest, no family, no proper job, no aspiration, no dreams, no reason to leave the house apart from getting drugs or getting money. It's a little like being a writer.

At this point you know you're an addict, you know you've fucked up; you may even start to see why. By then I knew that my childhood was fucked up and that my means, mode and methods of integrating with the world weren't helped by my childhood experiences.

I knew this not only because of my addiction, but because two of my siblings were also battling with their own addictions. On the odd occasion when we came together, we did so to do drugs, usually heroin or crack cocaine, but anything to hand really: opium, morphine, speed, acid, microdots, any number of pills.

T sold ecstasy for a while, I popped them like they were aspirins as a way to resolve my drug crankiness. We were like some mid-American couple, him out to work (albeit in the kitchen) and me, bored, frustrated popping pills in the bedroom.

I seldom saw my siblings, doing hard drugs with them felt very messy. I can't explain why it seemed so messy but the three of us doing drugs together felt hopeless, dystopian. We became a landscape. Three parts to a puzzle that none of us could face at that point.

In the relatively few moments when the drug staves off the constant withdrawals, you have to focus on getting money for more drugs. That's all.

It's exhausting.

When business was lean, my lean spotty arse and mouth plugged the gaps in our (il)legitimate drug-dealing earnings.

I'd often work with a friend out of their flat in Euston. We placed ads in magazines for massages, punters turned up, we'd take it in turn to 'massage' them, then score and use.

As the drugs rushed in we'd laugh about punters, or the floorboards which we thought looked chic and French but were really just floorboards without carpet, like being cold on the street without a coat. I once gave a well-known art critic a hand job and he offered to pay me in ham sandwiches, homemade, white bread with the crusts cut off.

We laughed about that for fucking ages. My friend once got given a kitten by a punter who had taken a shine to him, it seemed romantic and silly, but we loved that kitten. We did give it a name, but I think it was only Kitten. Like I called Pup Pup.

We'd roll up foil or empty condom packets and flick them across the floorboards for it to chase, its tiny, innocent kitten paws pattering to and fro, racing to scoop up the foil, rolling onto its back and playing with it like a ball. We'd laugh and talk about getting clean and moving to the countryside where we'd run an animal shelter for cats like Kitten.

I had a special knock to use on my friend's door, a code. I'd rat-a-tat-tat on his door to the beat of 'Finally' by CeCe Peniston until he answered. He kept trying to get clean, often I'd bang out the whole song, even start humming. Truthfully, I was his enabler. I pushed and he hid behind his door with the kitten.

'I'm trying not to use,' he'd call out through the letter box.

'OK, I understand, just let me have your dealer's number,' I'd reply through the slit.

Knowing full well that it meant we'd both use.

One day I rat-a-tattatted and hummed for an age on his door, for almost the whole of our song. A woman shouted down from the balcony above, 'Shut the fuck up, he's dead, he was in there for a week with the kitten chewing on his fingertips until the police came, the fucking poof overdosed,' she called out. 'Poor kitten's gone to the PDSA, probably be put down, who'd want a junkie's kitten? Probably got AIDS.'

'Keep your voice down,' I shouted up, 'have some fucking respect for my mate.'

*Respect*, like I'd had every time I'd got him to score when he wanted to stay inside with the kitten and get clean.

I'm not telling this kitten-laced story to seek redemption, it's just the way it was. It could have been any one of us. Addiction has a very hard edge at which you can fall away.

Addiction masks an overwhelming sadness that has become intolerable and makes you dream of darkness, of death, but addiction itself becomes intolerable and when you reach that intolerable point, you don't know where to go.

Back then, to the burning duvet.

## Twelve

## Egypt Part One: Two Drug Addicts Plan a Five-Star Getaway to Egypt

After the calamity of the burning duvet, we decided that we needed to get away. Ever the creative addicts, we set about concocting a plan. We decided that we'd get some cocaine on tick, which to anyone not in the trade means goods upfront without payment, from the only medium-size dealer who would still sell to us, keep it as powder and sell it on as quickly as possible. Then we'd run away to somewhere where we could lie in the sun and start over. We looked each other straight in the eyes, through our pinhead-pupils, looked deep into each other's souls and said, *we'll get clean by getting away*.

A holiday to end our addiction.

Junkies never take holidays unless they are trying to get clean. Junkies never leave sight of their dealers. It was never a great plan for us, it was always a sandcastle built at the sea's edge. More often than not, that's the only place to build a sandcastle.

Obviously, we'd take enough heroin with us so that we

could withdraw slowly and gently, emerging on the other side, in another country, with less pallor and perhaps a suntan, a glow. We'd have to take a sizeable amount of gear for that nonsense to materialise.

When we were kids, Mum said that a suntan always makes you look better, and if you look better then you are better. So committed to this paper-thin truism was she that when we were babies she'd wheel the pram out into the street, drag the hood back, pull off the blankets, slather us in vinegar and cooking oil and let us roast. *I couldn't stand the thought of pale, pasty babies*, she said, *babies who might look ill.*

T asked me where in the world I'd like to go, *anywhere* he said, *anywhere you want in the world, we'll go.* It is one of the few romantic memories I have, and I still have love for him for creating that memory. He was the first person in the world who asked me, *what would make you really happy? Say it, and I'll make it happen.* Forget the drug scenario or the nightmare that would ensue, it was a moment. An *Eat, Pray, Love* moment.

The 1963 film, *Cleopatra*, starring Elizabeth Taylor is, visually, my favourite film because of its fabulous campy sets. It's a close-run thing with the 1968 musical film version of *Oliver!* As a kid I imagined being in that East End attic space, being Nancy in that red dress, singing with Fagin, then dancing out into a sunlit square full of milkmaids, window cleaners and strawberry sellers, then back to the attic via the fishmongers, butchers and flower sellers plying their trades on the straw-covered street. The happy chirpy noise of Hollywood Cockneys and not the angry noise of my dad, who people said looked like Bill Sykes.

But the sets of *Cleopatra* always won out. Liz in gold lamé entering the set of Rome on her golden Sphinx is monumental. She's wearing kitten heels. As if!

Because of that film I'd dreamt about wandering through the temples of Egypt ever since, admittedly a film-set version of Egypt. When T asked me where, I knew, in my mind I already felt like a firefly, shimmering with energy, about to follow in Liz's kitten heel footsteps. I'm from south London; we're drawn to gold.

I've created a life from pilfered bits, snippets from film sets, magazine covers, magazine shoots of interiors, exteriors, gardens, looks, estate agents' windows. Olivia Laing's Instagram.

Lines from books, words I've learnt from listening to others. Like a magpie or a righteously indignant matchgirl peeking through the windows, then smashing a pane and reaching in to itemise, classify, memorise, own. I imagined that one day I'd put all of the fragments of beauty, colour, materiality, texture together to form a life. An actual physical life and a physical space to live that life in. Years ago, I fantasised about the house I have now but I only saw it as fragments that belonged to other people. *I made it happen, Ma, I made it happen.*

I told you I would, Mum, and when no one believed me because I was a junkie on the edge, you did.

T said, *anywhere you want to go, we'll go.*

Just like that, he gave me something I'd never had, a wish. It seems childlike to talk about wishes, but in my childhood I had only one wish, for the noise and fighting to stop and it never did. It never has. That single wish never came true.

I said to T, *my wish is to visit the Valley of the Kings and the Great Pyramids of Giza.*

As a seventeen-year-old, I'd got a simple tattoo of the Great Pyramid on my right shoulder. It was the seventies and there was no three-dimensional detail or gradation of shade, just a triangle with a few lines to indicate hieroglyphs, which I deduced said something about the passage of life into death.

I made it up: a bird shape and a wavy line indicating a river, the Nile, or perhaps the Thames, an onwards journey down the river to the afterlife. I made it up but at the time people were having anchors, cocks, tits and names, so frankly kudos to me for trying. The tattoo always felt like a sign that my mind was searching for signs. I already felt outside of everyone and an anchor might have firmly lodged me within their stratospheres, but no, from day one even the tattooist said, *what's this shit?*

The tattoo of the Great Pyramid was inked in an Elephant and Castle tattooist's in the shadow of the Great Shopping Centre, the candy-pink behemoth to modernism in south London. I love the connection between the two great architectural statements, albeit reduced to a tiny illustration on my shoulder. It's still there, faded, aged, like a notation of three very separate histories: mine, the rise, the fall; the rebirth of south London; and the rise and fall of the Great Pharaonic dynasties. I should donate my shoulder to the Victoria and Albert Museum and label it *Naive Globalism.*

Back to the uncouthness of drug money.

We'd book a two-week holiday. Earnestly we talked about how we'd need that amount of time to get clean, one week to withdraw and the second to sightsee to take our minds off it. You have to realise that up to this point, we'd never attempted to get clean; we were now going to try to accomplish that in Egypt. No less. My wish, no less. Being poetic is so expensive.

I can laugh now at our neat, razor-sharp get-clean plan, but back then we were deadly serious. It was a plan made with furrowed brows, scrawled notes and numbers written down carefully.

Junkies always think that A + B = whatever they need it to be.

Fuck me, the joyful delusion of drugs, it's a different universe. A different ordering or reordering of the stars, the planets, our gods and our values. You are now in the service of a chemical response in your body, a reaction in your cells, a response created by a drug; a natural substance harvested thousands of miles away from poppies. You worship the opium poppy and the coca leaf.

The seed pods and leaves controlled my life for over ten years. That's why philosophy matters, because we don't make any fucking sense.

We worked out that if we ran away using the money from the cocaine deal, we'd have enough for the holiday and some money for essentials like booze, maybe we'd even rent a pedalo down the Nile. We were so fucking tiny minded that we thought you could pedal a pedalo down the Nile. All hail the joyless delusions of seed and pod worship.

I said, *I'll need some money to buy tiny tin or ceramic models of Tutankhamun, Cleopatra and the Great Pyramid of Giza.* I had a vision that if we got clean then we could have a proper Christmas and I could put the models on the tree. I always believed.

We bought £800 of heroin. With the money left over we bought a few rocks of crack to smoke as a treat, a holiday treat, like a new bikini or sandals. Others order dinky bottles of champagne; we'd smoke crack on the balcony. We'd withdraw from heroin and then smoke crack to celebrate. Some plan, out with the seed pods and in with the leaves. All hail the leaves!

A day after the 'should-be our last ever drug deal', we went down to the local travel agent's and booked our trip to Egypt.

A five-star holiday, not any old trip.

*None of your old shit*, they'd say, the women I'd grown up listening to, talking about pieces of jewellery, a sovereign or a half sovereign, or a 'good' fake handbag that by definition was shit. A good fake is still a fake. I sometimes wonder if I'm a good fake, like a Joseph Cornell box about love, an expression of an emotion he never expressed. A model of an emotion or a film set, I've always felt an affinity with both. A similar set of concerns.

We booked a five-star hotel, the Hilton in Luxor. The Luxor Hilton no less.

Addict-drug-dealers who've never had any money often feel the need to overcompensate for feeling like the world is looking down on us – they were, so like lottery winners, we spunked cash on high-ticket items that we'd sell a day later to pay for more drugs. It was a cycle. Look at us, we're as good as you; don't look at us, we're fucked up again. Look, don't look.

We didn't think that we'd look like junkies in a five-star

hotel, why would we? At one point in our lives we'd been fresh-faced.

Now, a few years on from fresh-faced, his head was shaved, mine was an unruly dry mass of overly bleached blonde hair which I yanked back into a ponytail thinking it looked classic. I thought I was Patsy Kensit in *Absolute Beginners*. In later years I thought, if I pull my hair back and pout I'm Kate Moss on the cover of *The Face*. That cover.

I didn't look anything like that cover.

We both looked like sparrows, scrawny, taut, greyish-skinned sparrows. We could have weighed ourselves on the drug scales in grams. Our clothes were a motley crew that we'd stopped seeing years before. We didn't realise how distraught they were, jeans screaming, clawing for patching and patching screaming, begging for retirement. Our clothes all had a grimy sheen. Years of addiction doesn't allow you to prioritise cleanliness and trips to the launderette.

Our tiny, bird-like bodies were topped off with seemingly huge pale comedy heads. Like those wobbly footballers made of plastic that lads would stand on their dashboard in their first car. We were the nodding heads with real nodding heads.

God love us, we'd lost sight of ourselves years before, but losing sight of ourselves was a blessing, a protective addiction mechanism. A way to stay in the here and the now enough to enable you to get out the door to sell and score. To source new contacts and to connect with existing ones.

I love the resourcefulness of junkies, I'm not externalising or romanticising, it was me and I was there. The way they weave a narrative of normalcy around their being like a great fat duvet coat, a protective coat they sling on, pulling it close to their skin every time they leave the house and then letting it fall when they re-enter, and the gear floods in. They have to face the world every day, most days more than once.

To score is to leave the house, to leave the womb. Dealers don't come to you unless they are medium-size dealers dropping off product to smaller dealers to deal, but even that's rare. Dealers have a pecking order that keeps everyone brutally and often cruelly in check, everyone on their nervy, blood-deprived, bony toes.

Every day an addict has to gussy up leave to the house and face the world.

Bang, the door shuts and it's out into the world with you, head up, find some pride.

This is your life, live it. Scrape back hair into scrunchie, pull on oversized Rubenesque protective coat over unwashed lounging wear, throw freezing cold water (there's no money in the meter) on your cheeks to draw reticent colour temporarily to the surface. Skin that lost all joy and gave up long ago. Your body hibernates. Your stomach, your digestive system, your emotions, your brain.

Slam the door and face the world. A high ponytail, acute angles snuggled beneath a duvet coat, she's got her shit together. She's leaving the office for the office.

It's a performance resurrected daily, the same outerwear left by the door to go over the same innerwear, worn day in, day out. I've started the same fashion regime again during these COVID-19 lockdowns. It felt thrilling to shop in the supermarket with what I'd worn to bed under a slightly more expensive version of the duvet coat. I eroticised my own drug past in the aisles of Lidl. I once bought a coat in Lidl, a duvet coat, a little like the ones I'd worn before but with a completely different context, a coat without a shimmering emotional resonance. A coat simply to keep me warm in the winter mountains.

The outer layers are a performance that lets you face an unkind world which has often treated you very badly in one way or another. Most addicts I've met were hiding in pain from pain. Pain extinguishing pain. Pain disguising pain. Pain concealing pain.

Most found the first hit of heroin anesthetising, the only thing that had ever taken away the pain. Leaving you empty and painless. A virginal vacuum. Briefly, heroin made me feel that I could start over. The empty painlessness felt like joy. Nirvana. Religion. Belief. Love.

The next set of hits after the first few only chase away the pain, but you soon start to feel its presence again, shimmerings of pain return. Like shadows. But soon the pain of chasing the pain away and the pain of withdrawal allows you to transfer the focus of your pain to the substance itself. Heroin becomes the problem, the pain. The daily accrued bad memories. It was heroin what did it. It fucked me up. Heroin personified as the one who fucked me without consent.

Before heroin, I was doing all right, I'd say to endless drug counsellors who held both the lock and the keys to my daily methadone script. The pain of chasing away the pain of heroin withdrawal cancelled out all the other pains that had gone before. There was an equanimity of pain. A balance wrought from the chaos, like *The Lord of the Rings*. I never could watch those films. The endless journeys and hairy feet. T had hairy feet. I'd call him a hobbit, he'd get hard and we'd fuck. How whimsical.

Almost every addict I knew would occasionally let slip a memory of pain, of abuse, of rape. T, as a child, had been handcuffed to a radiator on full heat by a stepfather who went on to commit murder. Not told off, not tied to a chair, or slapped, or even punched. But handcuffed with handcuffs, proper police handcuffs, heavy, brutal ones, to a radiator in his bedroom for hours at a time, until the radiator burnt his skin. He hated radiators, we always had them turned off, even when we had the money to have them on. What with his hairy feet and the cold it was like living in Middle Earth.

We bonded because we both understood what violence could do to a young mind. We never needed to explain that part of our lives. We never needed to talk about it because our pain balanced out each other's pain. Our pains linked hands, entwined fingertips and hushed.

There was a tenuous, sinewy balance around the things we knew and the things we didn't. Like a tightrope, a washing line off of which hung our individual bad memories. Out to dry, evenly spaced, never jostling for prominence or attention. Being with him strangely allowed me to view my past as if it were a flat open plain. A great territory over which I gained a sense of control, or perhaps distance. More likely distance.

Next time you walk past an addict on the street with a sign asking for money that you think to be a bullshit sign, please don't judge them, just give them enough money to score drugs and wish them safety in doing it. Trust me, they'll get there in their own time or they won't, but your crass, unthinking purchase of a vegetarian sandwich from Pret won't help a jot. Not a tiny pinprick jot. You deciding what is good for them and what isn't good for them isn't the answer, it's just another version of our foreign policy. Somehow social media, especially Twitter, has encouraged everyone to become a minor expert on everything from addiction to sex work, each with their own tuppence-worth of expertise, how depressing.

Unless you've really experienced addiction or actually engaged in sex work, then don't speak. *Just support*, as my mum would say, *just be there*.

That addict on the street might not get a bed for the night with your donation, but they might score, which will be as good for them as a bed for that night.

Trust me, I've had so many people spit at me and call me all kinds of junkie-scum-lowlife. I've begged on the street and felt utterly disheartened by offerings of sarnies or words of comfort; my body, painful from withdrawal, needed drugs.

When, at my most wretched, I still had to earn money and woo punters on the street, you were quick to call me a dirty whore when I said no to a sandwich. I couldn't win, addicts never can in your eyes, any which way they try to support their habits. Begging with little white lies, selling drugs or sex work. Always the same, us deserving punishment.

Thank fuck for Go Fund Mes, which have allowed people having a shit time to write some words down, create a narrative and be seen as human and not as excrement. Go

Fund Mes are a form of democracy that truly allows dignity or dignified distance from the class of people who used to consider themselves charitably generous.

Most people want to give conditionally, which isn't giving.

Go Fund Mes have helped to liberate some trans surgeries from the arms of people who make us wait in lines and who don't give a shit. I always donate to trans surgery appeals because I was turned away for years because of my HIV status.

It's not like sickness benefit has ever been available for those people suffering with addictions; if it weren't for the hypocrisy of capitalism it would be. Addiction is an admission that life within our punishing structures is too tough to manage without substances – leaves and seed pods, to dampen and dim the pain of struggle, failure and purposelessness. Hopelessness.

Addiction is self-diagnosed, self-administered mental health care. Often knowingly self-administered by those who know that the system has failed them from the get-go. I knew what pains were being dampened down by heroin and stamped on by crack cocaine.

I knew that throughout my young life no one had ever stepped in.

When we were kids and taken to A&E, no one questioned our cuts; when we were misbehaving, doing drugs, fighting or drinking at school, no one questioned why a whole family was behaving this badly, they just labelled us 'wrong 'uns'. Can you imagine your name becoming a badge of dishonour when all you're feeling is pain and isolation?

Little wonder I've worked like stink to get where I am. I remember the looks people gave me when I was a junkie on the street. Like I was worse than dog shit.

That's why we booked a first-class holiday with our tick-drug money, because we were sick of people thinking that we were worthless when all we were doing was covering up the pain that others had often neglectfully inflicted on us. We weren't born in pain, we were born from pain. As were my parents, each from their own pots of pain rather than gold. My dad wasn't a nasty violent man but a boy raised in fear, taught that violence is the way to become the king of your street. Kings don't suffer poverty or powerlessness.

We booked a first-class holiday because of generations of that – failed kingship and stumbles in and out of pain.

By the time I was planning my Egyptian dream I had already blamed myself for everything that had ever happened to me. I tried to seal myself away, vacuum pack my emotions, hold them in tight, scared that if they got out I'd ruin the space around me. Damaged kids often blame themselves – who else can they blame? Parents they love, structures they are taught to respect – the house, the school, the family? Kids blame themselves, thinking that they are toxic. When HIV infected my cells, I thought it might cleanse me. How mad/sad/terrifying is that?

I thought one of the most lethal viruses the world had ever seen would cleanse me. That's what society taught me.

# Thirteen

# Egypt Part Two:
# Becoming Cleopatra

What a sight we were, two heroin addicts, me thinking I looked like a bleached version of Audrey Hepburn, my hair pulled back, a black polo neck jumper covered in spliff burns, thinking I was booking a jaunt to somewhere romantic where we'd hop on and off a scooter and wander through age-old ruins. Throw a penny in a fountain, make my wish, make it so, get clean and smoke a rock.

T, his head roughly home-shaved, looking a tad Gulag, shades of grey-green skin pulled taut over fine cheekbones, gorgeous cheekbones which cupped his huge brown eyes, eyes so big they made him look like a nocturnal frog-eyed gecko. He had a great tongue. A gecko's tongue.

He was braver than me, in that moment I thought he was a god. He was small, tough, feisty and damaged. We enabled each other to remain on drugs for many years. Constantly toing and froing, oscillating between plans to get clean, plans to get money, plans to sell ourselves, and then plans to sell each other.

Detailed plans to increase drug sales, and occasionally plans to get rich quick or die trying.

That never happened, we never held on to any money for longer than a day. We might have thousands in the morning and by that night be scraping the floor for pennies or the illusion of crack chippings. I'd put anything light, white, cream or yellow into my crack pipe and smoke it if I was high and saw it glint in the carpet.

We cut deals and we cut drugs. All drugs are successively cut, diluted, from the field to the table. Anything in powder form would be cut with other powders – baby powder, baking powder, sucrose, anything that you thought wouldn't kill you. We rationalised the immorality of cutting drugs by inserting a neat paragraph of morality into the wider narrative, convincing ourselves that what was delivered to us was too pure for general consumption, therefore by cutting it and diluting it we were in fact saving lives. Such bollocks, this unwritten falsehood enables many dealers to feel easier about cutting drugs to increase their margins. By the time the powder gets to the lowest rung of dealership the margins are slender, the grains of powder replaced almost one by one.

Anyway, back to my Egyptian dream.

The travel agent was in Stratford, but it could have been in Hackney, or maybe Whitechapel, I can't remember where exactly, but I do remember that we could barely keep our eyes open, nodding off in turn, our heads, full of drugs, resting on each other's shoulders, at one point my head slipped into his lap. I wanted to sleep but felt his cock stir very slightly; if he needed to use, every nerve ending in it would start to fire up.

Cranking up slowly but surely. Beneath my cheek his cock started to swell, I lifted my head away. I felt nothing. I was high, I didn't want cock, I wanted to be Liz in Egypt.

At the start of our relationship, when we were fledgling addicts, we had filthy sex; he was spitefully dominant and I was greedily submissive. We'd smoke crack, pop pills and he'd burn wax on my skin, pull my head back and force dildos into me. The more dominant he was the better the sex. I think it was its own form of forgetting. Another pain to balance out the pain, but it was also pleasure.

Maybe we knew that it needed to end, that kind of sex, maybe we didn't. But it did end. Heroin took over and became both our master and mistress. Supplicant to it, both on our knees to the drug. I only had sex in those years to get drugs, never pleasure. If I'm really honest, I'm not sure that I ever enjoyed a flesh-and-blood cock again. I like the ones I can switch on and off and put in a drawer.

Maybe it's just cis cock I don't want any more. If I were younger I'd date trans men, I think, but now I'll stick with my olive-tree fantasies. They seem harmless. Famous last words, as someone tries to extricate a branch (plus olives) from my cunt, at least it's moisturised.

The travel agent looked past us, talking endlessly about the hotel amenities and airport transfers. She had a script and was determined to sell us day trips, despite our being asleep for at least half of her pitches. Bless her.

Eventually she stopped still like an engine that's run out of fuel and T handed her a block of cash for us to visit temples and tombs thousands of miles away. He paid for the dream.

That travel agent was great at her job, she never batted an eyelid, even when we stood up to leave and he had a hard on. The subtle difference, the drop in drug-level producing an innate cellular reaction. Sometimes I'd cry spontaneously if the gear ran dry in my bloodstream. Just cry, floods of tears, then inject heroin and the tears would stop. Instantly. Automatic tears. Automatic hard cock. He once came in from scoring drugs, heavily withdrawing, desperately needing to use. Sitting down he said, *I spunked in my trousers running up the stairs, the motion of running made me cum. The slight friction, the slight reawakening of emotions and pleasurable feelings.*

Instantly dampened down by the heroin, his cock returned to sleep like a Cyclops in a cave.

After the travel agent, we walked home, used, and his cock returned to slumber. High, we flicked through some old Marvel comics deciding what our superpowers might be. I said, *I'd like to not be scared of flying,* he said, *not being scared isn't a superpower, it's a right.* And I thought, that's deep for him, but he was right. Deeply profound, I thought. I sucked him off.

Afterwards he said, *we're gonna need superpowers to explain to the dealers where their money is. Another day,* I thought, *we'll deal with them another day,* the money already spent.

I would always have become an addict, it was written in the stars, preborn logistics making it so. Looking back, I'm warmed by the fact that we found one another to go on that drug adventure with. I felt safe with him and I think he with me, even though we constantly led each other further into danger. We took chances, bought and sold far too many things to remember, had fights in the street, had bad drug turns, supported each other, held each other's head and hands, and knew each other's pains.

In the last few years, we became almost envious of each other's intimacy with heroin or the crack pipe. The drug becoming the lover, the other lover, the other man, the other woman. The greater commitment and loyalty.

One weekend we binged, again at the expense of drug dealers higher up the food chain. We started by taking a £3,000 delivery of cocaine late on a Thursday afternoon, when cocaine is amassed to sell for the weekend. We'd have a stream of suited and booted coming to the flat to buy powder for their jollities.

I said, like I always did, *shall we wash up a tiny bit of powder just to test the quality? Just a tiny bit* are the last words a crack addict utters on the edge of a very dark precipice.

The edge of an Escher ledge.

By Sunday night we'd smoked all of it and done a couple of hundred quids' worth of heroin to try to level out. I'd drunk a bottle of whisky trying to flatten myself out. It was as close as I've ever come to the edge, not to overdose, but to madness. I lost control.

By Monday morning, as the sun rose, I sat shaking like a deeply damaged rescue dog that hadn't been rescued. A dog in a secret perpetual pandemonium. I swigged bottles of Night Nurse to try to ease the shakes and settle my heartbeat, which fluttered dangerously – manically, erratically. Since Saturday night I hadn't left the room, I hadn't pissed or shat. Just stared at my partner so much that I'd started to hallucinate that he was secretly doing drugs every time he turned his head away. My eyes started to flicker like I was watching a film about him through a magic lantern.

We were listening to Brandy. Brandy on repeat for fifty-six straight hours. 'The Boy is Mine' on repeat. I hallucinated; the voice in my head said, *the boy isn't yours, he belongs to someone else*. Everything turned a little shady and then a lot malevolent. My mind unhinged a millimetre or two, which doesn't sound a lot but a mind unhinged is a mind unhinged. I know that from my mum: slight differences in her chemical intake turned her baking from love into weaponry.

The hallucinations worsened. I thought I could see him talking to someone, I couldn't quite see who. The drug, crack, had become a person he wanted more than me, a person he wanted to fuck.

'Do you want me to leave the room?' I said, with absolutely no intention of leaving the room or any idea why I was saying it. That paranoid inner voice rising up and out of me, that voice that even on crack didn't think it was good enough for crack. I was possessed by every single failed personality trait and every single fear.

I knew that if I gave in to the paranoid hallucinations that I'd be royally fucked. But I couldn't help it; the words came out. Every time he left the room I, me, not him, stole fragments of crack from the table. Squirrelling it away in the space that would become home to my neo vagina years later. My habit slipped down another notch, I was thieving from him, I was a mess. I was the one being fucked in the arse and the head by crack. I was the one with knickers full of rocks.

The words spilled out, 'Do you want me to leave you with

them, you obviously prefer them to me, shall I leave you both alone so you can fuck each other's brains out?'

He looked at me and I knew from his expression that I'd stepped off the ledge; he looked scared. He shook his head and smiled. 'No, what are you talking about, there's only us here.'

'Fuck off is there,' I said, 'you know if I leave the room you'll be fucking in a second.'

His smile stopped. He scanned my face for any signs of sanity. None.

With each word, my pulse racing. I looked at my wrist and the vein seemed to be breaching the skin. Pushing upwards and out. *I'm going to have a heart attack*, I thought, why, *because I think he's fucking crack which is an inanimate substance.* I've gone crack-mad. That's an edge you don't want to find yourself at on a Monday morning. People think a crowded tube is a Monday morning issue, try overloading your brain with crack cocaine.

I was talking to him about the manifestation of crack cocaine as a person he'd rather fuck than me. She was she, obviously. My gender fuckery always rose to the surface on crack, it's that kind of drug. It seeks out and inhabits your darkness, your insecurities, your fragilities, and squats in them like punks in the seventies. That's not actually true, punks in the seventies were largely a middle-class bunch playing at being tough rather than being tough.

The people squatting in my insecurities had no fear of death. That's when people are truly scary, when they aren't scared of dying. Crack doesn't care about you dying because it knows a gazillion others will pop up instantly in your place, it doesn't need you. You will spit yourself out for it, unlike heroin which slowly milks you year after year. I'm not sure which is worse, the drug that can take a whole lifetime or a drug that quickly takes a life. Obviously far better to get on a crowded tube on a Monday morning than do either.

Crack has no redeeming qualities, it doesn't soothe, or ease, or allow distant troubling emotions to rise to the surface and settle, mist-like, upon your skin. Heroin can and does, gently evoking, loosening difficult memories. Crack is designed to finish you off.

One drug is carnivorous and the other parasitical.

With crack, only the first pipe, the first ever rock, is blissful. An ultimate moment, an ultimate high which offers nothing afterwards but hellishness. It takes everything, then knocks at the door, screaming, *I left the floorboards, give them here.*

When people tell me I'm brave, I smile and I think, *yes, I survived crack, where's my badge, my OBE?* Please don't, I hate the Empire. The Empire created the global drugs trade, the processing of leaves and seed pods into addictive substances to establish mass control.

That weekend I imagined that my partner was leaving me for *her*, for the impalpable memory of the first time with crack. I was losing my mind. At that point closer to the edge than I'd ever been. Crack bettered me, and I'd grown up seeing all kinds of gore, all kinds of shit.

Things weren't always so messy.

At the start of our relationship, we were fresh-faced twenty-somethings who imagined they'd be able to dabble and dive in and out of any drug they chose. Drugs were our currency and the language we'd chosen to debate the world in – a little like Valium for Mum, drugs became tokens of love. We felt invincible and powerful for maybe the first time in our lives. Drugs, and the money we made selling them, gave us a bold presence in our lives that we'd never felt before. We'd only felt like shadows in other people's lives. Drugs gave us an identity.

At the start the downers were smooth and the uppers steady. Every deal straightforward.

Ten years on, everything had become bloody and splintered.

By the last day of our relationship, we were half dead, physically and emotionally, both of us had full-blown AIDS diagnoses, and both of us were struggling to know if there would ever be a way out of addiction. Was there a place for us in this new world, a world which over ten years had changed? We entered drugs childishly hopeful with pagers and phone boxes and came out the other side, albeit discarded with the arrival of mobile phones.

Being addicted is a little like doing time, being out on licence, tagged. But it's you that tags you, that jails you. You put yourself into the smallest box and then, day in, day out, you brick yourself in, until it's just you, the foil, the needle, the pipe, and the need to use and to make money. That's it, you don't need or do anything else. Food becomes inconsequential, some days I might have a yogurt or some chips on the run, or half a pack of cheap pink wafer biscuits whose sugar content gave my poor belly a false sense of motoring up.

I was constantly empty but never had the time to notice being hungry. At the end of addiction, I was structurally anorexic, my digestive system having closed down years earlier and moved on to greener, lusher pastures. Even a little food made my belly feel like a sluggish, broke mountain.

Leaving him, leaving T, my long-term drug love affair, was the hardest thing I've ever done; he was the drug and the addiction at the end, because he was the only human who had ever been emotionally intimate and vulnerable with me. We were everything and nothing to each other.

We walked in each other's footsteps for ten years. We listened to each other breathe for ten years, almost every night. Deep breaths, orgasmic breaths, dying viral breaths and the last breath of goodbye. I left in the middle of the night, secretly packing a case and putting it in the boot of my old red van. I drove away to a new life, a life with books, words and silence. A life without him.

But back then I was nowhere near walking away yet, we still had years to go before that would happen.

A week or so later, the tickets to Egypt arrived in the post. Actual tickets, that's what happened then. Actual paper tickets, I stared at them for hours. Us on a plane to a place called Luxor, which according to the guidebook was the town next to the Valley of the Kings. The brochure said that most rooms in our hotel had balconies that overlooked the Nile and the Valley of the Kings beyond. Luxor had its own spectacular temples and Karnak was only a short taxi ride away: *if you want to really experience Egyptian culture as it might have been in the time of the pharaohs, why not take a horse-and-cart taxi to Karnak alongside the Nile?*

I thought, *I'll do that, I'll take a horse-and-cart ride alongside the Nile towards Karnak, as the heroin is leeching out of my body for ever, I'll feel a warm wind cleanse my soul.* It's child-ish, maybe childlike, but I was so excited. I felt like a proper human who deserved respect. Fuck that this was drug money, and fuck that everything we were about to do was illegal and potentially incredibly dangerous. I believed in the beauty of the world even if I'd received that beauty through the gold click, click, click of Liz Taylor impersonating Cleopatra. I didn't want to spend the money getting high in Ibiza or some other drug-fuelled destination. I wanted to see the pyramids and the temples, to breathe them in.

I honestly thought, as I was nicking watercolour paints and a pad of watercolour paper from the art shop in Soho, that I was like any other late-nineteenth-century traveller planning to make small, beautiful watercolour sketches of the Nile.

Only an addict could ignore the chaos around them and believe enough in the wonder of life to spend stolen drug money on a holiday to see the Valley of the Kings and then to nick watercolours thinking they would document the adventure. *Was I really that person?* I miss that person sometimes, they were so carefree and fabulously stupid and ridiculous.

Looking at our travel tickets, we joked about how impulsive we were, how bold we were. So bold that it might, just might, herald a new age for us, a new age of normality. An age without drugs.

We'd get clean. We'd go cold turkey in the shimmering, mystical Egyptian heat.

By some silly pseudo-scientific-reckoning bollocks we assumed that going cold turkey shouldn't be too bad in the heat, should it? The heat of the sun balancing out the cold of the turkey. Always seeking balance in bodies that sought out chemical imbalances.

We closed our eyes, nodding off, full of opiates, and imagined that the sun's rays would be soothing, the heroin leaching out of our pores. Dripping out in individual beads of sweat, unnoticeably. We'd sleep on the balcony overlooking the Nile, sip wine and smoke the remnants of our duty-free crack. We'd be just like any other traveller, but the addict versions, so not like them.

I hate writing those kinds of cancelling statements, but they're true: we were and we weren't.

I once saw a large toad flattened on the road; it was flat but still a toad. The next day some bluebottles that had been tucking into the flattened toad's flesh had also been run over by a car and become embedded into the toad's back. The toad now looked like a piece of jewellery, the bluebottles like sapphires, deep, rich sapphires glinting in the sun. It was beautiful, in that moment as beautiful as any Boucheron brooch. The following day it had dried in the sun and was then only a dead toad with barely visible shit-eating flies.

We were like any other tourists but we weren't, and as the holiday went on we became less like them and more like flattened toads replete with turkey skins.

Before we embarked we didn't think about being addicts or looking like addicts, we just dreamt about the Nile, the balcony, sipping wine and maybe making love. Over the years our bodies had been torn into shreds by the unrelenting demands of addiction, my body peppered with the spunk of strangers, unholy waters shot all over my torn surface in order that I find the money to press the tip of a needle into a vein. Dreaming about ordinary things felt like such a kindness.

I closed my eyes and dreamt about sketching boats on the Nile and the horse-and-cart taxi in a warm breeze. I dreamt about the clean, unsullied space we'd find thousands of miles away.

We saw our holiday as a step towards living again. A surreal step considering that we intended to smuggle drugs into a country which had the death penalty for drug smuggling. We were so devoid of any reality that we didn't even think to hide the drugs beyond the childlike and rudimentary, *put them under our caps, no one will look there.*

And they didn't. Can you believe it, they didn't?

Like a gilded journey, a myth, us led by the gods to a place where we'd find redemption and forgiveness for all we'd done as addicts. We'd recover in the shade of palm trees and temples, smoke crack and contemplate how best to live again.

It wasn't gilded, perhaps it was simply luck, but we walked straight through the airport, through security, passed through the police and border controls, all seemingly blind. We took enough heroin and crack to last two weeks, neatly tucked into the brims of our baseball caps and between the cheeks of our arses.

I've often been stopped since, walking through security. Stopped, pulled to one side and searched, I've had shampoo taken away because it was over 100ml, been asked endless questions about who packed my case. Once, the time I made it back to Egypt to really see the tombs, I was dragged out of the airport by the military police who took my passport away and questioned me about my political beliefs, in a building that was part of the airport but wasn't part of the airport, scarily adjunct. A short 4X4-ride across the tarmac, away from arrivals.

The head man questioning me wore civilian clothes, but a military beret lay on his desk, next to an ashtray full of Camel dogends. I saw the packet, I'm not trying to conjure up any fag exoticism. The beret was a sign, like an evil eye on the desk's surface. Intimidating. He didn't know my past, bless him.

He had great hands; I love hands. I had a moment in which I imagined his fingers entering me. No wonder I've ended up in such scrapes, I'm such a fucking sucker for chunky knuckles and that's definitely my dad's fault. His imprint.

He waved my passport in my face, asking me if my family was Irish, had I been to Ireland?

*For fuck's sake*, I thought, *I'm a teacher and when ten years ago I walked through here loaded with Class As no one even flicked a look.*

My friend's waiting outside by the taxi rank, panicking, thinking that my drug past had caught up with me – for years people never let me forget my drug past. The man with the beret and the hands insisted that I have a cup of hot apple tea with him and accept his apology. Accept it out loud, he demanded smoothly, say it, say I accept your apology.

I did.

He handed me my passport and told me to enjoy the sights of Egypt.

Ten years earlier, when we arrived at the airport, we bought cigarettes and a small bottle of brandy in duty free, took a handful of Valium each, drank the brandy and snuggled down into the coach journey, the warmth flowing. Excitement encased in blossoming layers.

We arrived in Luxor, drug mules, our holiday stash hidden. We did what we did every day, we kept our drugs on us, next to our skin. We'd never risk anyone taking them away, heroin was as important, if not more important than the air we breathed, much more important than sex, relationships, housing or family. More important than life itself.

Addicts take daily risks with their lives because the drug is the life and without the drug there is no life. That's how an overdose happens, there's no calculation of risk, just need, which outweighs any risk. I've knowingly used dirty needles because I needed to use a needle. I've knowingly and dangerously mixed opiates and synthetic opiates because I felt that I needed to. I cannot remember ever having an internal conversation about life or death connected to drugs. Selling sex, yes, but even then the need for drug money overrode any sense of safety.

I once took thirty ecstasy pills, one after the other, because I couldn't get high but I needed to get high, so I just kept taking them until I did. I didn't, I collapsed and people walked over me. Hours later I heard someone say, *are they breathing? Yes, I am*, I replied, *but I'm not fucking high, so fuck off.* I was truly awful around any substance that could alter my emotions.

We would never have hidden our drugs in suitcases that travelled separately from us. Had we been caught I can say with almost certainty that we would have swallowed the drugs in one go, the whole cling-filmed wraps, biting them open to allow the powder to seep into our bloodstream. Then they could have done anything to us. There is no perception of time or consequence in the moment after you take a hit. The hit is the full stop.

Although I can't be sure, I think my partner did some heroin in the toilet on the plane, snorting it, taking just a little bit more from the pie than me. He came back from the toilet with that shady shimmer of heroin. A cocky glow, eyelids heavy.

His head falling asleep on my shoulder.

*Cunt*, I thought as I necked a couple of Valium in a pointless act of revenge.

It defies logic that we walked out through one airport and in through another transporting heroin and crack cocaine, yet no one blinked an eye, no dog sniffed us, no one searched us. We looked like addicts and I'm sure we moved like addicts do when they are half-cut, half un-cut. Half-down and a little up. Jerky and smooth, like a piece of middle-class student dance that's aiming for urban.

We walked straight through both airports with every other traveller (or smuggler) on our Egyptian adventure. My Cleopatra, my Liz Taylor as Cleopatra, dream.

Just like Liz without the gems or the kitten heels.

I wrote a piece for an anthology about love, commissioned by a high-end jeweller's. Throughout the piece I hinted that no one had ever given me a diamond, or a gem of any kind. I ended the piece with the line, 'Maybe I'll buy my own yellow sapphire set in the narrowest of gold bands and inside have the words inscribed, I'll always believe in love.' I naively thought they might pay me with the ring, but no, it was for charity.

I'm nothing like Liz, she'd have had the chutzpah to get that in writing before she wrote a single word.

Instead, the words I had were on lined paper, which we'd used to make wraps for the heroin that was now hidden under our caps. I remember unwrapping the last wrap in Egypt and seeing something written about 'for day fourteen', and let's just say, day fourteen it wasn't.

You know what's coming and it ain't pretty.

# Fourteen

# Egypt Part Three: The Little Red Camel

We arrived at the Luxor Hilton and lay on luxurious 400-thread cotton sheets. I adore crisp white bedsheets, they embody fruition, if that's possible. Our room had a mini-bar stacked with sparkling water, chilled white wine, natural yogurt, orange juice and packets of cashews. We only ate what was in the mini-bar.

Yogurts and cashews.

The room had a beautiful terrace that overlooked the hotel gardens and out across the Nile to the Valley of the Kings beyond. It was perfect, it was stupid, it was reckless. It was beautiful, and dreamy and after we opened the curtains and shutters, I glimpsed the landscape I'd so often fantasised about: beautiful gardens; palm trees, each with its own bird song; and in the distance, the gentle lapping waves from feluccas that drifted by on the Nile. For a moment there was quiet and hope. This was the dream.

I thought I was worth the dream even if in that wishful moment it was absurd.

The first night we closed the curtains and never opened them again. I only glimpsed the Nile and the gardens and the valleys beyond through the great sheaves of bronze-coloured fabric. Noting only that we were in Egypt and not east London, the curtains framing the Nile as if it were a photograph in a magazine. The drugs soon demanded our complete attention.

It was brave and stupidly creative for two working-class, fucked-up queers to have the audacity to think that the tombs of pharaohs long dead might be the kick-start to their redemption. When working-class people do succeed, nothing can stop them because they reach way out into the realms of *anything can happen if you think it can*.

We never left the room until our drug supply ran dry. That was on day four, terrifyingly only four days in to a fourteen-day stay.

The heroin was the first to go.

In the heat, heroin rapidly rushes through your system, evaporating out of your body as sweat. We knew it was happening, we could feel the panic rising, so we shut the shutters and pulled the curtains tight, trying to keep out the sun's heat. Removing the last sliver of Egypt from our view. We turned the air con up to its coldest setting.

The room became Siberia, Siberia in Egypt. Those Siberian measures bought us maybe an hour or two's grace. The truth of an addict's intake is that if there are drugs available, you can't, and you won't stop. You'll stay awake and consume whatever drugs you have until the last grain of powder or splinter of rock is gone.

You'll start crushing up pills, dissolving them in water to swallow or inject them, you'll start injecting water to convince your brain that you're injecting something. You'll start to scrape the chase lines off the foil and smoke that, even though your mind knows that you're only smoking charred foil. Your addiction thought processes become unhinged. A cavern opens up between reality and fantasy.

That happened in that room; we fell into the cavern and the cavern wasn't a tomb, a tomb would have felt far easier.

We started to play stupid addiction games just before the heroin ran out: *we'll have a small amount every other hour up until lunchtime and we'll wash it down with sips of wine from the mini-bar which will keep us on the brighter side of wrong until teatime, then we'll make a cup of tea and wash that down by smoking a grain of crack and chase a single, one-grain-of-dust-wide line of heroin, then, withdrawals held at bay, we'll go for a walk in the beautiful world beyond the shutters and curtains, through the landscaped garden paradise.*

We tried that for a day or so but never made it out to the garden because one or other of us would say that they wanted to stay behind and sleep and we both knew that that was bullshit addict talk meaning, I'll take bits from the edge of the bit that remains – like kids do from a birthday cake, thinking no one will see. Neither of us could let the other one out of our sight.

So the curtains and shutters stayed closed and the Nile and its wonders out of sight. I dreamt about them though, how bizarre is that? That they were the other side of closed curtains but still only accessible through my dreams. Maybe that's the truth of wonders, that they are only ever fantasies in your mind. Perhaps the film would always be more real to me?

When I did make it back to Egypt and Luxor years after that first time, the most beautiful experience wasn't walking around temples, staring at hieroglyphs or caskets surrounded by a thousand and one other tourists, but sitting alone in the scorching mid-afternoon heat in the Temple of Luxor, closing my eyes and listening as the call to prayer emerged all around me. The chants emerging from mosques all around the temple, which sits at the centre of Luxor. The sound like birds flying into the sky from different trees, singing the same song but ever so slightly differently. It was a monumental moment.

But on that first Egypt trip we stayed in a dark, chilled room. Like any crack den back at home but smarter, with heavy bronze curtains, air con and a mini-bar.

The Luxor Hilton crack den. Will I be sued for calling it a crack den? It was beautiful, but that's what we needed the room to become. The room suffered no damage, only us. I never broke or stole anything ... actually, as I'm confessing, there were the sheets.

We didn't piss or shit until the drugs ran dry and then we couldn't piss or shit because our bodies started to shut down. Your intestines do that when you are using, and they do that when you're not using, your innards shut down, assaulted by the toxic strength of opiates. Like brass valves on a church organ, different bodily functions stop and start in accordance with your drug intake.

I wouldn't shit for weeks until whatever was there was so compacted that it shot out like pellets. Like a Gatling gun. I'd stop drugs and the shit valve would open again, like pressure from a dam. Sorry to focus on shit, but heroin addiction and your stomach become entwined in a narrative of constipation and variously ill-formed shits.

So our two-week supply of drugs lasted four days, then we started to get sick. Really sick. Really fucking extremely sick. The heat, the bastard heat crept through the cracks in the shutters, forcing us to take what little we had and forcing what little we had taken, out through our pores. I licked my arms to catch the sweat, trying to reprocess heroin back into my system, *don't leech out, recycle*. The intense heat and humidity drew out every sweaty, shivering response possible from our skin.

Our minds tried to avoid the frenetic panic mounting in each and every corner. *This can't be happening, we can't run out of drugs here, don't think about it, think about temples or Liz's gold kitten heels, think about anything, but don't think about the drugs, which are almost gone*. Your body turns your mind against you, you find yourself apologising to your inner addict and begging them not to hurt you, telling them that as soon as you can you'll feed them drugs. You plead with your inner addicted self as if you are an errant baby. *Don't hurt me, I've got a plan*.

As always in the very first throes of withdrawal, in the first couple of hours you imagine that you are strong enough to get clean, to get through it to a long-since-forgotten place of sanity and serenity. We lay on the once crisp laundered sheets, our skin prickling and shivering, hair follicles standing abruptly in waves of painful panic, then lying flat in false calm. We looked into each other's eyes and said that this was the perfect opportunity to get clean once and for all. He held my face. His beautiful hands allowed my head and my mind to momentarily disconnect from my jarring body full of fears. My head came to rest as my body was readying to fuck me up.

We had no drugs, no dealers, no shady or otherwise connections, just an almost empty mini-bar and grubby white sheets which needed pressing. My mum's OCD would climb the temple walls.

We'd banned housekeeping so the room was a mess. A complete picture. If William Burroughs or any other addict had visited the Luxor Hilton and run dry, it would have looked identical. Despite the myth of finding yourself on a personal inwards journey, on some opium or ayahuasca Western meandering, there is no unique drug experience. With heroin, crack cocaine or any other Class A addiction it's just a set of very predictable chemical reactions that always beget or lead to the same or similar physical, emotional and economic outcomes. The room was a mess, no outsider mythology, just dirty sheets, used drug paraphernalia and sheer emotional collapse.

No one from Hollywood was filming, it was just us and a dirty, messed-up, once beautiful hotel room. Two very fucked-up individuals whose sense of power was gleaned from the streets of a city far away.

We were so deluded (or desperate) that we could use this hideous situation as the impetus to get clean from drugs that we booked ourselves on a day trip down the fucking Nile to visit a temple. The Temple of Hatshepsut, the woman-would-be-pharaoh whose face was cut away, erased, from every statue or symbol.

How we came to that day trip decision is wildly beyond me now. But one minute we were talking about getting clean, him holding my head in his hands, and the next we were flicking through a booklet of *things to do while you're here withdrawing from Class As*. Two minutes later, T was on the phone booking two places on the *exquisite historical trip down the ancient Nile*.

Truthfully, that decision, more than any other in my whole marriage to drugs, makes me shudder and feel sick to the back teeth. It was the riskiest and the most exposing drug decision ever made by us or me. It made smuggling or selling drugs, or selling my arse, look like a trip to Ikea to buy a Billy bookcase that you know you have to assemble.

On the bed, my head in his hands, I felt protected by him. He could always make me feel safe, which was lucky considering the amount of danger we got into. When I was a kid I couldn't stand the idea that the socks at the back of my sock drawer might feel rejected, left out. Every morning I would change the order, bringing the socks from the back to the front, pushing them neatly together like peas sleeping in a pod, a family of socks. His hands made me feel like that, like a pea safe in a pod.

We booked the trip.

Withdrawing from heroin always made me throw up violently, it affected me physically much more than mentally, whereas T seemed OK physically until he lost the plot in his mind. When he lost the plot, he really lost the plot.

Maybe I was already partially lost in the severity of my bodily responses to withdrawal when I agreed to the day trip. Not that I'm blaming anyone. A part of me did see it as a solution. A part of me thought that the best place to withdraw from heroin would be on a boat with tourists jauntily sailing down the Nile in one hundred degrees of heat. Ignoring my dilemma by trying to act like them, like the rest of the world.

The minute I got on the boat I started throwing up, surrounded by polite clusters of middle-aged white heterosexual folk from Surbiton and one or two couples from Germany and Sweden. I know this detail because on the coach we had to do a jolly introduction. *I'm Juno and I'm fucked from fucked*, I didn't say.

The nightmare of withdrawal started as if I were at a summer fete in a small village the other side of the M25. Boat trips, however cruddy or small, encourage people to mix and mingle with their boat-trip tribe. We were not part of this tribe; we were from a different planet.

The polite folk clustered at the edges of the boat to wave to the children who rowed small boats and swam after us, selling trinkets and T-shirts adorned with hieroglyphs. I thought, *the kids don't want you to wave to them like you're the fucking Queen, they want you to lean over and buy something. This isn't 1880, you're not royalty just because you can afford a day trip down the Nile on an ageing tugboat pumping out diesel fumes and fuel which is polluting their river.* I felt suffocated by the amorphous mass of middle-classness around me. Hemmed in by their well-meaning wave of waves. They looked at us as if we were foreign, which I think queerness is in those settings, forget the addiction, forget my throwing up.

However I might judge them, I was just as bad. I hadn't respected anything about the country or its culture, I'd dreamt about visiting Egypt because of Liz Taylor in gold lamé and kitten heels. I was the one hemmed in by fanciful dreams. Were these tourists any different, thinking themselves royal? Secretly, didn't I want to be just like them, with a husband and a kinky session on a Friday night after a glass or two of Chablis? Wasn't my Liz Taylor dream just that, seeking normativity even if it were the gold lamé version? *Wasn't I on this boat trying to be them?* I was the junkie throwing up, they were capturing memories, click, click went their shiny new 35mm cameras.

I tried to extricate myself from them and moved slowly and carefully to the upper deck, trying not to puke over the polite people coming down the other way. When I reached the upper deck, I threw up into the waters of a ridiculously small, crystal-clear swimming pool. A swimming pool that would only hold one or two floating bodies, it would feel like you were in bed with someone. It was a couple's pool, a lovers' pool. *A fuck pool*, I thought.

I threw up into the pool and not into the river, which might have seemed more logical, but when I looked over the edge of the boat I saw kids swimming in the water and I knew that they didn't deserve my rancid outpourings, the spewed years of addiction. The years of toxic stench built up in my belly. No one deserved it, but the kids looking up, laughing, smiling and haggling, certainly didn't. Being sick in the Nile was a no-no because local kids swam in it and local men fished in it. I did have some morals, even if they were frequently skewed and sold for a fiver.

Throwing up in the pool, the lyrics to my favourite Joni Mitchell song, 'Little Green', rolled through my mind. When I announced to my friends about my impending gender realignment, one of them said that I should stand still and not change because I'd make an ugly woman. When I walked away from them and their stinging rebuke, I hummed 'Little Green' to myself and thought, *fuck you, I'm Joni*, which became Juno. In my mind I'm Joni, The High Priestess of words and things.

I looked up from my expulsions floating in the pool and watched as a young child, maybe eight or nine, was helped up from a rowing boat to sell his goods on deck. Oblivious to my drug dilemma, he was soon stood in front of me displaying an armful of beautifully handcrafted animals, and people riding horses and camels. Despite the sick dribbling down my chin, he politely asked me if I wanted to buy one, I said yes and handed him some Egyptian pounds.

'Which one?' he asked. 'You choose,' I replied.

He handed me the most beautifully handsewn man riding a camel, a man wearing a red hat and a red net skirt. The camel's neck made out of silver-blue lamé, its eyes sequins, its body a piece of upholstery velvet with a swirling 1970s pattern. The stitching, big, bright-red cotton stitches that I was reminded of years later when I looked at my freshly delivered neo-cunt in a hand mirror. I thought, *the men and boys who give me cunts and camels aren't great at stitching*. My cunt's always reminded me of an outsider work of art.

I've never let go of that camel, it's as perfect today on my shelf in Spain as it was the day I bought it, with sick dribbling down my chin.

After my camel purchase I carried on throwing up in the miniature tourist pool. My vomit sploshing around on the surface of aqua-green, chemically induced clarity, the petrified contents of my stomach, years in the making, starting to break down, sloshing violently as the boat hit wave after wave created by the endless tourist traffic. The number of boats making the Nile seem like a tributary in Oxford, full of punts of cunts.

Once I started throwing up I couldn't stop, the vomit shooting out in whatever direction I was facing. I became a fountain into the intimate two-person pool, which now had a scummy surface like the images we are so used to seeing of the detritus, the mountains of flip-flops and condoms, the fun of the West, floating on once perfect seas.

Addiction is essentially selfish and destructive. People right down the narcotic production line suffered for me to dull my pain. Narcotic production is surrounded on all sides by intense violence and abuse, people enslaved, communities destroyed, often indigenous. So that I, little old me, fucked-up me, could dull my pain.

No, I would not throw up in the Nile. It's the very least a selfish fucker could do.

I moved to the very edge of the boat, the hot metal gunwale pressing into my flesh. I ran my finger over its newly painted surface, feeling years, tens of years, of painted layers, accumulated to cover its history. I pushed the tip of my finger into a mound of encrusted paint, it easily went through the layers of paint and rust and found the hull. Touching the hull momentarily felt like my lover's hands cupping my face. I hummed Joni and hoped.

A brief moment of respite, then sickness again. I tried to cover my mouth, horrified, mortified, but the vomit shot through my fingers, running over me as if I were a lemon drizzle cake.

I looked over at T, who was now sitting on the edge of an even smaller Jacuzzi, his legs dangling in the water, trying to look relaxed, doing his best to distance himself from me and my explosive expulsions. Fucker. He looked like a frog at the edge of a lily-pond.

To everyone else he looked fine, I was the mess, but I could see a demonic twinkle in his eyes, an empty blackness to his pupils. Pupils that expanded and contracted like terrified black holes in space; I could feel myself being sucked in.

Through the smokescreen of my vomit, I watched him unhinge in his pupils. I knew that in a few hours the shit would truly hit the fan. *Please let us have left these people and this boat behind by then, oh my goddess, Liz, please make it so.*

We were stranded on a boat in a myth that we had created back in London with a cupboard full of drugs and an easy ability to buy more. This wasn't quite the first-class, redemptive, sun-splayed experience we'd laughed about being bold enough to book, staring at our travel tickets as if they were golden tokens of salvation.

It was nightmarish. Us withdrawing from heroin on a boat on the Nile surrounded by tourists who wanted nothing more than a slice of history and spoonful of houmous wrapped in a vine leaf.

They hadn't paid for the company of withdrawing addicts; we weren't part of their myth-making, we weren't a tale they'd recall as part of a wedding speech like the Whirling Dervish who, because of the cramped space, kept his whirling to a minimum. The dancing and finger food were laid out inside the formal dining room, which was on the lower deck. We stayed on the upper deck in terrified silence. I think we were in shock and perhaps even disbelief at our predicament. There was nothing to say, I couldn't stop vomiting, his pupils were now resolutely demonic. We couldn't look at each other, let alone speak.

After lunch, the tourists, fed and watered, wandered back up to the upper decks as the boat pulled in to a small cranky jetty. Tight friendship groups had obviously formed over lunch, everyone part of one community now, one community and us. Our guide said, *here's where you get off to visit the Temple of Hatshepsut, the most important of all the female pharaohs.*

So important that her fragile nephew had had all traces of her erased, her face wearing the traditional male beard, chipped away. *Was she transgender?* I wondered in a moment of historical landgrab and cultural appropriation. But trans is my word. She was a woman who couldn't be a pharaoh while also being a woman; history tells us nothing about her feelings about gender.

I said to the guide, *I can't move, I think I've eaten something bad; I need to stay onboard.* But that was lost in translation and he said, *no, everyone needs to get off the boat to see this wonderful temple.* As if we could look at the temple's grandiosity and not notice the violence meted out onto the carved faces of Hatshepsut. As if the hieroglyphs surrounding the beheaded woman could mask the violence that men have always perpetuated against women. It's called her temple but she's been all but erased. It should be called *the temple of the woman that men never want you to see*. At least then you'd be forewarned about the horrific scars that lie in wait.

Strange, no one else seemed to mind. And I was fragile that day.

The rest of the coach party kept their distance from us in our long crocodile file. I continued to throw up. They sensed something now, but they couldn't put their finger on it. The bleached hair, the shaven head, the eyes, the pupils, the copious amounts of sick floating in the lovers' pool. Signs.

Every other step I'd retch and throw up what remained inside of me, my childhood memories and fish fingers I'd eaten in 1979. Then I threw up bile, acid-yellow-green bile. I felt alien, I was an alien among tourists, an addict who should be scoring in Hackney or sipping methadone as an aperitif, but who instead was dying of shame in the temple of no faces.

The endless faceless statues and bleak burnt interior felt like a sign that in some way I'd defaced myself, desecrated myself and my body. I thought of all the cocks I'd sucked, cocks that made me gag because they smelt, or were unclean. Men whose names I didn't know who came over my face – old spunk, young spunk, salty spunk, watery spunk, globules of spunk as thick as bread dough, dripping off my nose. I wish I could go back and remove that face.

It was tortuous listening to the guide pointing out one chiselled-off face after another.

I wanted to say, *I get it, the men didn't want her in charge, they never do. The number of weak men who've abused my body enjoying the feeling of control, I get it.*

In that temple I was losing the battle of withdrawals, my past rushing from one side of my brain to the other, like kids playing Bulldog across a concrete playground. Each time leaving embedded footprints, traces of what had been, of what I'd been. I'd never thought about the stuff I'd done, because I'd never allowed withdrawal to get to this point, not in ten years.

My head was overwhelmed by shame, regret and fear. By the unknown fears of what would play out in the following hours and the shame of all I'd ever done. *What will be? What have I done?* Again and again, from one side of my mind to the other. I suddenly saw Hatshepsut's missing features as a calmness, away from here, I imagined her gathered in a place much better, much kinder than here.

I wanted to die. Those moments, those minutes felt impossibly bleak. The temple, stifling hot, dark, part burnt and full to the rafters with mutilation. You couldn't withdraw from heroin in a worse place. But it happened. That's the gig when you're damaged but creative.

In those moments there wasn't a single part of my brain that could see anything good, only everything bad that I'd done that had brought me to this point of heroin withdrawal in the Temple of Hatshepsut.

It felt like my head would split in two, cleaved by the intensity of my shame. It would have been easier to roll behind one of the temple walls and stay there in the shade. Hiding like a child. Staying there until I died alongside Hatshepsut. I felt an infinity with her and I can't describe why.

But our overly eager guide was not allowing any of us to

linger, he ushered us along at pace, spitting out different versions of *this statue had its face chipped away, this statue had its face smashed off*. He had done this trip so often that he didn't even notice me, like one of the dead accompanying Hatshepsut on to the afterlife. His autopilot was a blessing, because no one in the group was anything but a tourist. He had no time to investigate my woeful addiction.

That afternoon was completely surreal; when we were back on the boat I would have been content to slip over the side and drown silently, like an unnamed pebble, into the murky depths of the Nile. My vomiting subsided for a brief moment before chugging up again like an ancient steam engine.

I looked over at T, his feet back dangling into the Jacuzzi, his legs white, his hair jet black, the bubbling water aqua blue, his face a pale apple green. It wasn't painted by Hockney, but the colour palette was as beautiful as any Hockney spring landscape. All throughout this current pandemic, a publisher has posted Hockney landscapes every day on Twitter. Each one, genius, made me happy.

On the coach back to the hotel my vomiting became horrific. The couple sitting in front, desperately trying to avoid my vomit, turned and said that they thought I needed hospitalising for food poisoning. *It's OK*, T said, *she's got a very weak stomach and the silly moo tried to eat the stuffed vine leaves*. I looked over at him calling me *she* in public and a *silly moo*, his eyes were bulging, his withdrawal had properly started. I'd never heard him use the word 'moo' before, it was a very worrying sign. 'Cunt' would have been far less worrying than 'moo'.

The mention of stuffed vine leaves made me throw up even more.

Getting back to the relative safety – let's be clear, there was no relative safety – of the room, made little difference to the severity of what was happening. We knew that we were royally, up the jacksie, fucked. We were withdrawing from heroin in the middle of Egypt with no drugs, no dealers, no streets to score on, and only a couple of small, half empty bottles of wine from the mini-bar to try and alleviate the nightmare that was now fully kicking in. As addicts do, we concocted a plan, a ludicrous plan which seemed perfectly plausible to us and utterly doable.

*The Plan*

*We will do the following, in the following order, try to memorise.*

*Ring the reception desk and ask them to call a doctor, a private doctor. Then invite the private doctor to visit us in our plush suite and convince them to sell us drugs by acting like innocent, well-meaning travellers caught up in a nightmare for which we had no responsibility.*

*Apologise profusely for our stupidity and try to blame it on our Englishness, mad dogs and all that. Tell the doctor that a couple of months before travelling we had been involved in a traffic accident in London and that my friend (T) had broken some bones which although now mended were still very painful, especially in this heat. Make small talk about the temperature, everybody knows about London and the rain, perhaps connect the traffic accident to the rain? Perhaps not, don't get messy!*

*Tell the doctor that because of the pain of past broken bones, my friend (I think it's best to go with friend despite the obvious mess of a shared bed) needs strong pain medication, opiate based please, thank you. Be polite.*

*Please, if you could give us the opiate-based medication it will really help him and thus me to relax and explore this wonderful country of yours. To relax in this wonderful Egyptian splendour.*

*He shouldn't worry, because we know the names of the drugs that work as they have been prescribed by our doctor in England, an old responsible family doctor, but silly us, we forgot to bring them with us as we had left in such an excitable rush to see the tombs. I've been dreaming about this visit for years, has he ever seen the film* Cleopatra *starring Liz Taylor?*

I genuinely thought that might help – who doesn't love Liz Taylor in gold lamé? To a doctor in Egypt, I was going to bring up the most culturally insensitive, offensive depiction of Egyptian history ever made, along with every other film made in Hollywood about anywhere other than Hollywood, thank fuck I never got the chance to mention her.

*Also,* I'd say, splurging out more rubbish in our plan, *the heat is far too much for me, I think I might have heatstroke, which is why I look so awful and keep vomiting, could he please prescribe me some Valium as they had always helped before when I'd had heatstroke in London, that one time it didn't rain. Make joke about rain, people love the idea of English people being wet and cold after all we've done. Who can blame them?*

I'd continue, *I normally take 10mg Valium for heatstroke because my doctor, the family doctor who I think goes to church every Sunday, said it was the best drug to lower your body temperature. Who would have thought, Valium and body temperature, it really is multi-faceted, does he prescribe it often?*

*Maybe leave off the last statement about Valium and its medicinal properties.*

*Thank him for his kindness and offer the last remining packet of cashews as well as a sizeable tip if we get the goods.*

*End of plan.*

This was as good a plan as any gets when it's hatched in the minds of withdrawing heroin addicts. It seemed reasonable to us and likely to succeed. I kept saying to T, *I'll pull out the angelic and lay the pleases and thank yous on thick.* Not realising that the angelic act had departed my exhausted face to search for more gainful employment a good few years before.

We started to laugh a little and guess which opioid they'd be most likely to give us and then to decide what we'd do with them – swallow, crush, smoke. Like kiss, marry, fuck, or is it kiss, cuddle, fuck?

I'd have written down the plan and our options in the watercolour pad, but I'd left that next to the pool on the boat which was now probably being dredged. I tried to learn the script in my head, repeating key words and phrases, somehow the fictitious doctor with a family and regular church visits seemed to become more important in the story than us.

I suppose that said something, even in my mind, about our believability. Even I believed in a fictitious doctor more than I believed in myself. That should have been a sign. Frankly, if being on heroin and coming to Egypt wasn't enough of a sign, then it really wouldn't matter if I said I was Jane Austen.

I even said to T, *we must remember to ask them for a repeat prescription, as we're here for another ten days.* Completely delusional.

We started to make a mental list of the pills we would accept if he couldn't give out medical-grade opioids. We actually believed that we held some cards. Oh, dear god, the fucking absurdity. In my mind I really was Jane Austen, or any other number of characters floating around in my head. This was the entirely shit *Sex and the City 2* film and I was a mash-up of every fucked-up one of them, CarriCharmanthrandalotteeSaaMi.

We started to set the stage for scene one, the doctor's arrival.

In preparation for his arrival, I wrapped a white(ish) sheet around me like a full-length modesty gown. I'm not sure if in my addled brain I thought I was being culturally respectful. Probably, and I know it's awful but God love me I was a trier, I got more wrong than I ever got right.

After preparing my costume (addicts always do costumes) I positioned T (my friend) on the bed, carefully covering him with the other white(ish) sheet to make the outline of his legs look pained. It was all method acting with no method or acting.

'Make your legs look like they're hurting,' I said. 'For fuck's sake, like this.' I demonstrated post-broken legs by crouching a little and saying ouch.

'They'll never believe us if you don't.'

By now the preparation had become the preamble to a bad drama lesson: take two white sheets and create a scene.

I rang reception, put on my best voice, and booked an appointment with the private doctor, who, they told me, was attached to the hotel for the sole use of the guests. *Brilliant*, I thought, *he comes with the room*. You don't pay through the nose for nothing. Your own private doctor, an addict's delight. Briefly I imagined he'd restock all our Class As with a smile.

I didn't notice the mess around us, the stained sheets, the empty yogurt cartons, the empty miniature wine bottles. The homemade, *Blue Peter*esque crack pipe. The drug parapher- nalia pushed into a neat pile under the bedside table as if a neat pile of addiction wasn't a problem. I honestly believed that our plan would work. I brushed my hair back into a ponytail, tightened my tomb-like wrap, looked in the mirror and mouthed, *you've so got this, you're fierce as fuck.*

Five minutes later, a knock. I go to the door and let the doctor in, my white(ish) gown trailing behind me, wafting across the floor like I'm in a posh LA suite getting ready for the Oscars, wearing Givenchy and the doctor turning up is actually part of my glam squad, arriving to do my hair and make-up.

He comes in, all suited and booted, smiling at first, expecting Luxor Hilton-standard guests. Then he sees me in my Givenchy sheet and T in bed, under the covers with an overly emphasised pained expression. He's overdoing it, I think, he'll give us away. Less of the fucking acting, I try to mouth to him.

The doctor's face changes completely. Not slightly, but completely, like a sky that goes from turquoise blue to lead grey in a moment, heralding the arrival of a storm. A tornado, a tsunami, a flood. His face becomes biblical. His going to smite us down. My sheet falls a little.

It takes him seconds to work out that we were fucked-up, queer addicts. His hands shake with anger. I'd forgotten that to him we were not only drug addicts but queer drug addicts, sharing a vast, dirty, mucky double bed. At that point in my life, I still had a cock, so this was a bed that housed two cocks. My transness hadn't completely surfaced yet, and even if it had, this would still have been a very messy cartouche.

I start blurting about family doctors and opiates, my robe falling even more, exposing my huge stainless-steel nipple ring. *Fuck it*, I thought, *that's blown it, he's seen the nipple ring*, like the ring of steel was the game changer and not all of it, all of us and all that we were. No, in my mind the nipple ring would be the problem.

I offered him money to write us a prescription. I scooped up a wad of notes from the bed, garbling the story that my friend needed opiate-based pain relief for recently mended bones after our terrible but not fatal, don't worry we're not dead, car accident. A terrible accident that happened in the heart of busy London town, a city full of cars and buses and huddling people, it happened when we were travelling to our very respectable jobs in the city. Under my breath, *I suck cock and he deals the shit that's got us into this mess, please, please cough up the drugs, I'm dying here.* I thought afterwards, *Where the fuckery did the line about city jobs come from?*

I continued to spill out bollocks after more bollocks until there was no more bollocks left to spill.

I think it was my absurd request about the specificity of needing 10mg of Valium for heatstroke, that pushed him right over the edge. He looked appalled and angry in equal measures, his expression concrete, stormed. In a quiet and calm yet threatening voice he said that if we weren't packed and out of the hotel in thirty minutes he would call the police and have us arrested. We should leave Egypt – not just Luxor, but Egypt.

It wasn't a suggestion; it was an order.

*We should be in jail*, he said, we were no good in his eyes, in fact it was an insult to people *like him* that people *like us* had somehow got into his country. On some level he wasn't wrong. On some level, our privilege had allowed us to believe that we were untouchable. That we could smuggle drugs (for personal use, please don't ban me) into a country with the death penalty for drug smuggling.

Then precede to get entirely fucked up in one of the plushest hotels in the beautiful, historic town of Luxor.

Who the fuck did we think we were, thinking that we held some cards? That's white British privilege, right there. Me wrapped in a white sheet, smashed, frayed, thinking I held some cards.

He left repeating the threat about the police with me still pathetically offering to pay him more money. Look, I said, take it all, all we want to do is be well enough to see the Valley of the Kings and the tombs. A part of me did. A little nugget in me, a little nugget that would expand and grow and enable me to move to these mountains years later.

I started to weep withdrawal tears, which are real tears, ones you've held onto for many years that now flood out uncontrollably.

Why the fuck did I think he'd need our money, he was probably a good doctor, a decent man with a decent job. I'll never know anything about him because an addict never sees anyone or anything apart from their insatiable need to get drugs. It's beyond white western privilege.

In the ten-odd years of drug addiction, I must have spent over £200,000 on drugs and drug paraphernalia. That calculation is conservative and based just on my heroin use. I dread to think of the house that crack could have built.

With the door closed and the doctor gone, we stared at each other, shell-shocked. All acting methodology fallen away, lying on the floor, snuggling up to the useless empty crack pipe. An empty crack pipe isn't a crack pipe at all but a set of small, adapted household objects cobbled together. The kind of object that people who aren't crack users think is a bong.

T's face and eyes had now changed; he was in the first full notch of fucked-up-ness that wouldn't subside until he either went completely cold turkey, which would take at least two or three weeks – I couldn't be sure because we'd never allowed it to happen – or he got drugs into his system. It dawned on me that our situation had gone from privately very fucking bad, to publicly absolutely fucking awful and dangerous. I didn't want to end up in prison for drugs, I'd seen *Midnight Express* and I'd been in jail abroad once before, very briefly, so I knew it was a nightmarish vision with overflowing toilets, nasty guards and stifling heat.

I knew the doctor was being serious, his face told me so. I was good at reading men's faces; it was a vital protective sixth sense. *This fucker means business*, I'd often think. Or *run, this one's got harm running through his capillaries, don't get on your knees, Juno, stay on your feet and wank him off.*

I knew we'd be in hideous trouble if we ignored his threat. We were in big trouble unless we could leave Luxor pronto.

Big trouble in little Luxor. You'll know the reference if you're old enough to know the film.

I sat on the edge of the bed, just missing T's once damaged legs. I apologised, like a fucking idiot, I believed our story more than the doctor did.

I said, *we need to get out of here fast, like now*. However awful we felt we had to run. Not metaphorically run like we said we'd do daily from our addictions, but literally run. Scamper, scurry, scarper, dash. We needed to leave the country and the first stage of our escape was to leave the hotel and Luxor. Shit got real in our lives. We were both scared, that never happened, one or the other but never both.

Writing this has made me scared all over again. I thought, for research, I'd look at photographs of the gardens of the Luxor Hilton but it made me feel physically sick. All these years later I can't even look at the rooms online.

Our suitcases had fortuitously remained unpacked, we'd hardly left the room, so we just threw in a few things and zipped up the lids. I stole the once crisp white sheets and recklessly tried to stuff the feather pillows into my case. They didn't fit. Even in that moment my brain on junkie-autopilot was sussing out the money we need to score at the other end of wherever our journey would take us. You can always flog good pillows.

At that point we had no idea where or how we'd go when we left the room. *Our holiday*, I thought, *has not fucking panned out the way I thought it would*. We never sat on the balcony sipping wine and smoking crack. Such potential romance utterly ruined.

We were queer drug addicts from London in an upmarket

Luxor hotel withdrawing from heroin. Addicts who'd insulted the hotel doctor by trying to buy illegal drugs. He saw us for what we were, our idea that we appeared *just like the rest of them* was frankly ridiculous.

I looked at us hurriedly dressing and I saw that we looked like we would if we were at home going out to buy or sell drugs. We didn't look like tourists, we looked like long-term junkies, which is an entirely different look to short-term junkies who can still blend in, until they don't.

We weren't short-term any more, we were junkies, we'd nailed our colours firmly to that post. In that room in Egypt, I realised for the first time ever that I'd become entirely lost to drugs. That made me unhappy, which sounds stupid in a cesspit of unhappiness, but in that room I saw myself clearly. I saw waste.

The fear of Egyptian incarceration partially halted our withdrawal, at least long enough for us to leave the *do not disturb* sign on the door on our way out. The doctor was at reception speaking to the hotel management. He didn't see us as we left.

We jumped into a taxi parked on the rank outside the hotel and a few minutes later we pulled up in front of a pharmacy to buy whatever drugs we could to alleviate the shakes and vomiting. We told the taxi driver we needed stomach pills for travel sickness. Fuck it, even travel-sickness pills might help, we rationalised. Anything.

I caught sight of myself in the taxi mirror, I was grey-green, a kind of tanned sallow grey-green. Deep, dark circles cupped my eyes like ceremonial bowls about to overflow with grey liquid from inside. The rims of my eyeballs were red, bright, fiery orange-red. I've always loved that colour, the colour of Crocosmia 'Lucifer', my favourite perennial.

My fringe, bleached straw-yellow, peroxide dreams, lay in coarse tatters on my forehead. The driver looked at me in the mirror and smiled. In that brief moment, with all of the madness going on, I thought, *I know, I'll offer him a blow job and ask him to take us to a dealer.*

Dumb fuck, but I'd hustled for years, on drugs you have to, and without shame.

He looked away and I slumped against the window, my breath obscuring T leaving the pharmacy, returning to the taxi with several boxes of over-the-counter Valium (yes, Valium over the counter), some painkillers and some anti-sickness pills. On the way to the airport, we consumed one whole strip of Valium between us to try to level out.

I thought, *who the fuck knew that you could buy Valium over the counter?* If only our fucking stupid plan had included, *maybe before you start talking seven shades of illegal shit, visit the local pharmacy?*

Enough Valium might have held us long enough to have stretched out on the terrace and maybe, just maybe, we might have got clean. We might have got clean in Luxor. Sipping wine and taking copious amounts of Valium. We might have. But we didn't.

Addict-talk when it truthfully and self-deceivingly wants to remain as addict-talk is always just full-blown nonsense. *Call the doctor, talk about car crashes, Jane Austen and country doctors, wear a sheet as a robe, offer money.*

Instead of, *let's calmly walk to the chemist and buy some*

*fucking Valium*. You couldn't make it up. Valium over the counter, I hate Valium for its inconsistency.

Out of the taxi window I saw signs to the Valley of the Kings and signs to Karnak and signs to the Temple of Luxor. Places I could almost touch. There was an intensely warm breeze that hid my tears. The pain of having to leave forced my eyes open but shut, my mind refocused on scoring. It felt kinder to let go, easier, maybe I wasn't the kind of person who would do nice things, I was the kind of person who'd do drugs and suck cock. I wasn't Liz.

He dropped us off at the airport. Our eyes half-closed, tired, full of Valium.

We flew to Cairo in business class; it was the only flight we could get quickly. We didn't want to spend too long at the booking desk or hanging about in the airport, terrified that our messiness would show or that the incensed doctor would come looking for us with a platoon of police.

Our holiday spending money was still intact, we'd bought no trinkets, no models of pyramids or miniature busts of Tutankhamun. Only the fabric man wearing a red net skirt riding a camel I'd bought on the boat, from the boy who was polite enough to ignore my vomit. We spent almost all the money on the flights, one to Cairo and the next to Heathrow, keeping a little money back for a taxi and hotel in Cairo.

We'd stay there overnight, before getting the connecting flight back to Heathrow the next morning, that one was economy, I prayed that by cramped economy, my vomiting would have ceased.

*

I was sick all the way to Cairo but because we were in business class, rather than question me, the stewardesses fussed over me and made me sweet mint tea. It helped a little. T's eyes looked manic, so I leant over and whispered in his ear, *keep your eyes closed, you look like something from* The Exorcist.

He seemed to fall asleep, but I know he didn't, withdrawal doesn't let you sleep for weeks. Behind closed lids his body was raging, synapses snapping taut, firing, and misfiring, creating ripples of stabbing goosebumps across tired tense skin. Everything and nothing runs through your mind when you start to withdraw. Emotions, memories, dreams, wishes, stupid, clever, bizarre, and very real. Everything cranks up and then everything stops and you think, it's over, that the worst is over, and then it cranks up again and you realise it's hardly begun.

His eyes were closed. I kept mine open. It was an unwritten pact about protection between us. Keeping watch. A watchful eye over each other. It often felt like love, maybe that is love. We cared deeply about the shit we were in because we understood exactly what shit we were in. We always did. Silently I counted through my withdrawal out-of-body moments, feeling detached, out of my body and out of my mind and then back in my body, feeling like the withdrawals were easing, stopping. But I knew this was only the start, because I counted only seconds in my body and minutes being over there. Wherever there is.

It was a one-hour flight from Luxor to Cairo. Twenty seconds in my body and fifty-nine minutes and forty seconds over there, wherever the withdrawals dragged me. T's eyelids were closed for the whole flight. That was a little disconcerting, weird maybe, like him calling me a silly moo. A sign that all was not well. Even when the stewardess asked if we wanted a soft drink or any food, he'd shaken his head but kept his eyes closed, like a cowboy in a Spaghetti Western with his booted feet up on a bar-room table.

I never asked him where he'd gone on that flight but wherever it was it held him; he didn't freak out.

He just motioned *no, no juice for me, thank you*, with a slight shake of his head.

Leaving Cairo airport, we were searched by security but clean of all drugs, other than the legal ones we'd bought in Luxor, and so we passed straight through and out into the warm evening air. Cairo chirped with life. I felt like a tourist, I did. Like a tourist and that was blissful. I closed my eyes and breathed it in, leaving my partner to watch over the next part of our journey. His eyes now open. Wide as an owl's. I felt safe with his all-seeing eyes.

We slipped into a taxi, the driver suggesting a hotel nearby run by his friend, he said *he'd recommend it to his own family, it was that nice*. And it was. Being able to trust a complete stranger in that moment has always stayed with me. We were the ones on the make, trying to rob everyone blind and he, the taxi driver, was a sweet man who took us to a lovely hotel twenty minutes from the airport. Like the doctor who'd actually given us a chance to escape.

Gracious really. Kind. That doctor, he took a risk for us, a slight one, in letting us have a head start. I suspect if we'd been caught and it had come out that he'd come to our room and not instantly reported us to the police he would have got into trouble of some sort. Who knows? But now we were somewhere no one from the town of Luxor would ever find us. I felt safe.

That night we ordered room service, ate hamburgers and fries. The first real food I'd tasted for months, if not years. I kept my eyes closed as I ate, tasting meat and pickles and the soft white bun. I felt like a tourist. The burger, a wonder, a monument.

I ate. I tasted food. Slowly I chewed and swallowed and chewed some more. I was a tourist in a hotel in Cairo eating room service, for a night I was like them, the people in the room next door, the couple in a hotel in Paris, London, Marbella, I was them, ordering room service, eating a burger and fries. We shared one large bottle of icy sparkling water and another strip of Valium, before lying on two single beds that we pushed together to face each other.

I said, 'I can't do this any more, I'd rather die.'

I'd said that exact same thing a thousand times before, but never after eating a burger and fries in a hotel in Cairo. The noise of the city, the chirp, chirp, chirping of the cicadas and crickets, the hoots of cars and taxis and shouts from the shops and restaurants down on the street encircled me. I'd said it a thousand times, but never when I'd been close enough to touch the Nile.

I started to cry and then so did he. Valium only eased the very top layer of withdrawal, we both started to slip down into our very own turkey skins. Like onesies before onesies. We interlocked, hugged, he got hard and then soft, we cried and then for the first time in many moons we slept with only Valium in our bloodstreams.

The next morning, we paid the bill and got into the same taxi from the night before. He said he'd be there for us in the morning and he was. We were very shaky, almost out of Valium, the withdrawals kicking back in hard. Him being there was everything that morning.

He became the man I trusted, and as usual with any man I thought I could trust I started to fantasise about him, fantasising that I'd stay with him in Cairo, late at night after his taxi shift ended, I'd make us supper and read him poems I'd written that day about our love.

So, so, fucked up. That's one of the dangers of growing up not being able to trust your dad. I'm not blaming him, I'm sure he'd have wanted anything but the mess I was in then, but my dad was a boy, an angry boy who couldn't cope with children, so when I grew up I only ever looked for angry men. A man who wasn't angry with me surely didn't love me. I was my dad's child, I realised, fantasising about cooking for my taxi-driver lover in Cairo.

Our connecting flight to London took us back to the pointless minutiae of our tiny addict-lives.

Lives stuttering on still. Oscillating between new and used twenty-pound notes, the optimal drug currency; a twenty-pound wrap of heroin, or a twenty-pound rock of crack cocaine. It was such an exhausting life to run back to, imagine running away from the wonders of Egypt towards harm, towards a grubby vanishing point.

My pointless existence centred around money and drugs. Nothing grand, philosophical, creative or revelatory. Just money for drugs.

Whatever people say or fantasise about drug addiction, and people do fantasise about addiction, they romanticise it, it is ultimately the most mundane, mind-numbingly tedious existence. Whatever I'd seen and romanticised in the film *Christiane F.* years earlier didn't do justice to the utter point-lessness of heroin addiction. On heroin there is no space to be alive, no space for emotion, sex, intimacy or personal growth. No space to see the pyramids or even, stupidly, to pretend to be Liz Taylor playing Cleopatra in kitten heels.

When we were on the plane coming back to London, T leaned over to me and whispered, cowboy eyes still closed, *I've just come, the plane made me shoot my load.* I looked down at his crotch and saw the darkening outline of pent-up spunk flowing outwards like a graphic on the news about the extent of a flood, or the retreat of glacial ice. He hadn't come for ages, we hadn't been sexual for ages. I realised I missed it, and then I felt envious that the movement of the plane had made him come and not me. I was envious of the plane. I was still lost. I knew that my envying a plane was a sure indication that I'd be using heroin again by sundown.

Twenty-four hours of travel and I'd been in my body for enough time to know that I was damaged, that I was the prob-lem now. Whatever traumas I'd ingested along the way, now it was my mind that made me fall in love with a taxi driver in Cairo and my mind that made me envy an aeroplane whose rhythm had made T come. In those few minutes of being in my body, I realised the work I'd have to do if I wanted to stay in my body. To be alive. To be present. It sounds a little Joni, but I was tired of being absent in my life.

We fled Egypt to buy heroin to stop us from withdrawing,

twenty pounds' worth. A twenty-pound wrap of heroin. I can see me now, buying it from the dealer with fucked-up knuckles, as clear as day. I can see us using heroin, it flooding in and us, full of opiate bullshit saying, we'll stop tomorrow. There are almost 2,500 miles between Luxor and London. I was close enough to touch the Valley of the Kings, barely half a mile away, close enough to reach out across the Nile and feel their wonder. But instead, I had to travel back to east London for drugs which were, in that moment, the centre of my world.

In those four days I only briefly glimpsed the Valley of the Kings from across the river. Like a line from a Springsteen song. A perfect philosophical conundrum. A turning point at which I didn't turn, but at which I knew that I *could* turn. I'd seen me in that hotel room in Luxor, I knew that I wanted and needed more, I knew that I was worthy of more, of beauty and safe adventures.

I did drugs for a few more years, but the man in the red net skirt and red hat on the camel made from upholstery fabric became my touchstone.

I'll get there, I'd tell him.

# Fifteen

## Take a Breath

I fell asleep in the sun today; even early in spring the sun is really too hot to fall asleep in. I should have been in the shade but I'm so exhausted that sleep unexpectedly dragged me off.

Inside I look in the mirror, my face was burnt a deep reddish brown. I yawned and caught sight of my yawning reflection; it wasn't pretty.

I've aged this year, my hair, now grey, is home-cut and very uneven – I tried to cut layers but I cut steps all the way around, like a craggy mountain path. I scoop it up at the back so it isn't noticeable and I try to be more exacting with the fringe cut. I watch videos on YouTube, searching for *at home hair styling*.

They either make it seem ridiculously easy (there's a clever trick or two) or disastrous. I try the quick cheats and tricks but with blunt kitchen scissors there's only so close you'll ever get to a sharp cut. I've had the same hairdresser in Bethnal Green for over twenty years, I miss him and his nifty scissors.

I catch sight of my neck, it's caught the sun and burnt to

the same shade as my face, perhaps a tad darker and redder. All the way down its length are white, horizontal wavy lines that appear when I put my head back. I lift my chin up and down a few times, my neck like the concertinaed body of a jack-in-the-box.

My skin is slackening, these white lines and my grey hair are new phenomena I'll have to live with, alongside the hairs on my chin, coming through thick and fast now. I've found masks to be a blessing, I don't care what people say about feeling hemmed in, I like my chin hairs being hemmed in. Hairs like stray cats popping up all over the village.

My neck looks like an elephant's leg, criss-crossed with lines, I wonder if a fortune teller could read them. I try not to get caught up in that narrative for fear that Tom Hanks comes rushing in looking for clues to hidden Knights Templar treasures. My dad was a Freemason, he joined the legal lodge for obvious reasons. Only they could repeatedly help him out of troubling corners.

It's a strange truism that many of the upper-class structures in England are held aloft by working-class men running away from being working-class men. Their shame at being working class making them blindly entrapped to yet more service. He once showed me his Masonry case containing his apron and apron accoutrements; I thought, this man who dresses up in this ridiculous garb for his lodge is also a racist who's battered his wife and kids. The legal lodge was headed up by a minor royal, who apparently did fuck-all work.

The lower half of my face and neck is ageing at a different speed to the upper half. Perhaps I should have a half facelift, my sister always talked about having one before she fell into her current depressive crisis, a space beyond facelifts. Apparently half facelifts are quite common and in the latest method they insert threads under the cheeks which can be pulled tight, and then, as the years go on, tighter still. Ruched by the ears like a 1980s Roman blind. My mum thought a Roman blind at the kitchen window said everything that you ever needed to say. It was an absolute statement. I suppose that threads under the cheeks are also an absolute statement, a pulling back of time. I will not age!

I've always thought that anti-ageing products or surgery are a slippery slope, but I don't want to emerge from this lockdown as a person who's detached from their skin as well as any future potential. We live in an ageist, sexist world, to age openly in our world isn't at all Instagrammable unless you age like an ex-model or a *Vogue* editor-at-large without it really showing. Age swathed under layer upon layer of gentle filtering, great lighting and delicate light grey cashmere. I might think it's a slippery slope, but I so covet that look.

Nearly everyone I know has had work done, I sometimes feel embarrassed about looking old next to them, perhaps that's why I never post photographs of me on Instagram, flowers only last a day or two, faces are supposed to last a lifetime in one static position.

Ageing is a series of detachments; however much we kid ourselves that age doesn't matter, that's what happens. *It's only a number*, they say, until that number goes over fifty-five. And then it's not a number, it's legit permission for the world to be ageist.

I look in the mirror at the lines gathering around my mouth; they genuinely shock me, I look like I smoke a hundred fags a day, I don't. I try not to be freaked out by the lines, but the ones across my neck, the elephantine white wavy lines, the ones that might entice Tom Hanks, are a little disconcerting. I must learn to love this new face I'm growing into as it becomes looser, baggier and much more lined.

My mum used to be athletic and five foot six, she's now as round as an apple and four foot eight. I decide to start measuring the decline of my stature on a door frame like parents do with their ever-growing toddlers. Perhaps if I hit five foot I'll sell up and move to an easy apartment by the sea with low-slung kitchen cupboards.

I like the idea of drying out by the sea like a starfish.

Good sleep has always evaded me, in photographs of me as a young child my face is dominated by large dark circles around my eyes, dark circles accentuated by a mop of white-blonde hair. People notice my dark circles first. I wonder if I was already having nightmares then, I can't remember because the time awake was bad enough.

Restful, rejuvenating sleep has always evaded me, but this past year every reason for not sleeping has come back to haunt me almost every night. I've hit back and tried to grab sleep the only way I know how. At first I tried herbs and soft tinkling music or the sounds of whales bellowing a thousand fathoms down. But none worked. Why would whales or the sound of rain be relaxing? I need silence.

So, I turned off the whales and tried to grab sleep with chemicals and alcohol. I haven't drunk alcohol for years, but this year, this past year I've slipped into a melee of late-night drug decisions, indecisions, weaknesses and fears.

I've tried to self-medicate using a single substance – a Valium or a stronger sleeping pill or a combination of alcohol and pills. I never risk anything; this isn't suicidal ideation but a desperation to sleep without nightmares, terrifying nightmares that make me sleep with the light on.

In the evening, when I move from being outside to being in, from working in the garden to sitting on the sofa, from doing to not doing, I skirt round benzodiazepines like potholes in the road. I sense them looming and calling to me before I see them. I try not to take them because I know that they are black holes into which I'm tumbling more and more frequently in this catastrophic year. I understand my current proximity to addiction.

If I don't take anything, I have brief snatches of sleep which are filled with nightmares. The snatches of sleep are trapdoors to somewhere deep in my psyche. The snatches of nightmarish sleep are more tiring than not sleeping.

A nightmare – the man from next door is clearing out my garage and then my front room. I look on, apparently invisible and shout at him that *I'm still here, I'm not dead yet*, but he carries on regardless. I look down and don't have a body, at least I do, or I did, but it's vanishing from the feet upwards.

Out loud I say, *don't take my cunt away from me, I want to make babies*. My neighbour lifts his head and says, *no one cares about your cunt. I want a family*, I say to him, but he's throwing everything into a skip and can't hear me. There's a bright red skip outside my front door which reminds me of a show I'd seen at the Baltic which was shit. I had a panic attack in the Baltic lifts because they're so high. I decided then and there that I was done looking at art in real life; galleries started to play with my anxiety, they became treacherous.

Just for a second, in my dream, I think it's not all bad, at least my possessions have become an art installation. I move towards the skip to artfully arrange them, but then a big metal arm comes down and crushes all of my worldly goods, flattens them into a single leaf, like a page in a book. I scream, *no fucking way; I don't die here alone.*

I peer into the skip and in the flattened single page of my life I make out my dogs, they're dead but their eyes flicker and follow me, and the photograph of my mum as a teenage bridesmaid in the early fifties, her eyes move and blink, did she just wink at me, and the piece of wood I found in the mountains with what looked like an evil eye etched into it. I stuck it above my front door, ever superstitious. That eye doesn't move.

I want to avoid that nightmare, and taking a benzodiazepine helps me avoid it.


Tonight, I went to bed late and didn't take anything. I was hopeful, but now I can't sleep for thinking about Christmas, well, Christmases, all Christmases. The last Christmas, the pandemic Christmas, was horrible. I felt bleak. My dad's wife sent me an open packet of pocket tissues and a half-empty eye cream sample from Boots, as part of a surprise present. It was *that* all right, but an awful surprise; I felt degraded, it was the height of the pandemic and I needed to feel loved or at least respected. Opened tissues made me feel long discarded.

I missed people on Christmas Day, it hurt.

I notice the time on my small bedside clock, which I bought

to replace the mobile phone that I blamed for not sleeping; it's gone two in the morning. The dogs have sneaked in and squatted the lower half of the bed. I look past them, up to the top of the wardrobe to the Christmas box.

The Christmas box I've always been so ridiculously proud of, chuffed about its contents.

I get up to get the box, the dogs don't move. Max, the pit bull, is lying on his back, his legs splayed wide open, Ruby's and Pup's heads rest on the warmth of his belly. They all snore different snores. Such a life.

The large cream Ikea box is falling apart because although it looks like leather it's made out of card, it's faux leather. It's the box that holds all of my Christmases – past, present and future.

The top of the box is covered in a layer of dust, everything gets dusty in these dry mountains. Even a recent Christmas. Even me. The dust settling in my lungs makes me cough and my asthma wheeze. My dead neighbour always coughed, years before COVID-19; I sense the same cough in me. Millions of dust particles swept up on dry Saharan winds have come to settle in my lungs, building new adobe dwellings. Perhaps that's where my HIV ones and twos live, deep in my lungs, in small dwellings made from spittle and dust.

For thirty years I've collected baubles and trinkets from partners, ex-partners, ex-lovers, lovers, friends, my mum, things I've found, things I've stolen, things I've borrowed.

My Christmas box is full of hope. Family hope, motherhood hope, connection hope, romantic hope, love and life hope.

The contents speak to my deep-seated desire to become a

more embedded part of this world, to be lodged in the world rather than adjacent to it. It's a box that speaks to feelings of emptiness despite ironically bursting at the seams, overflowing with the gaudiest and glitteriest of Christmas trinkets. Desperate trinkets, trinkling out year after year, each doing their party piece, glittering, shining, glowing.

My thoughts stray to Valium, I want one. I feel queasy, uneasy, stressed. I decide to try to sit with the *I want one* feeling for a while.

Fuck it.

I get up to take one. I wonder if I could possibly count the number of Valium I've taken since being a kid. I bring strips of pills back to bed with me.

I pull the cream Ikea Christmas box close to me on the bed and start to sort through it.

I pop another Valium, it might help.

The first Christmas after my AIDS diagnosis my mum bought me a Christmas tree. It was a splendid tree, large and symmetrical. It made the whole flat smell like a pine forest. She gave me a single bauble to put on the tree. 'There,' she said, 'hopefully you can collect one every year and as the years go by your tree will tell a story about your life.'

When she left that night she told me that she loved me and I told her the same. That was our AIDS conversation. Incredibly beautiful. She wished for me to have years of life.

'Have a good Christmas, Mum,' I said, closing the door.

I hung the purple sparkly bird on the tree alone in the centre. It lit up my flat like the North Star. I was an addict and alone that year, apart from the virus, which never left my side. My present to myself was a wrap of heroin and a fat rock of crack cocaine. A science kit of experimentation and self-subjugation.

By Boxing Day, I was empty of Christmas, so when I went out to score and be scored I was cool about it, accepting. Two days after Boxing Day I threw the tree out and wrapped the purple bird in protective reams of toilet paper.

I put the bird in a drawer.

I search around in the box and find the bird, now thirty years old and ageing badly. One wing, one eye and most of the purple glitter now missing. Its polystyrene body peeking through like a balding white scalp. Its head full of bite marks from the year that my Jack Russell decided that Christmas to him was a tree full of chewable objects, nothing more.

I feel a draft and realise that I've left the doors to the court-yard slightly open. A cold breeze drifts in. I push my feet deep down under the covers either side of the box. My toes trying to find warmth. The box now held between my legs, my knees pushed wide by its girth, the box like an enormous fledgling. I feel weighed down by its contents, like they're now a burden. Hope is a burden.

I lift out the purple, one-eyed, one-winged, glitterless bird and put it to rest on the bed. I decide that I should get rid of everything that feels punishing the instant it's hung on the tree. If the instant it hangs it symbolises loss or my failure to build a family then it should go.

I examine each bauble.

I take half a clonazepam and an hour or so later, the pile of discarded shiny objects that I've held on to religiously for years as if without them the magic will disappear, has grown into a mountain.

I get up, go to the kitchen, and pull out a black bin-liner.

Grabbing handfuls of decorations, baubles and ornaments, I throw them away. The cream Ikea box also goes. I take out one string of fairy lights and keep back three ornaments, then put the box on the floor and jump on it, it makes a loud noise like an explosion.

The box I've held onto for years easily collapses in on itself like a folding universe that once held planets and stars and now holds nothing but floating spectral dust. Like a black hole that sucks matter into anti-matter, it looked like an cream faux-leather Ikea box but it was so much more.

Now, whatever it was, it's gone. I don't need to be punished by my past at Christmas.

I take the bag and put it in the garage. I feel freer, lighter, like I've disobeyed a part of me that held me tight in sentimentality and sadness.

I've kept three ornaments.

The venerable purple bird from my mum, from all those years before when I was deeply gripped by addiction and sadness. It symbolises resilience and strength. I'm still here. *I made it, Mum,* I'm not dead, not of addiction, not of HIV, not of stupidity. *I have a house, Mum and I've paid for every part of it. You're proud of me, I know. This bird is your pride of me.* Slightly tatty, but still here.

I keep the hand-painted, limited-edition bauble, numbered 276 of 1,752, year 2005. A gift from a man who I think I loved and who loved me, but whose spunk felt like bullets on my skin. I was so incapable of love back then, but now I still believe in it, and that's no bad thing, is it? The bauble, lovingly hand painted with Monet's Garden at Giverny, represents my openness to love. I believe in love.

And the last ornament I keep is the least gaudy. It's a small – maybe an inch high and two wide – knitted Christmas tree. An emerald-green tree in a knitted scarlet pot. A fine red cotton thread comes out from the top, so the tree can hang on a tree.

I stole it from the last school I worked in. Christmas was upon us. I was sat in the whole school assembly right next to the Christmas tree and spotted the small, knitted bauble hanging from a low branch, almost hidden. So unremarkable was it that I wanted it to be at the front. It felt so sad that it hidden away. It was the most perfect ornament I'd ever seen. When I saw it, I felt like the matchgirl again, but now I was a teacher and I had a classroom.

This small knitted tree will always remind me of that. I'm not just a fuck-up.

Next Christmas, if I'm still here alone in the mountains, and that's a distinct possibility, pandemic or not, then I will decorate a small almond branch with these three objects and a single string of fairy lights and know that I've made some peace with myself, with my desire for family. I have a queer family of people and assorted dogs, that'll do.

I take the other half of the clonazepam and fall into a deep sleep. I'll deal with my addiction tomorrow, I think, as I drift off.

# Sixteen

## Searching for Family

'*Almería capital es la que sale peor parada, al sumar diez fall-ecidos. Tres son de Albox, dos de Níjar y también ha habido muertes por COVID-19 en Benahadux, Viator, El Ejido, Antas, Los Gallardos, Turre, Vélez-Rubio y Vera. En el recuento total por municipios aparecen veinticuatro muertes, ya que se han reubicado dos anteriores que aparecían como "municipio sin especificar".' Diario de Almeria*, 9 February 2021[*]

I had a benzo nightmare last night about Egypt; I think writing about it has jogged something about being scared. Perhaps a shred of that fearful memory came loose and lay next to me in bed, poking me throughout the night, asking me to re-examine the sense of flying to Egypt, or taking the boat trip. I'll never write about it again.

---

[*]   The city of Almería comes out the worst, with ten additional deaths from COVID-19. There have also been three deaths in Albox and two in Níjar and further deaths in Benahadux, Viator, El Ejido, Antas, Los Gallardos, Turre, Vélez-Rubio and Vera. In total there have been twenty-four deaths across all municipalities, now that two earlier reported deaths that had been reported as 'unspecified municipality' have now been located.

That chapter ended that chapter. I'm not that kind of addict any more. If I was fascinated with that time in my life, it's been with the mundanity of the days, and who I was in that mundanity. I've been clean of street drugs for years, which isn't saying that I'm not an addict, I am, I still struggle constantly with prescription drugs, but heroin, crack and smuggling into Egypt are done.

The village is silent this morning, apart from the sobs of a man who's lost his wife to COVID-19 after seventy years of marriage. His sobs have silenced the village; out of respect, everything that might have happened today, in a village like this, has stopped. Even the birds seem spooked by the sounds of his wailing. He's been sobbing since dusk yesterday, his tears still strong, he's nowhere near being cried out. His is a torrent of despair.

They met when they were fifteen years old, at a local fiesta, apparently they wowed the village by expertly dancing the tango. It was a sign that the marriage would last. They danced the tango every year at the fiesta on the village square, the square upon which sits my house. The traces of their tango light up the square. Like the traces of a sparkler. I have a film on my phone of flamenco dancers dancing in front of my house, it reminds me when I'm away that I live in the land of flamenco. When I'm here it reminds me that I'm alone.

Last night I heard a terrible sound from my kitchen, it sounded animalistic, so I went outside onto the terrace to see what the noise was. I looked across the pathway to their house and saw him through the window, hunched over, in front of a fire without flames, sobbing uncontrollably, screaming out in pain. Like an animal.

Visceral. It's the sound my mum made when Dad walked out.

My neighbour's tears got under my skin; they chilled me and not because they meant that COVID-19 is here in our tiny perfect village, or because death has arrived with claws unsheathed to take us one by one, but because the sound of loss is terrifying. He wasn't allowed in to see her in the hospital or to look into the coffin, no one is with this manner of COVID-19 death. The coffin will be delivered today, shut firmly, nailed down. She will not be seen by him again. His tears are that wrench, that dragging her out of his arms. A brutal death and an even more brutal burial. It makes me realise the importance of a decent funeral.

I poopoo the pomposity of death, but having the time and the dignity to say goodbye is a blessing.

The usual Catholic funereal rites unobserved in these harsh times.

His love gone.

She died on a ventilator; the oxygen forced into her lungs was not enough to save her. They don't own a mobile phone or an iPad so he couldn't say goodbye in our new normal way. This virus snatches those moments.

At least I had the chance to lay my head on T's chest as the oxygen was pumped in. I rested my head and cheek on his belly, smelling and feeling the familiarity of his skin, feeling him come back to this place and not that. Even AIDS, in all of its brutality, allowed for intimacy. Pockets of intimacy grew deep around the beds of AIDS patients; even while society was trying to cut us adrift, we floated and held each other. Those pockets became AIDS activism and AIDS support.

The silence of COVID-19 and the swiftness with which it tears through our need for intimacy is shocking. It's airborne, the very stuff that sustains and exits us with each and every breath. Each and every breath now high-risk behaviour, they'll never moralise that.

It doesn't even allow for intimate structures to evolve around the beds of the dying. We all have to breathe, therefore we are all complicit in this one. We all have a role in saving us.

I said to my mum that this virus will be far tougher on us than HIV, because fluids are actually extremely easy to retain within the confines of a body, but air, air inhaled is also air exhaled, breath. Breath becomes dangerous. We contemplate and process air as a weapon now. Air weaponised by the virus. My HIV has never escaped from my body, never seeped out, never leaked out of an ill-fitting mask.

God love 'em, the virus has come to occupy our bellows.


Love and intimacy, our bedrocks, have become dangerous activities best conducted through a glass screen. I read a story about two parents in Florida with a young family – two school-age children. Both parents had underlying conditions. Under Trump, the virus wasn't a virus, it was a macho stand-off, so for a time, schools carried on regardless, and parents with underlying conditions kissed their children off each morning. *Why wouldn't they?* Their president said the virus wasn't a real thing.

The photograph that accompanied the piece was of typically Floridian parents, jolly, tanned, chinoed, slightly chubby, smiling. Dead.

One of their children had contracted the virus before anyone would countenance the idea that the most loving of relationships, the most intimate, could become lethal. *What are we without intimacy?* I think and then realise, *lonely. I'm lonely.* I don't have anyone to tango with.

My neighbour hardly ever left her house or the village, her husband is worried that it must have been him who unwittingly brought it into the home. He's also crying because he knows she would have said, if she could have spoken to him from her deathbed, *It's my time, you silly man, no tears and look after the trees.*

She was a decent woman. She was always kind to me, she taught me how to pick and bottle fruit to last throughout the winter, she taught me how to get rid of the bitterness in olives and when to pick the capers. If I made a cake and gave them a piece she'd send him over with a bottle of preserved apricots or peppers in oil.

With HIV, we knew that fluids from one body had to enter another body by penetration – a cock, a needle, a transfusion. Often entering with, or needing permission, *I give you permission to enter me with a needle, your cock, or a transfusion.* Air doesn't have permissible or contended boundaries, it flows all around us, it is the stuff of life. It is everything and everywhere.

We cannot put a condom on breath, we can only wear masks, and look how angrily people have railed against that, talking about their loss of freedoms, possibly the very same people who condemned the marginalised for not having safe sex in the early days of HIV and AIDS.

My neighbour couldn't say goodbye to her love of seventy

years because her last exhaled breath might be deathly to those gathered around the bed. Her goodbye might drag them with her. HIV's mode of transmission is comparatively a kitten with soft rounded claws.

When T was first diagnosed, I'd lay my cheek on his chest and feel its wiriness inflate, his belly lifting my head. I closed my eyes and enjoyed the ride. The most intimate of rollercoasters on what we thought might be a bed of death – he survived. I think if only my neighbour could have said goodbye by resting his head on his wife's belly his grief may have been lessened, but perhaps not. Their intimacy was forged talking, laughing, and tending their fields and trees, not just in physical closeness. I only saw them kiss once, after a dance, but their fields and their trees were tended with care and love. They were so proud at harvest times, like parents they displayed their crops.

I have no comprehension of how a seventy-year relationship must feel. I know that even if I met someone tomorrow and we fell in love, at best we'd have a third of their time. As I'm impossible to live with, I have to accept that it won't happen. I'll grow old with the company of HIV.

Listening to him sob I realise that my longest relationship is with my virus.

With HIV and with the fear of death – of an AIDS death. In a sense my life has become a narrative of death. I'm sure in years to come that some people's lives will have been completely written by COVID-19 in the way mine has been by HIV and AIDS.

I've struggled to ever really leave it behind. My HIV

medication simply makes it hide away in undetectable pairings, clusters of virus. My neighbour sobs for the loss of his beautiful wife, and I mourn for the relationship that I know I'm incapable of. I can't blame AIDS or HIV for my being alone, AIDS hid the shame I felt at being incapable of being in love. COVID-19 has allowed me to feel normal in my isolation.

I met a man during the second lockdown, a tall man who bought fresh tomatoes on the vine. He was tall, he could reach every shelf.

That's where we met, over the tomatoes at the same time every Monday morning in Lidl. We shopped as the store opened, we started smiling with our eyes, as you do in a mask, and then we said hello. Quick, snappy hellos, hellos said in a particular please-let's-not-talk way.

We said hello, just single hellos, over tomatoes for about month, and then he stepped into the space after the hellos and asked me how I was doing.

Taken aback, I said, 'It's tough, I'm finding it difficult.'

I'd intended to make a joke about tomatoes, but somehow the way he asked me how I was made me realise that he wanted a real answer. Or at least that he could cope with a real answer. He said, 'I feel the same, I'm on my own here.'

'So am I,' I replied, feeling ridiculously tearful. Over tomatoes. Tearful. That's why I'd wanted the hellos to remain as that, as perfunctory dots of Monday-morning politeness, I was surviving this pandemic by pretending I was surviving.

He said, 'I see you every week on a Monday at this time.

It feels safer when the store's empty, doesn't it?' I nodded, scared if I talked I'd cry. Tears over the tomatoes.

I'm still this needy around men and the bridge they form to a fantasy father figure, a fantastical protector. A saviour.

One Monday by the tomatoes at five past nine, he said that maybe we should meet up some time and go for a walk. I said, 'Yes, that would be nice.'

We did. We laughed, we talked, we realised that we had past messiness in common and a shared belief that living a brave life felt at least hopeful, even if reckless. For the next few weeks, we'd meet at his house or mine, or go for a walk or mountain biking, although to be honest we're both quite unfit and have bodies shaped from addictions and the illnesses that addictions bequest, so mostly we walked and pushed bikes and freewheeled down inclines. But we talked freely and easily and laughed. I suppose I started to dream something.

At the last of our few sojourns, we had lunch at his house, an omelette, which was a little greasy, and a salad, which was lovely and made up for the omelette. We sat socially distanced on his terrace which overlooked the most beautiful mountains. I asked him if he was happy here and he said, 'That's a silly question, but most days I feel a kind of contentment which is enough.'

He then said to me, 'I don't think you'll ever feel safe enough to let a man get close enough to really get to know you and that makes me sad about whatever's happened.'

I hadn't told him anything that would lead him to say that. I didn't need to, it wears me, my history, like neon incendiary cladding. It must warn people away.

I said, 'I think you're right, I still don't trust myself to do right by myself with another, so being on my own feels like the only way.'

I wanted to say the opposite but I couldn't. And then I said, 'I should go now.' I didn't finish the salad.

I've never seen him again by the tomatoes, maybe he's gone off them, or me, or maybe he's just gone. I'm still that needy that I linger by them, especially those on the vine.

The next morning, after the crying has subsided, my neighbour tells me he's leaving the village to go and live with his family in Barcelona. The village starts to feel like a place that everyone leaves, I feel panicky.

I say to him, 'You can't, you love it here, it's your home. Whenever I used to travel to London you'd say, "Why go there to be crushed by all those people?" I thought you loved the mountains and the trees. Your trees, the almonds, the olives, the nispero and fig.'

He tells me, 'There's nothing for me any more here in the village, I can't be here on my own.'

'But I am,' I say pathetically, 'I'm here alone.'

The words come out before I realise they are out. I hope they're lost in translation. Was I a child talking? And if I was a child, who was he to me, was he my dad in that moment?

A stand-in?

'You'll be OK,' he says, 'you have your books and the dogs.' He goes inside his house and closes the door. The door closing is final, something about here for me has changed.

But none of them talk back to me, I think, watching him walk away. The dogs, the books, the mountains, the Instagram account, the posts, the likes, the comments are all silent. You were a voice I could hear that made me feel safe. But his door is already shut, he's already left and my words, like my world, are silent. Words in your head are silent words, even if you speak words aloud to yourself they are silent, words need people to hear them. He's almost the last villager.

My world feels like a tomb, the air being sucked out slowly. It's not just him. This feels like an end of a relationship, a relationship with a childish dream, the dream about a family, of being at the centre of a village, the village being my family. A stand-in. I thought this village would save me; I live in it like a photograph in a magazine. Like I'm in a photograph in a magazine.

I scan the houses. Opposite my house is a row of three old farmhouses. Records in the countryside started to be kept in about 1930: any house built before then cannot be altered or added to in anyway, because they are deemed historical and rustic, which means that they get to hold on to their charm but often remain empty, no one wants to inherit a house you can't modernise. That's the way of things, endless programmes about barns being rescued by architects and hundreds of thousands of pounds.

Seems silly really to spend all that money rescuing a barn. It seems absurd that someone might spend a million rescuing a decrepit barn when so many live in slums. It makes sense to allow some houses and structures to fall back into the earth. In these villages, most houses are adobe, made of earth, sand and stone. When they die they are welcomed home, back from where they once came. Only a small pile of plastic Pyrex dishes gives the game away, like headstones on ancient houses that now sleep happy back in the earth.

The large detached farmhouse opposite me is empty, he had Parkinson's and she had a series of heart attacks. They used to come down from Barcelona for the summer and at harvest times – the almond and olive harvests. She was a fabulous woman who'd dye her hair bright rust red for the fiestas. Every day she'd work in the fields, her red head bobbing between the branches like an Amazonian parrot. Her husband became ill a few years back and he'd sleep all day in the shade of the false pepper tree, his straw hat pulled down hiding all of his face except his chin. His chin jiggled, moved like a separate animal.

He'd doze in the shade for most of the day, his snoring intermingling with birdsong and the chirping of crickets. At night, everyone from the neighbourhood gathered in their garden, talking and laughing well into the night. It was Spain when I came here, now it's a village dying somewhere in southern Europe. It's a statistic.

The women with the rust-red hair and her dozing husband haven't been here for two years. Their children aren't interested in looking after the trees so no longer visit. The trees are less visible now in the grass, which is slowly engulfing them. Birds have moved into their farmhouse, flocking down the chimney, apparently the upper floor is full of shit. The slow process of decay is happening, I can see it through the photographs I've taken. Things revert to nature very quickly here when we stop managing the land.

The middle farmhouse, the middle *cortijo*, is almost always empty now. It's owned by an English couple who are simply too old to visit, but always thought that they would, so never made any plans to sell the house. It sits there as a ghostly reminder of more youthful ambitions. Like a corpse with its innards being eaten away, the beams throughout the house are apparently being munched by hungry termites. Someone said that unless they're careful (the people, not the termites), the house will collapse. Houses do here, they collapse. Termites bring the roofs down first and that's always the end of a house. A roof is the lid.

The houses are becoming like my siblings and me.

I once had a conversation with the older English couple about their plans to buy a motorhome and travel across Europe, visiting all the places they'd marked on a map; they seemed so intent on making it happen, but then ageing takes over. You'd think you'd get a warning with age, but you don't. One minute the world sees you and then you disappear into the invisibility and struggles of age.

The next house, the last, belonged to my departed neighbours. She and her husband lived in the house for seventy years. It's hardly changed. A small, traditional country village house, dark inside, small windows to keep out the heat and the cold, half the rooms given over to storing and drying produce. Almonds, onions, tomatoes, peppers. A smoky dark interior, he grew and rolled his own tobacco, he once gave a roll-up to my mum and she coughed like a cat with a furball. I thought, *if it makes Mum cough, imagine what seventy years has done to his wife's lungs as a passive inhaler of his homegrown.*

She always coughed; this dry arid landscape begets coughs. I knew she was really ill because ironically she could no longer summon up the energy to cough. Her mouth appeared to cough, but no coughing happened. I said to Mum, *she's ill, she can't cough any more.* Ironically, her coughing was life.

Her husband, my errant father-figure, is in Barcelona now, surrounded by his family. I hope he's found a café and a group of men to play dominos with.

When people die, the ones left behind say *I'll never forget them, I'll carry them in here, in my heart for ever.* I wonder if he's in Barcelona with her in his heart or here still, his body in Barcelona but his mind in the fields and fiestas with her. Perhaps he's still between places. Like I feel, constantly between my childhood and trying to be an adult in my present.

Only she has definitely left.

The row of farmhouses sits empty now, like three silent ageing people on a bench whose edges are starting to peel. I have three siblings, the farmhouses remind me of them, of us.

The houses are lightly encased in render, and once the render begins to peel and fall away the innards start to pour out. Slowly at first, in trickles like a sand timer, then, after rain, whole sections of the walls spill outwards onto the ground, revealing dark interior spaces in which humans once fucked, laughed and made babies and paella. Once a house loses its occupants it becomes silent. A memorial, an epitaph. A Rachel Whiteread.

I wonder if that will happen to my house; the years since being fifty are flying by. Will I make plans to leave but never leave, or will I just stay because there's nowhere more beautiful, even with the dying houses? Will I become trapped here in my one-dimensional dream?

My house sits at the centre of the village, the house next to me, to my left, is occupied by an older couple who are so terrified of the virus that I haven't seen them for over a year apart from rare sightings as they leave the house dressed like surgeons to do a weekly shop. I wonder if they've dug tunnels.

No one else is here, all the other houses are empty, the Belgians haven't been seen here for a couple of years, the old priest's house with its beautifully ornate window coverings is completely falling down now, only home to a couple of wild dogs who seem to be in a committed relationship. Rambla dogs who dart out to bite you and then snap back into the gloom of their romantic apostolic dwelling. They remind me of Cerberus guarding the Underworld – that makes me laugh and not be scared of them. I was once attacked by a friendly Labrador who tore a chunk out of my shin. My leg pulsed with infection for weeks, perhaps that Labrador was Cerberus.

When I first came here I thought it was life affirming, a rural idyll clutched lovingly in the fifties, but now I realise it's the kind of place that wild dogs inhabit and people leave, even if they say they never will, they always do. A village that was already dying – *do all villages eventually die?* – but I couldn't read the signs of impending death because I'm an outsider, an immigrant from a huge city with romantic ideas and flattened dreams about the permanence of the countryside. I dragged my needs and emptiness here with me.

I turned up needing it to be my dream.

I saw rustic, dishevelled and characterful, but also believed that to be permanently so. Fixed. Unmoving, perfectly unchanging. I thought its edge was permanent.

I supplanted onto it what I needed it to be and what I needed it to give me.

I needed a family; I can see that now. These houses and maybe their occupants were family. I was at the centre of a circle of buildings. Alive buildings, now dying, seem more like us, more human. Have I moved anywhere, or am I still there in a structure of family, desperately looking for family?

This house was my secret garden, the denizen of the Borrowers, the sanctuary I spied in magazines years before. The kind of beauty that only existed for me wishfully and wistfully in my dreams.

I bought this house within five minutes, I didn't think twice, I heard laughter and loud happy Spanish voices around me, I interpreted that as family. I was coming home.

Buying the house at the very centre of the village would be like becoming part of something, a family. I moved to be at the centre of a family. I bought my way in, perhaps barged in. My fake family. For much of the early years I was the silent, mute kid in the family; as I came out of my shell through the acquisition of their familial language, they started to drift away.

Like a child, I never stopped to think that it might end. I never thought that the noise of their lives around me would stop. I needed permanence. For the world to stop still. Unhappiness does that, keeps you there at the point of unhappiness's creation. The inescapability of family, of blood ties. I'm in this village desperately wanting my family to be a family.

Now they've all gone. When I learnt to talk to them, they'd gone.

# Seventeen

# The Violent King

My dad left suddenly when we were in our teens, although in truth he'd never really been there, not as a dad or a father, just a man who was emotionally distant and who had a terrible temper, a temper we all tried to avoid but couldn't. We all have scars and a plethora of bruises which now reside, disguised, in our skin. Bruises always make you feel ashamed.

A vain man who thought that women were for fucking and that white skin was superior to any other. He wasn't very likable. Sadly, though, he's what you might call my dad, the only one I've got and the only one I will ever have. The least he could have done is to have wanted us. But he didn't. He never wanted children.

When he was young he had all the cockiness of an Italian-American film star, handsome, model-like almost, and stylish. His charisma hid a spiteful underbelly, but to outsiders, especially women who didn't really know him, he could be charming and funny and generous with compliments. People would say, *your dad's a right charmer.*

A charmer. Tell that to my broken psyche. Tell that to my sister's lost child.

Mum discovered Dad was having an affair with her friend, who was also the mother of my older brother's fiancée. She found a letter in a locked, wine-coloured, leather-look briefcase.

In the letter, Mum discovered that the affair had been going on for years and that not only was her friend sleeping with my dad but also with my older brother, the fiancé of her eldest daughter, cue much violence and, frankly, head scratching. It was the late seventies, strange times with duplicitous streams of morality, but even so, we never quite understood how our dad could leave our mum (despite the fighting) for a woman who'd been sleeping with our brother too. Who had been sleeping with her daughter's fiancé.

My dad's then mistress (now long-standing wife) looked like Elizabeth Taylor, circa 1960. Curvy, beautiful, always perfectly made up and very glamorous. Big brown eyes and softly curled, subtly highlighted bouncy hair. Everything about her was soft and undulating. There's not a hint of anger about her, but it's there. You don't sleep with a father and son without some turbulence.

Mum, Ann 1 we say, always looked like Mia Farrow in *Rosemary's Baby*, crumpled up in her New York apartment, broken, sharp, angular, short flaming auburn hair. Quick to fly off the handle and throw the words *fucker* and *cunt* at my dad, basically because he was both.

But his wife, Ann 2, accommodated him and his ways from day one and she never called him anything but pet names that allowed him to act like a boy. He was never violent around her or her family. He changed for them or with them. He became a family man.

None of us saw that coming or even imagined it possible, it made the violence we'd suffered even more unbearable. I didn't talk to him for almost twenty years, because I missed the father he'd never been but so clearly was capable of being. I envied his new children having this version of Dad.

When he left, he said we all took after our mum, that we were all mental like her. That's why he couldn't cope with us. He left us for a woman who was sleeping with his son and called us mental. Deep.

After he left, what followed was an unmitigated nightmare, a nightmare in which he already had another family and a nightmare in which Mum completely fell apart, broke into smithereens. Splinters splintered all over us kids, Ann 1's kids.

A tirade of violence followed that lasted almost twenty years, it was like a bloody civil war. A family that never was a family, split in two or three or four and pitted against each other because of a paucity of love.

It's hard to explain it to people, you really had to be us and be there.

It was unremitting, unyielding. We fought over stale crumbs.

Doorstep fights, screaming arguments across streets, hollering down phonelines, in shops, in offices. My dad, like a pimp, having dinners at both houses, bedding both women, trying to placate both, trying to keep them and the violence apart, lacking the courage or the desire to create an ending. I suspect he really enjoyed feeling like a pimp. It played into his version of street Kingliness.

*I fuck 'em both.* I once went to a barbecue at his new house, his friends turned up, like him, working-class men with a bob or two. They all got pissed and then, ignoring that I was sitting at the same table, he started talking, or more precisely frothing and spouting, about all the Anns he fucked. Pissed, spitting with excitement about his conquests. *That's my mum you're spitting over,* I thought. I left.

He went from one set of comforts to another, one Christmas dinner to another.

My mum told us we weren't allowed to say anything to make him uncomfortable or angry because he was going to come home. If we kept our mouths shut, he'd come home. We were blamed because we were the kids that got in his way.

He never wanted kids. At least not us, and that's not a cry for sympathy; we weren't kids in his eyes, just part of the intractable problem of a bad marriage that was set to stop him from being crowned.

My sister wondered recently if her mental health issues come from Dad punching her in the head when she was a teenager. That punch was hidden for almost fifty years behind a succession of stage props we'd wheel out to hide his violence. We were ashamed of being his victims, of being victims full stop.

Telling this story has made me realise that we've kept so much in, and for what? He's never liked us, whether we are silent or loud. Speechless or speechful.

My poor sister having to deal with mental health worries but also the memory of being punched by her dad. Of course, she wanted to be Daddy's little girl. She wasn't though, she was a punchbag.

None of us saw his departure coming, although all of us had always wished it would. Wished that the violence and arguing would stop. I remember feeling guilty for the number of times that I'd said, *I wish he'd just fuck off.* And he did and Mum fell into disarray, crying constantly, her behaviour become manically depressive and irrational, driven by the rational anger of rejection which morphed through a lack of sleep and uppers and downers into violence and revenge one minute and an outpouring of love the next. *Hate him, kill him, he loves you, love him, hate him, he hurt me.*

Him leaving broke her.

So deeply rooted in my mum's fragile psyche was their tacit agreement of dysfunctional everlasting commitment that she fell apart. Her body, her posture, her eyes, her gaze changed. She vacated her body for the next twenty years.

She fell apart, stitch by stitch, hems unravelled, buttons popped off, zips got stuck, pins and needles turned inwards as weapons to jab herself with. She self-harmed, attempted suicide, smashed things and retreated back to the Walworth Road and a job working in a two-bit gangster pub. In the dead of night, she'd drive out of London to where my dad now lived with Ann 2, wreck his car, throw paint up the front of their house, rip up their flower beds and push the torn flowers through the letter box, neatly stuffing them through one by one, cutting her hands to ribbons in the process, and scream like a banshee until the early hours.

She'd hammer on their door calling them every fucker

under the sun until the police would be called by a neighbour, charges would be made and then dropped to keep the peace. You definitely didn't want to take my mum to court then. She was so hurt that she lost any sense of an edge too far, had she gone to court I fear she would have killed them.

I'm not blaming the men who abused her as a child, but all of that powerlessness had driven her mad, the shame and the feeling that she'd never be good enough to exist in her own life had driven her to seek control somewhere. She thought the marriage was bad but thought it was tenable, I understand that feeling of impossibility, of feeling no control, of feeling vulnerable in a world in which you have no control. Smashing at the edges to see if you can feel.

We were all teenagers when he left but she lost control, becoming a tsunami that lashed out under the cover of night. She stopped sleeping at night, grabbing a few hours in the daytime and then after working, late under the cover of dark, she'd drive to watch him through his windows. Seeing him be a different kind of man. 'He sits on the sofa and holds her hand,' Mum said. 'Your dad never holds anyone's hand, what the fuck has she done to him, where's he gone?'

Deep down I knew that my dad, the child he still was, needed to hold hands, that holding hands was part of his process of repair. The pain of his childhood – poverty, abandonment, and the violence he'd witnessed – assuaged by the simplicity of holding of hands. Romance a comfort to him, 'like fucking lovesick teenagers,' Mum said.

But he needed to hold hands. Just a shame that before holding hands he'd punched us with them.

\*

As an adult I've learnt to forgive him, I've had to. Inadvertently, he's repaired parts of himself enough to be able to be tender in this world, even if it's never been towards us, his first family. The unwanted family, the punched family. But the child me still feels the rejection. When I hear the new family call him by his chosen nickname, Nobby (what a stupid name), when I see them come in and easily hug and kiss him and see him not flinch, I feel anger and I realise that I haven't really forgiven him, I've just allowed him to leave without demanding that he, at least, apologise for the punches. I wish he'd do that; it might set us free.

One night many years before he left, Dad came in late and we heard screaming downstairs. One by one we crept out of bed and watched them fighting through the slats on the staircase. My dad, obviously pissed, swaying, jabbed his finger right into my mum's tearful face. She was screaming that his trousers were covered in spunk: 'which whore did you fuck tonight?' she spat at him, tears mingling with her spittle.

As kids we couldn't properly make out what she was saying through her screams and thought she'd screamed that he'd slept with a sack of spuds, for some strange kid-like reason (nerves) we started to chant through the slats, *Dad loves a sack of spuds, Dad loves a sack of spuds, Dad's fucked a sack of spuds, Dad's spunked over a sack of spuds.*

'Get to bed,' he snarled at us, all Elvis wet-lipped. We did. We never crossed him when he was angry or crossed him when he was not angry because in a second he could become angry. His temper an on–off switch which you could accidently switch on by brushing against it. His temper wasn't logical.

This was the dad we got. A man who wasn't a dad but a man trying violently to get out of a commitment he should never have made.

The next morning, Mum had a neat row of stitches beneath her blackened eye.

'It wasn't his fault; I fell over, it was my fault for being clumsy,' she said.

Their violence made me clumsy, the violence slipped under my skin, making me scared of the world. Making me nervy and shaky. I was pigeon toed; always falling over and falling over made me more fearful of falling over. I was forever being whisked to the doctors for stitches.

I was so scared of falling over that I constantly looked down at my feet; consequently, I fell over more or was pushed over more because I'd accidently walk into someone. And that's the complete story of my school years in a sentence.

Bumping into people because I was scared of bumping into people while trying to learn something.

A couple of years after he left, Mum ended up being referred to a psychiatrist who believed her when she said that everything was OK, they never followed up with anything despite saying they would, just giving her more pills. She once rang me and in hushed, almost whispered tones asked me how I was. 'Why are you whispering, Mum?' I asked. 'Because they've turned the lights off on the ward and I shouldn't be using a phone,' she replied.

I tried my hardest to take away her pain, tried to replace it with happy simple things, like shopping down the Walworth Road and breakfast in local cafés, doing everything in my power to make her happy. *Life's great, Mum, look at how beautiful the sky is.*

'No, life's shit and then you die,' she'd reply, sparking up a fag. 'Your father's ruined my life, there's no point me living.'

Lighting one fag from the butt of another. She chain-smoked, sometimes leaving a trail of cigarettes burning in different ashtrays like coastal warning beacons. I was terrified that she'd burn her flat down.

Her frequent liaisons with Dad after he'd apparently gone often resulted in violence and uncontrollable anger. Desperate emotions whipped out of her snaring any one of us who was in range – we all learnt to get out the way. She once sent me a photograph of her fingers on one hand, swollen and bruised a deep, dead black.

'What happened, Mum?' I asked.

'He hurt me,' she said.

'Please stay away from him, Mum,' I begged.

She wouldn't stay away, so I had to. I needed to get away from the violence and fear but it came with me, followed me, preceded me, inhabited me. My stories, my past, my childhood experiences, all that had shaped me was riven with their violence, anger, and breakup. We were born into a thing that was already broken, ripped, smashed. We were raised by their coping strategies, ill-formed, maladjusted, often self-harming coping strategies in the shadows of which they birthed and raised four kids.

When I went to art college I thought I could let go a little, everyone did after a few drinks, it seemed everyone told personal stories about their lives and their hopes after a can or two.

One night in the kitchen of our shared student house people started to tell stories about their families. I didn't know any better so I told them that my dad and brother had a fight in which my brother's hand was cut almost clean off, hanging on by a flap of skin that looked like a snippet of chamois leather. Bloodied on one side. Skin the other.

There was silence, and horror registered on my fellow students' faces. Under the kitchen table, I turned my toes inwards and tried to climb inside myself. They looked at me but were silent, I looked down at my feet and my mind raced back to that kitchen of ours, the kitchen in which a hand was almost cut off, divvied up like a cut of meat. That was the dad we had; we had no nickname for that dad.

We'd moved to a new house on a small, gleamingly new estate. An estate deep in the shires. It felt hopeful and bold, like we'd left everything behind.

Each house had a postage-stamp garden and a white painted porch. It seemed like California.

Our kitchen was tiled white, floor-to-ceiling white tiles with a middle edging tile in electric blue. 'It looks French,' Mum said.

White tiles and a single electric blue line which zinged like a new horizon. We'd start over, things would be different here, French, and quiet. Mum said we'd plant an apple tree.

Things felt sane. Then.

My dad and brother Nick had a fight fuelled by testosterone, perhaps it was secretly over the same woman, Ann 2, they were both fucking behind Mum's back. Like Kirk Douglas and Tony Curtis in *The Vikings*, they brawled as if over a servant girl.

They fought; they always did, but this time it ended with my brother's hand being sliced almost clean off.

Shit had got serious; Nick was fifteen going on sixteen and challenging the silverback in the sheepskin car coat, move over, young blood coming through.

My brother's hand was cut almost clean off but for a flap of skin and a single bone which stopped the hand from falling and becoming an object on the floor alongside shards of glass and smashed mugs.

The flap of skin and single bone kept it attached and hand-like. Just.

In *The Vikings*, Tony Curtis's hand is cut clean off by Kirk Douglas; that moment in our new white kitchen was more than a little suggestive of that.

I was upstairs, I heard screams, came down and stood at the entrance to the kitchen. My brother was on his knees, his face the colour of soured milk, his mouth like a pained arsehole, tightened and contorted by shock and fear.

In the sea of white tiles, he seemed like a tiny ghostly figure in a Leonora Carrington painting. The fear hammered onto his face a ghostly doorway right back to our fucked-up-ness. Who were we to think that a new house would end the violence?

Mum had an armful of tea towels in her hands and was making a makeshift-tourniquet. Tea towels decorated with illustrations of places someone had visited.

My brother, his eyes tightly closed, his mouth scrunched tight in pain, was gripping the place where his hand met his arm, holding it together. Mum screamed at him to hold it up, 'hold your arm up please for the love of God hold it up.'

The man who would be called Dad, all colour drained from

his face, was standing in a pile of broken glass by the back door, atop a mountain of razor-sharp shards. Something had happened, a fight, a struggle, a loss of temper and the glass in the door had smashed, blood was everywhere around him.

He looked on with empty black eyes, he was still travelling back from his anger, from his angry place. He was still, his mind racing. His anger was a place he'd arrive at in an instant, *your dad's quick tempered*, they'd say. His anger a place from where he travelled back slowly.

So arduous was his return that it dissipated all of his anger, frequently he cried at the moment he arrived back and told us he loved us. He once smashed my head on the corner of the oven, stood silently for a moment or two and then pulled me in to him, hugging me until his anger subsided and then he cried. He told me he loved me and I thought, *love is a product of violence, they never show that in films*.

My brother looked up to Mum and mouthed the words, *am I going to die?* For a moment he looked like Jesus, and Mum Mary. He passed out, letting go of his wrist, slumping back onto Mum's legs. However lost to us and to herself Mum was, whenever she needed to be there, she was there. She's saved our lives many times over. Literally saved our lives.

As he slumped I watched his severed hand fall back, his wrist gaping open like an old-fashioned coin purse. It just came apart. I always wanted to dive into coin purses, they seemed like safe, kind spaces.

Strange, Juno, strange. A purse is a purse, not an island. Perhaps Dad was right, perhaps I was mad like Mum.

Each time his heart beat, a fountain of blood shot high into the air, splattering on the Artexed ceiling, then splashing down onto the white tiles. I thought no one would ever be able to clean the blood off the textured ceiling, I pictured Mum trying to bleach the blood away. Scrubbing the ceiling until she became dizzy. She did, later that night, when we were upstairs pretending to sleep.

'Get the fucking car started before he bleeds to death,' Mum bellowed at Dad like an elephant flooded with protective hormones. He moved to the car, brushing past me, I didn't feel any presence of him, he was like a ghost. I think he was scared that his temper had finally killed someone.

I think it was the Capri Mum was bellowing about, a tomato-red Capri – new car, new house. Whichever car it was, the blood stayed deeply embedded in the back seats for ages, like a Catholic shrine that bled a little onto whatever we wore. Staining us.

The blood from that day still seeps easily into my mind, I can still smell it, that much congealed blood smells. Our dazzling white kitchen now like an abattoir.

Nick's blood solidified like a Quinn head but a hand, lodged on the shelf in my mind marked, *really, is this love?*

The day Mum found the letter about Dad's affair she smashed her mum's mirror over his head, a huge mirror she had to yank off the wall. It cut his head open. I've always thought that in that moment she was hitting him and her own mother, both of them similar, both runners from poverty, both had helped shape her life. Both left her to danger.

It took them a whole day of surgery to sew Nick's hand back on. It's a useless appendage now, bordered, cut off from the arm by a great welt of a scar, a mountain range of gnarled keloid skin. The hand freezes, swells, full of arthritis and neuropathy and pain. It's hurt him his whole life, a reminder of our child-hoods. It was his left hand, he's left-handed, I suspect it was the hand he touched her with. Was that it, was that the reason for its removal?

My dad's in his eighties now. I visit him very occasionally. Watching him, looking at his body made fragile by his relent-lessly intensifying neurological condition. A disease that little by little is taking away all of his strength, autonomy and certainty. I study this new fragility which encases the same anger and the same reasons for rejecting us all those years before. He still freezes if I go to hug him. Not knowing how to respond to me, to us. I watch him soften with his new family so I know his body can, when it understands it can. How did we become a danger to him, to his body? He responds to us as if we are predators.

His anger still resides, simmering in every part of him. It's exhausting that he still flares up at the same topics.

He hates immigrants, queers, probably trans people, but most especially the Labour Party for it represents everything he wanted to leave far behind. He was happy with Trump and Farage, even when I told him that they'd both outlaw me if they could.

It seems impossible to believe that his was once a body that was strong and violent, a body capable of wreaking havoc. A body I was so scared of, a body that removed hands.

He can barely stand now without a relay of carefully placed Zimmer frames that enables him to move from one room to the next, or out into the garden. Like a child in a play centre, he slowly swings one arm from one frame to the next before taking hesitant steps. Like a ponderous gibbon.

His misfiring and dampened neurons make him shake, appear drunk and fall.

When we were kids, it often felt like his only purpose was to dominate us physically by fear. He was a strong man, square in shape with broad shoulders and big gnarly hands, fronted by squat, damaged knuckles, flattened by punching and physical work.

When he lost his temper, he was terrifying. But in families like ours, it was almost accepted that men lost their temper. A space was created for men to lose their temper in. We, the women, the children, the fledgling-trans ones, accepted, placated, moved and assuaged. Mopping up tears and blood.

They do it because they don't know any better. They do it because they're stressed. They do it because we ask for too much. They do it because they are men and men can't control themselves. They tell us we like it when they control the house. They say they do it because women annoy them and that's why women should stay with women and just give men what they need – feed them, have sex with them when they want, forgive them. Women running around trying to manage men's violence with the softest of kid gloves.

The list of reasons why no one said to my dad, *you're a violent cunt*, were long.

In fact, I did say it to him once, on a shitty rain-soaked holiday in a caravan. I was within spitting distance of him and as the words 'violent cunt' left my mouth they smashed into smithereens in the air in front of me, exploding like an asteroid as they touched his cannonball of a fist. I saw the words 'violent cunt' disintegrate just before his fist connected with my mouth. A villainous cartoon punch that sent me flying backwards across the floor, the caravan shook.

In his second family's house extension, I watch him sleeping on the wicker sofa, the kind you only find in summer houses or extensions. Next to him on a cushion were his hearing aids, left out because they make him feel old, he hates feeling old, he hates looking old. His vanity was one of the few things that as kids we all joked about. We'd say, he can't walk past a mirror or reflective surface without flipping out a comb and to make us laugh he'd take out an imaginary comb out from his pocket and pretend to be Elvis combing a quiff in an imaginary mirror. I still say that line to him and he still pretends to get a comb out, it's the only non-violent legacy. It's the only line.

It makes no sense to me that he'd rather be deaf than appear old, it makes him seem even older. He constantly says, *pardon, sorry, say that again, nope can't hear you, pardon*.

I used to think that leaving his hearing aids out was attention-seeking out of sheer boredom, his life reduced to sitting on a wicker sofa in a summer house moaning about Jeremy Corbyn. But actually, I think that he'd rather be left in silence or left with just the sound of his own angry internal voices. The racist, the sexist, the violent and the self-hating.

The voice that told me when I was a teenager that Black people in Africa didn't know how to run a country like white men did. I went to the library and took out a book on the history of the Zulus. At dinner a few weeks later, he started talking about Africa, which was often in the news because of the insidious Apartheid regime, and again he started to say that the country needed white men to show them how to be civilised. I said, *no, Dad, they did brilliantly before we came along and divided them along different lines, our lines, forcing them off their own lands and into townships to work for a pittance for the white men who stripped everything from the country. We did that, we were the monsters, Dad, we still are.*

No one confronted my dad, certainly not with a book. He was above books and facts. Very fucking Trump.

His face whitened, his fists clenched, he stood, walked round the table, and stood behind me. He smacked my face down into my plate of food. I lifted my head, with gravy dripping and a piece of hot roast potato squashed, burning, into my cheek, and I said, *you can hit me all you want but you're wrong*. We didn't talk much after that.

In my fifties, I'm trying to forgive him and show him he's loved, but I don't know if I do love him, I don't think love was ever in the offing. Perhaps in pity I'm allowing him to get off scot-free, without any penitence. Perhaps I'm still scared of him, perhaps I want him to love me. Perhaps all of that is true. Hopeless as it is. You only get one father. One chance at that relationship.

His view of the world has never changed, but he's weaker now so he no longer goes out looking for my sister to make sure she's not dancing or sleeping with a Black man. When we were young, he carried a crowbar with him to deal with that eventuality. My sister's head has a scar hidden beneath her hair. I remember the night it happened; her stack perm weighed down at the back with congealed blood. That was our dad, no nickname, no hugs.

In his mind, in his silent world, I imagine he's still punching.

When his neurological condition worsened a few years ago, I'd ring him after his hospital appointments to see what had been said about the progression of his disease. Almost always, he or his wife would say that they couldn't understand a word that the doctors, who were African or Pakistani, had said, and therefore they couldn't say how he was. It was a bloody liberty that these people were supposed to be looking after him after a lifetime of paying taxes. *What taxes, Dad? You spent a lifetime avoiding paying them.*

They, the non-white doctors, became the reason for his failing health, and not the diagnosed neurological condition.

He'd rant, 'the NHS is falling apart, it's the fucking idiot Labour Party for you, they've encouraged all these foreigners to come and work in the NHS and I bet half of them don't have any qualifications.' This from a man who's barely read a book and gets his world-view from the *Daily Mail*.

Many people running from poverty vote Tory, thus, the Tories. There aren't enough rich people in the United Kingdom to keep them and capitalism afloat, it's us and our stupid material aspiration and class shame that keeps them in power.

One day on the phone, when he could still easily talk on the phone, he said to me, 'you know what, a bloody miracle happened today.' I thought they've had a breakthrough with his condition, but no, he went on to say, 'we went to the hospital and a white doctor walked towards us and bugger me, you know what, everything he said made sense and I feel much better now, I hope we can see him again. What was his name, love?' he called out to his wife who was apparently separating a frozen prawn ring for dinner later that evening. Y the racist out of Bethnal Green but his racism stil a prawn ring from Iceland.

*

I look at him dozing on his wicker sofa, his hearing aids cast asunder, and quietly I whisper, *it's taken me years to say this, Dad, but I'm not mental and even if I were deranged like you say Mum is, it didn't give you the right to hit us like you did, breaking our skin, smashing our bones. It didn't give you the right to leave us without a single care in the world for our wellbeing, or us having to take care of Mum. My little brother was a kid when you left him with a woman who was falling apart, and I say woman and not mother because she couldn't be a mother then. Mum couldn't mother at that point, but you didn't care.*

*You didn't have the right to think that you could leave your violence behind, blaming it on us, on our mental health, telling us we were like her, like Mum. I'm glad we were more like her, at least she's faced up to stuff, you just remove your hearing aids and act like butter never melted. You're not leaving your violence with us, it's yours, I give it back to you and you know what? I'll even forgive you for not picking it up and taking it with you when you left, because I am a better person than you. We were never your kids, I see that now, we were part of a commitment you didn't want. So, there it is, I'm not sure if you can hear me, but when you put your hearing aids back in your violence is tucked in them, your violence is back with you and not with us.*

# Epilogue

I was born on the fifteenth of April 1964. A spring baby who came screaming into this world, into a room full of hope, a room lined with yellow rose wallpaper and a dark green carpet – almost a garden. I was put in an ivory Clydella night-dress – a bridesmaid in a rose garden. Dad was apparently fast asleep in the armchair; Mum, high on Valium, gas and air, was nodding off in bed, her auburn beehive almost toppling over like an accident waiting to happen.

I like to think that as they slept, I pulled myself up and looked out of the window. Already looking for somewhere to run.

I was born at 5.30 a.m., a weighty, ginger-haired baby. Screaming, apparently full of rage and frustration. A great pulsating red birthmark spanned my forehead, an archipelago of a birthmark. It still emerges if I'm upset or angry. Mum tells me it was like I was trying to say something. Gertie told Mum that I was the ugliest baby that she'd ever seen, and when I was three or four years old she also told Mum that I wasn't a boy but a girl. Mum remembers that moment as clear as day.

As kids, we were taught that to escape pain, to escape violence, to escape class, we should run, not look back, and not stop running until we were sure that everything bad was a long way behind us. But how would you know when to stop? If you

:d back how would you know if you were safe? I ran
he seven years of being here, I think I've still been
my mind.

I look out into my courtyard through the small wooden doors
and realise that here I have a beautiful space, a garden I can stop
still in. I can stop running now. I'm tired. This house, this place
is very much like the rose-filled room in which I came into the
world, the garden room, it feels full circle, this is home.

I must let that seep in, that I have reached somewhere. I
must stop the punishing journey in my mind. Perhaps this
book is an end to that. Telling this story is a destination.

I've started to have therapy, the endings that arose from
writing this do feel monumental, the realisation that I might
have closure called into question so much about the life that
has already passed. My therapist asked me why I wanted to
engage with therapy and I said, 'because I think I can be happier than this.'

I've also signed up to a poetry class, which felt fitting as a
response to the weight of the experiences that this book now
holds. I wanted or needed less on a page, more blank space
around fewer words. I'm editing a poem for my class, it's my
turn this evening to workshop a piece. It will be the first time
I've ever workshopped a poem. It's a small class, perhaps seven
or eight of us who meet every Tuesday evening and listen to
each other's work and discuss works by established poets. I'm
terrified, I considered taking a Valium but I rationalised that
the fear is probably the same for all of us so I'll go it alone.
Someday, I'd like to tackle my pill usage.

Home
my house balances on a pinhead held

tight between fingertips, a pinhead
carved from bamboo. warm
winds from the Sahara gently
blow the house.
there's a village atop the pinhead, a
small village, just them and me.
A single shop sits dead centre, a
boutique in which we buy and sell each
other's outtakes.
the winds whistles, it sings a song
I drag a chair out into the whistling,
a chair clad loosely in chalky bones,
bones painted yellow to mimic corn.
I snuggle into its embrace.
my house rests on me finding you.

The old story of my old life has to end in order for a new
one to begin, poetry and therapy will help in that. Therapy and
poetry aren't simply modes of creativity and creative thinking
but ways for me to end formally all that's gone before.

I knew I needed to document how I felt coming to the end
of writing this book – the sense of loss and finality, the sense
of a true ending – but I knew that I couldn't write anything
longer, not yet. Hour-long therapy sessions and short snappy
stanzas are like doors and windows I can open and close. They
assist me in clearing up, boxing up and putting on the shelves
all of the remnants that are left and that matter. My love for
Mum, for my siblings and forgiveness for the boy that my dad
still is and will always be.

I'm so fortunate to have run here, to this silent village in the
mountains. I feel content.

I get up and open the small flaking doors to the courtyard, the wisteria hangs, plentiful, purple racemes gently frame my perfect view. *Who'd have thought, Juno, who'd have thought?* You once sold yourself for a tenner in a phone box in Euston and then did the drugs right there and then, in full view, as people swarmed by, cutting their eyes at you, tutting at you. Someone spat on the window of the phone box and you watched their spit dribble down to the ground. If they could see you now, you and your beautiful wisteria framing your beautiful view.

I chuckle. I wish them all wisteria-well.

I look at a photograph on the wall of Mum sitting upright on a sun lounger.

Sitting between her legs is me, looking wistfully up at her, craning my neck to do so. I already have sallow deep-set eyes, a shock of white-blonde hair and pale skin. I look sickly, like a child full of gloom. I look like I was always going to become this overly complicated version of me.

In the photograph, Mum is looking off into the distance, into space, completely disconnected from me despite our skin-on-skin proximity, our mother-and-child proximity. I must be two or three years old. I'm chubby, my birthmark, a raised landmass on my forehead, is only partially hidden by the mop of blonde hair, hair grown long from the get-go to cover the birthmark.

She's wearing a scarf around her head, her auburn hair peeking out, framing a pair of Jackie O's. A striped shirt dress is belted tightly around her waist. She looks fantastic, like she's been painted by Alex Katz.

Two people captured in the same photograph with completely different narratives, painted so differently. I always felt so safe being close to her, but I can see from the photograph that she was always somewhere else. I wonder if being a mother ever made her feel better, or if were we always a reminder of her own childhood and then her failed marriage. A marriage that inadvertently blamed us for its failure.

Dad must have taken this photograph, he must have captured this moment of separate yet divided intimacy, that's how I'll explain us in the future, as separately intimate, as close but divided.

I miss her and I feel an overwhelming sense of love towards her whoosh up through my tired, sleepy body and gush out through my eyes. When I first arrived here I planted a pomegranate tree for Mum, this is the first year it hangs heavy with fruit. I hope she comes back and falls asleep in the shadow of a ripe pomegranate. That's a poem right there, her head in the shade of a single pomegranate.

I take the pillows out from under my head and rest them against the headboard. I pull my knees up tightly into my belly and whisper *thank you* to a dad who was never a dad. Thank you for making us happen.

Somehow you'll always be a part of this life of mine, even if you were only ever just passing through. Strange that it's taken me to move to the edge of my nowhere, to my event horizon, to realise that. Somehow that does allow you off the hook, allows you to be blameless in all of this because we were never your story. We were never your children.

I wish you as much love as I can muster in your journey to face the violence you left us with, the scars.

But this is my story, and from now and always, it only belongs to me.

# Acknowledgements

To Mum, thank you for all your unique, messy and bloody wonderful support. I love you more than I love the mountains and fuck me do I love these mountains.

# References

En.wikipedia.org. 2021. *Love letter – Wikipedia*. [online]
    Available at: https://en.wikipedia.org/wiki/Love_letter
    [Accessed 18 December 2021].

Rubenhold, H., 2019. *The Five*. London: Doubleday.

*Steel Magnolias*. 1989. [film] Directed by H. Ross.

*Sex and the City*. 1998–2004. [TV series]

*Eat Pray Love*. 2010. [film] Directed by R. Murphy.

*Imagine . . . Georgia O'Keeffe: By Myself*. 2016. [film] Directed
    by J. Nicholls.

Brown, H., 2016. Judith Butler in Belgium: Reflections on
    Public Grief and Precarity in the Wake of the Paris
    Attacks. *DiGeSt. Journal of Diversity and Gender Studies*,
    3(1), p.7.

Kolk, B., 2021. *The Body Keeps the Score*. La Vergne: Memories
    of Ages Press.

*It's a Sin*. 2021. [TV series] Directed by P. Hoar.

*Grease*. 1978. [film] Directed by R. Kleiser.

*Cleopatra*. 1963. [film] Directed by J. L. Mankiewicz.

*Oliver!* 1968. [film] Directed by C. Reed.

*Midnight Express*. 1978 [film] Directed by A. Parker.

*Christiane F.* 1981 [film] Directed by U. Edel.

Visiedo, V., 2021. Almería registra su segunda peor cifra de muertes a pesar de la bajada de contagios. *Diario de Almeria*, [online] <https://www.diariodealmeria.es/almeria/Almeria-registra-segunda-muertes-contagios_0_1545746197.html> [Accessed 18 December 2021].

*Rosemary's Baby*. 1968. [film] Directed by R. Polanski.

Bringing a book from manuscript to what you are reading is a team effort.

Dialogue Books would like to thank everyone who helped to publish *Roam* in the UK.

**Editorial**
Sharmaine Lovegrove
Amy Mae Baxter
Adriano Noble
Nithya Rae

**Audio**
Louise Harvey

**Contracts**
Anniina Vuori

**Sales**
Caitriona Row
Dominic Smith
Frances Doyle
Hannah Methuen
Lucy Hine
Toluwalope Ayo-Ajala

**Design**
Charlotte Stroomer
Jo Taylor

**Production**
Narges Nojoumi

**Publicity**
Millie Seaward

**Marketing**
Emily Moran

**Copy Editor**
David Bamford

**Proofreader**
Jon Appleton

**Operations**
Kellie Barnfield
Millie Gibson
Sanjeev Braich

**Finance**
Andrew Smith
Ellie Barry